Anne Coombs was born in Newcastle in 1956. After completing an Arts degree at Sydney University and working for several years as a journalist she took up writing full time. Her books include *Adland* (1990), the novel *No Man's Land* (1993) and *Sex and Anarchy: The life and death of the Sydney Push* (1996). *Sex and Anarchy* was short listed for the Kibble, N.S.W. Premier's and FAW Awards.

Anne and Susan live in the Southern Highland of NSW. *Broometime* is their first collaboration.

Susan Varga was born in Hungary but came to Australia as a child. After pursuing various aborted careers, including work in film and video and the law, she settled to full-time writing in 1990. *Heddy and Me,* her first book, won the 1994 Fellowship of Australian Writers Christina Stead Award for biography and was shortlisted for three other major awards.

Susan's first novel, *Happy Families*, (Sceptre) was published in 1999 and won both Braille Book of the Year and Audio Book of the Year.

Broometime

ANNE COOMBS AND **SUSAN VARGA**

SCEPTRE

This book may contain the names of people who have since died.

A couple of people's names have been changed and there are minor deviations in chronology, otherwise everything in this book is as we experienced it.

A Sceptre Book

Published in Australia and New Zealand in 2001
by Hodder Headline Australia Pty Limited
(A member of the Hodder Headline Group)
Level 22, 201 Kent Street, Sydney NSW 2000
Website: www.hha.com.au

National Library of Australia
Cataloguing-in-Publication data

Coombs, Anne, 1956- .
  Broometime.

  ISBN 0 7336 0990 2.

  1. Broome (W.A.) - Description and travel. I. Varga, Susan.
  II. Title.

919.414

The quotation on page 41 is reproduced by permission of Peter Burke,
author of *The Drowning Dream*, Freemantle Arts Centre Press, 1998

The lines from Jimmy Chi's songs are from *Indigenee* and *Heal Me O Risen Lord*,
('Corrugation Road', Angoorrabin Records, 1996) and *Town by the Bay* ('Bran Nue
Dae', BND Records, 1993)

Aerial photographs and gantheaume Point cliffs (inside front cover) are by
Out of the Blue Photos.

Mango in the rain (inside back cover) and Uncle Kiddo by Maria Mann

Jimmy Pike and Pat Lowe, by Brenton Edwards, News Ltd

Bishop Christopher Saunders, courtesy of the Catholic Diocese of Broome

Kevin Fong at Goolarri, from the *Broome Advertiser*

All other photographs by the authors.

Text design and typesetting by Bookhouse, Sydney
Printed in Australia by Griffin Press, Adelaide

Acknowledgements

First, our heartfelt thanks to the people of Broome, who made us feel welcome in their town and who, virtually without exception, gave generously of their time and hospitality. Thank you for many wonderful conversations.

Our particular thanks to Lyn Page, Gordon Bauman, Mary Tarran, Pearl Hamaguchi, Kevin Fong, Vanessa Poelina and Bishop Christopher Saunders for allowing us into your lives a little, and for your generosity and friendship.

We are also grateful to those who contributed in their various ways to the creation of *Broometime*: a special thank you to Perpetua Durack who was always ready to help us in ways large and small, and also to Wendy Albert, Wendy Attenborough and Bruce Sims.

This book is for the people of Broome. We hope you like it.

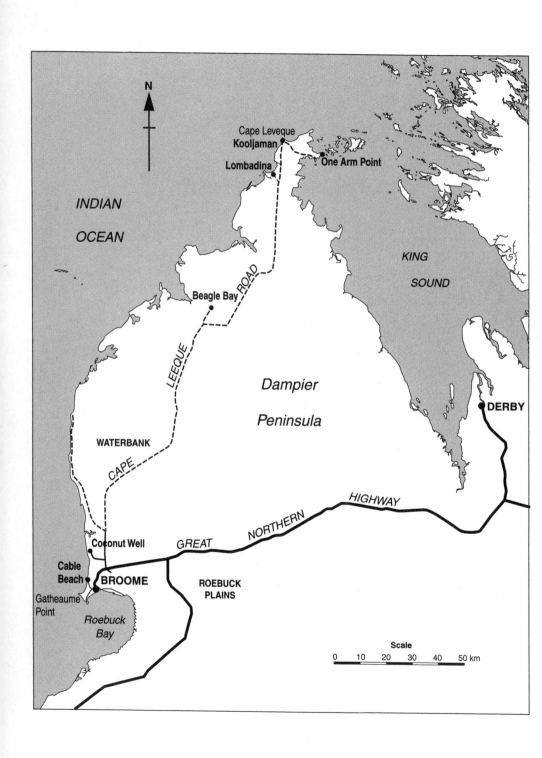

Contents

the cast

Stephen (Baamba) Albert—actor, singer and former bureaucrat

Mark Bin Bakar, aka Mary Geddardyu—Broome musician and radio personality

Phyllis Bin Bakar—Mark's mother and Broome identity

Gordon Bauman—Aboriginal Legal Service barrister

Jimmy Chi—musician and songwriter, half-brother of Pearl

Perpetua Durack—art gallery owner, daughter of artist Elizabeth Durack

Kevin Fong—managing director of Goolarri Media and budding politician

Peter Ghouse—Malaysian-born teacher, musician and community stalwart

Pearl Hamaguchi—former pearl farmer and Broome matriarch

Nolan Hunter—Shire councillor, director of the Aboriginal resource centre

Damien Kerr—Gordon's partner

Pat Lowe—writer and psychologist

Angus Murray—Shire President

Bob Noble—ex-butcher, old-timer and larrikin

Lyn Page—ex-Sydney socialite; businesswoman and Shire councillor

Jimmy Pike—renowned Aboriginal artist and husband of Pat

Vanessa Poelina—health worker and community activist

Bill Reed—owner of Linney's Pearls and prominent businessman

Eirlys Richards—ex-missionary and linguist

Christopher Saunders—Bishop of Broome

Marty Sibosado—Shire councillor and Aboriginal activist

Mary Tarran—prominent Yawuru woman

Shama Vanvaria- owner of Bloom's cafe

Peter Yu—executive director, Kimberley Land Council

For other characters, see page 293

the place

The first thing that strikes a newcomer to Broome is the colour. 'Where the red earth meets the blue sea' is a local saying. But that gives no idea of the glowing depth of the red or the iridescent aqua of the sea, or the way the colour changes as the tide moves in and out.

Broome is on a narrow strip of land that points roughly south. To the east is the wide, flat expanse of Roebuck Bay, a bay so large that tourists think it is the sea. To the west, rimmed by the silky white sand of Cable Beach, is the Indian Ocean. Bay and ocean meet at a stark red-gold promontory called Gantheaume Point, named by one of the French explorers who came this way in the eighteenth century. Gantheaume Point, or Minyirr as it is called by the local Yawuru people, is rich in spirituality, a place of associations so powerful that its atmosphere affects even the gardiya, or whitefellas, who visit it.

Gantheaume Point is only a few kilometres from town but one reaches it by bush track, a wide swath of red dirt that each year sinks further and further below the level of the surrounding bush. 'Pindan' is the name for this redness that stretches in all directions. Wherever you drive, you come upon that red ribbon of land topped by a band of aqua water.

In Roebuck Bay, where the water is shallower, its colour changes dramatically through the course of the day. The colour leaches out with a receding tide, so that as the water runs out of the bay so, too, does the colour. It fades from a brilliant blue-green, to lighter blue to milky blue-green. Even from a distance one can guess the height of the tide from the colour of the water.

Tides are more important here than clocks. Twice a day a massive volume of water, enough to fill Sydney Harbour, sweeps into the bay. And twice a day it retreats. Nothing here is done in moderation. It is a place of extremes and contradictions. The landscape seems to tell you this before the people have a chance to.

Water and pindan, sun and heat.

The second thing one notices about Broome, after the colours, is that you appear to have missed the town. You pass the main street before it has even registered. Then it's all wide verges and messy gardens, silvery tin houses peeping out from behind.

Back in the days of the pearling masters, Broome had several distinct sections. The European population lived in an area of well-spaced houses and shady gardens set back a little from the bay and laid out in a generous grid pattern. A few shops, banks, the post office, were scattered here and there. The local Aborigines mostly camped on the margins, or wherever they could. Eventually an area or two was set aside for their use, and they were expected to keep to them. The 'Asiatics'—the Malays, Manilamen, Koepangers, Japanese and Chinese who crewed the luggers and ran the shops and brothels and boarding houses—lived in a marshy area near Dampier

Creek, close to where the luggers drew up. This was, and remains, Chinatown. It was a lively, chaotic place, especially when the luggers were in and the crews had money in their pockets. Old men would sit around the stoop of the Chinese bakery in Napier Terrace smoking opium smuggled in from Singapore in hands of bananas.

A few of the old businesses still survive in Chinatown: Wing's store, where you can buy anything from a swag to shiitake mushrooms; Sun Pictures, the oldest 'picture gardens' in the world; Streeter and Male, agents for just about everything, a remnant of colonial times. In its heyday, European men strutted around Chinatown in their 'whites'. 'Young Kim Male' (no longer so young) still does, although today the uniform is not a white suit but white short-sleeved shirt, shorts and long socks.

Now Chinatown is being made over in imitation of itself. Now it is the new town centre. Rather than apologise for it, the civic fathers promote it—with half on eye on the past, but minds focussed on the future, on Chinatown as tourist drawcard. There is no high rise, no building taller than two stories. Old buildings and new are clad in Broome-signature corrugated iron. Many have verandahs. There is much use of latticework and red and green paint, seen as continuing the Chinese theme.

This new town centre still isn't very big, which is why one can miss it and spend half a day wondering where 'the town' is. In the centre of the main street are bronze statues of the three men who are credited with giving Broome its second chance. After World War II, Broome was dying. Its lugging fleet had been destroyed, most of the European population had left town, and people said the Japanese divers would never work in Broome again. Plastic was on its way. For sixty years Broome had thrived on the worldwide demand for mother-of-pearl buttons. But plastic superseded the lovely *Pinctada Maxima*. Plastic was harder-wearing, and men didn't have to dive fathoms deep into that aqua water to retrieve it.

It was pearlshell, not pearls, that made Broome. The pearl that was sometimes found when a shell was opened was a bonus, a mysterious stroke of luck. Such finds bred stories, stories that became legends. But it wasn't such pearls that paid the wages of the indentured labourers, the Koepangers and Manilamen; it was the tons and tons of pearlshell destined for European buttons.

In the 1960s, with plastic in control of the button market and the pearlshell lying uncollected on the ocean floor, the Japanese perfected a way of making cultured pearls. Slowly, and suspiciously, Broome watched the birth of a new industry. Pearlshell was gathered again, but not for buttons. Now the Pinctada Maxima was kept alive, to live in cages and to produce pearls on demand.

Again, the Japanese put Broome on the map. This is why there are three bronze statues in the centre of Chinatown, to the three men—two of them Japanese—who made it happen: Mr Kuribayashi, Mr Iwaki and an Australian, K.F. Dureau.

The third thing one notices about Broome are the faces in the street. And it is this which is constantly remarkable, long after one has grown accustomed to the aqua sea and the peculiar style of the town. Broome faces. Such a mix of races in any one visage. Often it is impossible to identify just what the mix might be—Malay/Chinese, Filipino/Aboriginal, Japanese/Thursday Islander or all of these? Six or eight races in a single family is not unusual. After a while it ceases to matter. They are just Broome faces, the 'mongrel breed' of Jimmy Chi's song.

Our ancients sowed their culture
Our ancients sowed their seed
So there is no pedigree
We're all one mongrel breed.

There is black and white in Broome, but the real Broome people are all those who are somewhere in between. In the old pearling days, the hierarchy was Europeans at the top, then the Japanese divers, then the Chinese merchants, then the other 'Asiatics' such as Malays and Koepangers (from West Timor) and, at the bottom of the heap, the indigenous people. But it didn't stay so neat for long. Few Asian men brought women with them, so there were countless liaisons between these men and local Aboriginal and half-caste women. These liaisons rarely resulted in marriage. More often, the man fathered a child or two, then went back to his own country, or was killed at sea. The children grew up together, played together in sprawling extended families.

The connections and cross-connections in this small town are constant and often surprising. Everyone knows who everyone else is—where they fit in the 'family'. Family is a wide, all-embracing concept in Broome. Although there may be many races in a family—a touch of Japanese blood here, a dollop of Malay there—the constant cultural glue is the Aboriginal blood, passed down from the mothers. And with that comes the Aboriginal meaning of family, which includes anyone, regardless of blood, who has a close attachment.

This is a town where any discussion of lineage and patrimony involves the telling of long stories, whispered gossip and gales of laughter. It is a forgiving town.

As the joke goes: 'What's the definition of confusion?'

'Father's Day in Broome.'

Arrival

One

The Rat Palazzo—Town Beach—Night of the rats—Real estate and other first impressions—Perpetua at the Thai tea house—On the fringe

S On trips large and small into the bush we have always been interested in country towns. Who lives in them and why? What can you learn about the mechanics of a society, and its heart, from **SUSAN** these small often half-forgotten places?

An idea grew for a book that Anne and I would write together—our first collaboration. For several years we searched, on and off, for a town to live in and write about. We even thought about Bundanoon, the little town closest to our small farm in the Southern Highlands of New South Wales, or an outback town, or somewhere in Tasmania—maybe even Tasmania itself…But not one of them took fire with us. Maybe country towns were boring after all.

Then we went to Broome on a holiday. Broome had never crossed our minds as a candidate town. A small isolated place on the other side of the continent, six thousand kilometres from home, it was just too remote and foreign. It was difficult and expensive to get there, even on a holiday.

But within twenty-four hours we knew this was our town, for better or for worse, and we began to plot and plan to get back to it. It occurred to us, too, that multi-racial Broome could be an interesting place to be at the end of the millennium when the nation was obsessed with a certain redhead and her politics.

Nine months later we packed our newly acquired aqua-blue Rav, the exact colour, as it turned out, of Broome's Roebuck Bay, and set off. We went roughly the way that the Duracks, that prominent pastoralist family, took on their epic journey north more than a century ago, starting in Goulburn. Our plan was to ease ourselves, day by day, night by night, into another atmosphere, like passing through a series of windows into a different world.

The journey took us two and a half weeks. The Duracks took months by dray just to get to the Channel Country of south-west Queensland, where they stayed for fifteen years before driving their cattle overland to that virtually unknown north-west tip of the country, the Kimberley.

As we set out on our journey, Anne and I kept a double journal. The large, spiral-bound notebook was the place where we wrote to each other or jotted notes, where we expressed our frustrations and fears. It was also the place where we played out a vague, more subterranean agenda: of stretching ourselves by leaving our familiar, loved surroundings for unknown territory, and pushing the limits of our own relationship, perhaps also grown too familiar, too comfortable . . .

Dubbo

 I haven't travelled like this since I was a child—the endless outback roads and dusty towns. The strongest memories are of the magnificent sunrises and sunsets, the cold still quiet of the campsite in early morning.

Now I am reminded of the charmlessness of most Australian urban settlements—these lakes of crass suburbs and messy commercialism spread out on the landscape—and how much they've always distressed me. Already I'm having flashes of homesickness for our soft green rolling hills.

And I'm suddenly nervous about the task before us and what it will do to us. There is risk in living as we do—in tying one's creative heart to the everyday loving heart.

Thursday, April 30

We might end up fighting every day—every hour?—over ideas, over a sentence. Yet I'm strangely confident. God knows why...

This kind of journey makes one think confused thoughts about time. Three days seems so slow, encompasses so much, because we've left our normal routines and all we do is drive, eat, peek into passing miniature worlds, then drive on again.

Yesterday, pushing on and on through that magnificent monotony towards Boulia was exciting and stressful and boring all at once. Boulia, a tiny dust-bitten town on the edge of the Simpson Desert, just 40 kilometres from the beginning of the Birdsville Track, felt like the real outback. Mount Isa, just three hours north, feels like an anachronism, with its modern Kmarts, Woolworths, and McDonalds restaurants. All from mining and mining wealth.

Northern Territory—Three Ways

A 'I don't know about this bloody Northern Territory,' you said.

'It feels barbarous,' I said.

'Deliberately barbarous, as if they're proud of how rough and uncouth everything is, as though there's nothing else to be proud of.'

The thing that gets me is the appalling slaughter on the roads—dead kangaroos everywhere. And tonight, at the Threeways Roadhouse, where we're staying in a very basic motel unit, we seem to be surrounded by it. Piles of rubbish, burnt-out caravans and other detritus everywhere. I heard a low rumbling sound that I couldn't identify. Then we walked around the corner and there, stationary in front of the roadhouse, were three enormous road trains, each with three double-decker trailers packed with cattle. The air was filled with the lowing and stamping of some eighteen hundred beasts.

We went in and ordered roast beef. There wasn't much else on the menu. I couldn't eat it. At the table next to us the road-train drivers joked and chiacked and hoed into their steaks.

Kununurra

S We're four-fifths of the way—a mere 1000 kilometres to go across the Kimberley.

As soon as we crossed the border and saw those proud, austere Kimberley ranges our hearts lifted. Now we're in a 'resort' motel, suddenly exhausted from the encroaching heat (in May!) and from the peculiar stresses of this trip. In a sense, nothing much happens, but everything is so different. Driving through these desolate places, sometimes little more than a roadhouse and a couple of straggly houses, I try to picture the camaraderie, the eccentric colour of local life, the legends . . . But all I see is people at the far reaches; isolated, often poor. And the Aborigines, despite the new health clinics and community police picking people up from around the pubs, still look sick, poor and disoriented. I'm aware of my own discomfort around them, even at times a bit of fear.

May 12, 30 kilometres from Broome

We're almost there and we've stopped to have a cup of coffee and eat the last of the 'traveller's cake' that our friend Chris made for us. I'm suddenly excited. What will the house we've rented (sight unseen) be like? How will we adjust to the town? I'm trying to forewarn myself—there will be ups and downs, it will probably take us months to settle to the place. But there's no delaying any longer. There is a continent behind us and only 30 kilometres between us and Broome . . .

Rat Palazzo

We knew it was going to be difficult but we didn't quite expect this! The shack we're renting—it really cannot be called a house—is twice as bad as we anticipated. It's brought us face to face with the softness of our pampered southern lives. Immediately I am having to confront my pathetic weaknesses—my fear of spiders, rats and other creepy-crawlies. There aren't even windows, just hinged flaps covered in sheet metal, which are chocked open with a long piece of wood. The walls and roof, mostly corrugated iron and some broken fibro, are unlined. There are enormous cracks and gaps everywhere.

Our friend Bruce, who has been here nearly three years, tells us there's no point fighting it—that the red pindan dust and mouse shit will never go away and you just have to learn to live with it. He's right, of course. Anyway, anything we try to clean too vigorously just falls apart.

This is what we wanted—a totally different environment, something to stretch and push us. And although the house is a mess, the garden is lovely. There's an enormous tamarind tree, under which I'm sitting now, and a couple of pawpaw trees with thick bunches of fruit, and a sprawling white bougainvillea by the back door. I might even get used to the frogs in the toilet bowl!

'I told you it was a dump,' Bruce says jovially. After many years at Penguin, Bruce came to work for Magabala Books in Broome. He looks more at home than he ever did in Melbourne. Here his long silver hair, T-shirts and tattoos don't merit a glance.

Perpetua, who found us this house, wanders in from next door, looking concerned but a trifle uncomprehending of our anxieties. She may appear genteel but she's from hardy Durack stock, and they braved far greater terrors than frogs in the toilet and rats in the night.

For us, everything is still new and has to be adjusted to, even the nice things: the funny upright lizards, heads and tails held high in the air, which scuttle in the undergrowth; the giant green frogs; the native mice that peek out from behind pot plants; the sound of boab nuts falling from the tree and hitting the roof.

I have discovered that the lizards are called Gilberts Dragons or, more commonly, ta-ta lizards, because of their habit of waving one front arm vigorously in the air each time they slide to a halt.

*

You've been furiously cleaning out cupboards, scrubbing surfaces, while I stand around helplessly. Sometimes I can see the house as a kind of raffish, down-at-heel weekender, but most of the time it is just a Dickensian hole —dark and crumbling, with fetid corners and spongy floors.

There are a couple of pleasant spots—the single bed next to the wide-open shutter where we stretch out at opposite ends during the hottest part of the day. It's on the shady side of the house and sometimes a gentle breeze comes through and you can hear the greenery rustling in the garden outside. Donny, our landlord, is passionate about the garden.

I quite like our bedroom, too, now that we've sorted it out. It's just a verandah, with corrugated iron to waist height and metal push-out shutters above. The shutters are kept open. There's no latticework or insect screens, so you feel as if you're sleeping in the garden. There's a big freezer at one end, which we haven't been able to move. There are ancient freezers all over the place. Donny is a keen fishermen and uses them to store his fish and bait.

Yesterday we tried to do something with the 'sitting room'—a dark, windowless hole in the centre of the house—by moving around the bits of furniture and throwing fabrics we'd brought with us over the split and sagging cushions. But even when it was done, I couldn't imagine ever actually sitting down in that room.

*

Today we went for a walk by the shore where some expensive new 'Broome-style' townhouses are being built. They look more like a line of tin boatsheds. There was an old man walking his great mastiff along the tide line between the mangroves and the new development.

'Wanna buy one?' he said, nodding towards the units.

'Nah, a bit of a rip-off.'

'Careful! I might be the owner,' he said.

We laughed. His name is Bob Noble. He lives in the ramshackle house next door to the new development—but a bit higher up and further back from the water line. He says the new houses will be swept away if there is a big cyclone.

'See that new sea wall?' he said. 'It's got a slope on it. The water will run right up. See mine? It's straight up and down—pushes the waves back.'

Bob thinks Broome will change out of sight in the next five years. He's been here since 1948. Says he has lots of stories. Next time we'll take a tape recorder.

Town Beach

Sometimes I fear we have come to Broome too late—so much about the town is changing—but at Town Beach I see that the old town is still there, just hidden a little. I know Town Beach is going to become a favourite place. The other day there were two groups of Aboriginal people sitting on the grass below the small pioneer cemetery. In one group sat the men and in the other, the women. One of the men started up a song, and it was taken up by some of the women, then the others joined in, clapping and swaying. They sat in two large circles, maybe fifteen metres apart—apart but together.

There is such a mix of symbols and images at Town Beach, which is perhaps why I like it so much. For a start, there's the cemetery; a small hillock with a dozen or so graves on it, some enclosed by rusting iron railings, some marked by just a headstone. A few trees give shade; and beyond is the blue of Roebuck Bay. There's one interesting grave which has a headstone at either end: Edward Chippendall and his 'friend and partner' Thomas Haynes. Haynes died 40 years after Chippendall, yet they lie here together.

In front of the tiny cemetery is the promontory that used to lead to the wharf, until the new wharf was constructed further south in the sixties. Now it is just a track that people walk out along for a better view of the bay, or to go fishing from, or to walk their dogs. At the opposite end of the beach—it is not a long beach—are the mangroves. At a very high tide, only the tops of the mangroves are visible and people swim among them. When the tide is that high, there is not much left of the beach—just a narrow strip of deep copper-gold sand.

At high tide, the water laps just below the Town Beach café, a simple affair of corrugated iron with a shaded area roofed with sails. Small palm trees have been planted just above the sand. The palms are not native but they look nice anyway.

Town Beach was named when this was the European end of town, with the jetty and the customs house and other official buildings nearby. The local people fish from the rocks here, or walk along the sand at low tide looking for shellfish. As the water recedes, you can walk hundreds of metres and still only be up to your ankles. On a calm day the water ripples across the sand in gentle milky currents.

The beach is a short and perfect arch, the mangroves at one end, the promontory at the other, the caravan park backing onto half of it, the public park onto the other half, and in between the two, the café. Cappuccino and caravans, paragliding and fossicking, fishing and sunbaking, car park and cemetery. All in the one place.

*

In no other town is one likely to find Aboriginal people so integral to the functioning of the place, so mainstream. Yet one can feel that even that is changing. In 1948, when Bob Noble came here, there were 350 whites. Those numbers have grown steadily. All the people who now flock to live in Broome, for part if not all of the year, are white. So white culture will end up dominating here, like everywhere else.

At the same time, many of the whites we are meeting are eager for rapport and understanding with the local people. For some of them it is the reason they are here: to learn and listen. Consciousness of the problem is like constant background chatter.

The other night at the Cable Beach Club I got talking to a bloke called Ted. He said how angry he was recently when he went to a beach he's been going to for years and was made to feel like a trespasser by the local Aborigines. He went on and on about how no-one really owns land.

'You and me only own land so long as we keep paying rates on it,' he said.

But then he told me that he had Aboriginal friends. He came here seventeen years ago to work for an Aboriginal band. He said that people in Broome used to mix in together much more than they do now. That divisions have been created.

You can't have a conversation in Broome without this subject coming up. This occurred to me again during the film evening at Perpetua's. The local film club, of which Bruce is an organiser, was showing *First Contact*, a documentary about the New Guinea highlanders' first meeting with white men. People here lean in masochistically on the problem of black/white relations, a scab they keep picking. Here, no white is allowed the luxury of forgetting.

∫ We're taking it in turns to despair. Depending on our mood, the house is a romantic if dilapidated charmer, or a hot tin box infested with mice, silverfish and red dust. Mostly the latter. Yet there is an untidy enchantment to the place: lying in bed at night on the open verandah, not even a flyscreen between us and the garden outside; sitting in the shady garden with a mosquito coil at our feet . . .

But during the day it is just a *hot, hot* tin box.

I still fantasise that we might settle to this old house, that its history and atmosphere will prove benign. It's a famous place in Broome; the family home of the D'Antoine's, one of the oldest Broome mixed-race families. Our landlord Donny's great-grandfather was a French beachcomber and, some say, a 'shooter'—that is, he shot Aborigines. According to Donny, old D'Antoine's business partner, Hunter, was the worse bastard of the two; at least D'Antoine didn't desert his many children by his Aboriginal 'harem', and made sure they got an education.

Donny is curly haired, with bright, friendly eyes behind glasses. He's charming, intelligent, and wonderfully easy to talk to. He finally turned up two hours late the second time we'd arranged to meet him. But talking to him was so pleasant that we didn't really get around to our long list of grievances and requests. We did ask him about the promised fence, though.

'Yeah, sorry about that,' he said, smiling easily. 'My brother was meant to help me but he's away in Darwin. Don't know when he'll be back. Would you like some fish? I caught a coupla big ones yesterday.'

Donny grew up in this house, although his mother and father only rented until the old Malay who owned it died. Aborigines didn't have the right to own property until the referendum of '67. Even after that, difficulties were put in their way. The Government owned large blocks of land all around Broome, and refused to give them up. 'But when Lord McAlpine wanted land for his zoo, he got hectares of it, cheap.'

Donny is bitter about the current land and property boom. For years, land was not available to his countrymen, and now they're watching Broome being sold off to developers and the white middle class. 'You go down to the supermarket and you don't know anyone any more. They smile at you, but you think, 'Who are you?'.

When Donny is here talking at the kitchen table, it's easier to see why his house is legendary. You can imagine it full of people, the garden with its chairs and open-air beds all occupied, the barbecue going (Don is renowned for his fish barbecues), the guitars strumming under the huge tamarind tree, the dozens of plants freshly watered, the garden raked. This is the place of many genial gatherings, parties, music making. The place where Jimmy Chi's hit musical *Bran Nue Dae* was conceived.

The garden is obviously the great theatre and living area. The house is nothing more than a roof and storage space. The large tamarind tree next door (subsumed by a new security-gated development, but still shading our garden) has a heritage order placed on it.

It's both living history and a dump, this house. Its soul is gone. Don has gone to live in his ex-wife's newer, more modern home (she's gone south), and the place feels its neglect and decay.

Night of the Rats

At about 3 a.m. you woke me, terrified. We'd finally put out rat-killer and the rats were having their last party, doing skids and wheelies across the tin roof and down the rafters. Chittering, chattering and fighting. The noise was extraordinary.

We got up, put on a light. We clutched each other in the middle of the kitchen as the rats raced about the open ceiling, dropping from the beams. You screeched; I screamed in reaction. We put all the lights on, got back into bed and listened to them till dawn, till their bedtime.

In the morning Donny explained that a whole colony of them lives in the date palm that scrapes the roof.

'I'm not staying here tonight,' you said. I agreed.

So we've moved into a little motel for as long as it takes to kill the lot of them. Every morning we return to what you've dubbed 'The Rat Palazzo' and we fight over who is to go inside first to find the newly dead rats. You hated them alive, I dread them dead.

But we did make a huge advance this morning. We got back to the Rat Palazzo before 9 a.m. and set up the computers. Me on a makeshift table in a corner of the verandah; you in the garden with an extension cord snaking to the power point in the laundry. But by 10 a.m. I was sweating. I peeled my top off and sat typing in shorts and bra. By 11 a.m. we both had to have a lie down, after a mere two hours of sweaty effort. Still, we've made a start and stopped obsessing about this bloody house.

*

On Wednesday evening we tagged along with Perpetua to the opening of a new art gallery at the Cable Beach Club, the five-star resort that Lord McAlpine created. It's a strange kind of gallery—displays of pearls and some mediocre art only a metre or two from the desk selling tours and toiletries. But there were a couple of good paintings by Robert Juniper, who lives in Broome part-time.

It was a hot, sticky night. The champagne grew warm in my hand halfway through a glass. The crowd—local money, tourists, gallery owners and art groupies—milled about sweatily.

Stephen (Baamba) Albert was there with his wife Pam. His was the only black face among the crowd. We met Baamba last year. He is all charm and intelligence, with a bit of bullshit mixed in, an impish grin under a big hat with the Aboriginal colours on the band. Very much at ease in the white man's world. Very much the professional black man.

Baamba used to be a Canberra-based bureaucrat until he became the star in Jimmy Chi's *Bran Nue Dae*. These days, when he's not acting and singing, he runs a little outfit called Baamba's Chinatown Tours. As you stroll through Chinatown on foot, Baamba tells stories about how the town used to be when he was a kid. Every few hundred yards Pam is there in the car, with orange juice and slabs of watermelon for refreshment. At the end, Baamba pulls out his guitar and sings a song.

Pam is an attractive white woman in her forties with a permanent harassed/resigned air about her. She's clearly the organiser, he the star. She looks tired—as if Broome and Baamba between them might be a bit much for her—but committed, too.

We wander around the manicured resort and share a pizza at 'Lord Mac's'. The place is pleasant enough; large, lush gardens, if synthetic—touches of Bali and India mixed in with 'Broome style'. Within yards of the resort, across the road on Cable Beach, we come across a beat-up old car with young joint smokers hanging out of it. Thank God for such contrasts.

*

We've started looking for somewhere else to live. The turning point came when I reached for the electric jug on the kitchen counter and found a huge not-quite-dead rat right next to it. So now the hunt is on for another house, flat, anything...At the brink of the full tourist season, an ordinary two-bedroom flat, in one of several dilapidated complexes around town, would be a lucky find. Just about everyone is temporary here, and after temporary accommodation.

And we feel more than temporary—precarious, and a bit panicked.

Yet some things about this town already feel well-loved and familiar. The precious soft coolness of the early morning (precious because you know it will be gone in an hour or two), the glimpses of calm aqua sea from suburban streets, the shock of red earth hard up against that spectacular blue, an afternoon iced coffee at Bloom's café on the main street, an evening beer with Bruce in the back garden, letting the quiet settle.

Real estate and other first impressions

Hunting around the real estate scene can tell you a lot about a place. In Broome at the moment there are at least four cheaply made, superficially smart complexes at various stages of construction. The target market is either investors-cum-holiday makers or local yuppies here for a few years to make a quick quid. There's also a large number of bland four-bedroom houses around Cable Beach, essentially suburban but superficially in 'Broome style' (corrugated iron walls, a verandah, some aqua-blue woodwork). The genuine old Broome homes are rare, unless tarted up enormously and selling for half a million.

There is a huge influx of newcomers. Most of the people we meet have arrived recently; six months ago, two years ago, a few weeks ago. All of them 'love it here', all of them want to stay. But some time in the next few years they'll be transferred elsewhere, or the dust and heat will get to them and they will move on. The rental rate is the reverse of the national average—65 per cent rental versus 35 per cent ownership.

Saturday we seemed to spend the whole day running around looking at furniture and second-hand fridges. Then a breakthrough—or so it seemed. We saw a little house, furnished, that would be perfect. But the agent couldn't tell us if it was available because the owners are overseas and out of contact. Perpetua, who knows the owners, tried to contact them for us, but without success. Stalemate.

Perpetua at the Thai Tea House

Perpetua is a slight, attractive woman somewhere in her fifties, part of the Durack clan which has such long, deep connections in the Kimberley. We first met her through Bruce when we were here on holiday last year. That was before the Eddie Burrup scandal broke, when she and Bruce were still good friends.

Some years ago Perpetua came up here to live and opened an art gallery in one of the renovated McAlpine properties. It's a lovely old place next door to the Rat Palazzo, with deep verandahs, oiled floorboards, no air-conditioning or other mod cons. It houses a discreet collection of quality art works

for sale. Perpetua 'camps', as she puts it, in a couple of small rooms out the back.

We both like Perpetua. She's an interesting blend of gentility and toughness, conventionality and adventurousness, the orthodox and the unorthodox, all packaged in a fluttery, polite, nervous manner and a trim, neat prettiness.

We had dinner with her at the Thai Tea House, which is nothing like the immaculate Thai restaurants of Sydney. Just metal chairs and tables in a concreted-over yard. No tablecloths, no decorations. The food is strong-tasting and a bit crude; no concessions to Western tastes.

Perpetua gave us fascinating snippets of information about her other lives—in Africa, Japan, here. But only snippets.

Her memories of Broome in the late forties and fifties are of a tiny forgotten place, where all the kids, black and white, mucked in together down at Town Beach. In the days when the whites were very much a minority, the races mixed more easily, and black people seemed to invite white people into their lives more. As a child Perpetua spent many holidays in Broome with her aunt, Mary Durack (of *Kings in Grass Castles* fame), and Mary's husband Horrie Miller and their six offspring. Horrie founded

Robertson Miller airlines, the pioneering aviation company of the north-west. He and Mary spent much of their lives apart, she in Perth, he in Broome, getting together as a family during school holidays. A pattern, Perpetua says, for many marriages in the north till very recently. The women hacked it for short periods, but sooner or later they fled back to Perth.

*

Miracle of miracles! Out of the blue, Perpetua has had a call from our prospective landlady. She was ringing from a hospital bed in County Galway, Ireland, totally unaware that Perpetua had been trying to find her.

We call her at the Galway hospital. We establish that we both have a dog called Scruffy. And the place is ours, in principle. But first, Lyn Page, another friend of hers, has to suss us out.

Lyn lives in a rather wonderful Bali-style house—no windows or solid doors, all timber shutters and open elegance. She's a local councillor, business woman and ex-Sydney socialite. Mad as a hatter in a loveable extrovert way. She is trim, dark and lively, with extraordinary black eyes, big tits and a small waist.

She does most of the talking, but we seem to pass the test. We go back to the motel, full of hope that we'll have somewhere to live soon.

*

Sometimes, for minutes at a time, I can forget I'm in Australia. I could be somewhere in the obscure and humid backblocks of South America or Asia: the rutted roads high with red dust; the randomly alternating messy poverty and manicured lawns; the high metal fences; the half-finished, already rotting projects of one kind or another.

It was actually coolish this morning, cloudy, a bit of rain—cause for celebration. We went for a drive around the area behind Cable Beach. From the car the bush is just boring scrub, but once you walk in it, it comes alive. The grey foliage turns the softest of green and the monotony transforms into lovely shapes and subtle shades, hiding a modest flower here, a grotesque seed pod there.

We drove towards Gantheaume Point. A few kilometres out of town down a wide swath of orange-red pindan dirt road is the racecourse, around which Broome's social life revolves for a few weeks each 'winter'. When you're driving on this road it feels like you're heading straight for the desert, then suddenly you see a well-tended race track and a grand-stand. On the other side of the road there are glimpses of the sea.

Just before the racecourse we turned off the road and saw a sweep of white beach, a sudden mysterious change from the fine red pindan. In the distance we could make out a couple of people and the forms of horses standing still in the ocean, the water washing over their haunches. This is the far end of Cable Beach, where the tourists don't come.

Further down the road, red cliffs hang directly over the sea. Large seabirds wheel overhead. On a small pinkish beach below the cliffs are hundreds of rocks, large and small—gnome-like shapes in striated bands of red, yellow, white, pink and mauve. This is Riddell Beach. We wander around picking up the occasional rock or shell. I strike a bargain with the resident spirits: if we take just two things away, a rock and a shell, and leave all the others we admire behind, will that be okay?

Bruce says that he won't go to Riddell on his own; there's a sense of danger and of spirits not altogether beneficent. It's also said that Riddell Beach is a women's place, so maybe that is why he is ill at ease there.

At night we go for a drink at the Continental Hotel's 'Lugger Bar', and we're back in Australia all right. Outside the drive-in bottle shop, there's a knot of black drunken 'countrymen' (as Aborigines sometimes call themselves here), and inside, a cacophony of sozzled white blokes.

We have a couple of drinks, then walk back to our motel in the windy coolness that hints of the next day's rain.

On the fringe

Broome is such a frenetic place, compared to Bundanoon, the town closest to our farm in the Southern Highlands. True, Bundanoon is smaller—a quarter of the size at best—and Broome is particularly busy at the moment, with the tourist season getting underway and the annual Fringe Festival starting. But it's more than that. This town is a highly charged confluence of energies—artistic, entrepreneurial, alternative, Aboriginal. It's a headquarters for the Aboriginal renaissance, the hub of the pearling industry, a burgeoning tourist town. It's on the edge of the 'last frontier' and a refuge from it, too.

At one of the Fringe Festival art exhibitions at the Durack Gallery, I met Desiree who had some lovely coolamons and feathered things on display. She's a lively, articulate young Aboriginal woman, if a bit overwhelming. Only twenty-seven, with jobs as an ABC announcer in Sydney and Broome already behind her, she's 'dropped out' and is living with a Dutchman north of Broome. They have become part of the Goolarabooloo community. Desiree is learning things from the Goolarabooloo—like how to make coolamons, which her own people on the north coast of New South Wales can no longer teach her.

The Fringe Festival program is full of art shows, events, workshops. Something every night for the last four nights. A mini film festival—independent and indigenous films—was held in the big grounds behind the Goolarri radio station. At least two hundred people of all sorts, straggling in with their blankets and cushions. Quite a few non-whites but still very much in the minority. Bruce was at the projector; he's the town's projector man. The films were a mixed bag. There was one we both liked—a simple story about an Aboriginal kid and his father.

Next day, at the People's Choice art show, there was a little composition that caught my eye—a swirl of red sand surrounded by a swirl of white, a bleached bottle and a palm husk. The inscription read, 'If only there was as much wilderness out there as there is within'. It was the creation of Marnie Hutchinson, local artist and sister of Tony Hutchinson, the real estate agent. The Hutchinsons have been here for twenty-odd years—a long time in Broometime.

Occasionally Fringe feels uniquely Broome, but most of the time it could be a Fringe Festival anywhere. It gets wearying. We long for a night in front of the telly.

*

Last night we dropped in on Lyn Page again. Yes, the landlady has confirmed that the house on Guy Street is ours, and Lyn is to get the keys from the agent.

Lyn was in a convivial mood. It was out with the champagne, and 'Stay for dinner!' A mad couple of hours followed. Tales of Lyn's socialite past in Sydney when she spent $500 a week on clothes; her years as a restaurant owner and mistress of a prominent Jewish businessman. One day she threw him over and abandoned the Sydney social scene. It dawned on her that it was all just a tad empty.

She has a more useful life these days. She runs a public relations/desktop publishing business, and has a seat on the Shire Council. She's running for pre-selection as Liberal candidate for the huge seat of Kalgoorlie, of which Broome is a part. In Broome she's a large fish in a small pond.

Lyn is erratic, playful, sexy. Also bright, and despite some hair-raising opinions and remarks, quite shrewd. We reeled out of her house well fed (she's one of those enviable cooks who whip up something terrific while chatting), the worse for champagne and exhausted from so much talk.

Two

Fringe finale—Sorry Day—Visiting Bob Noble—Film night—The Catholic Bishop of Broome—Seeing and not knowing—Bill Reed

Monday, May 25

We were a bit worried that Donny might be hurt when we told him we were moving. But he just gave a small, half-crooked grin and said, 'I'm surprised you lasted as long as you did.'

Now we're going mad with frustration, waiting to get into our new place. Lyn, who's been delegated to fetch the key from the agent, can't understand our anxiety. We're still paying rent to Donny for the Palazzo, plus eighty bucks a night for the motel. And we're feeling increasingly homeless.

Fringe finale

On the last day of the Fringe Festival there was a kids' concert at Town Beach in the late afternoon. A simple stage was set up near the café, with the palm trees as a backdrop. Families were spread out on the grass with rugs and picnics; children ran about freely. There were tourists and young feral lovers, arms entwined. Black and white, young and old, everyone in it together.

On the stage, Master of Ceremonies for the Broome High School band, was an energetic middle-aged man with a broad, alert face and thick black hair, greying. He was singing the praises of the local high school. 'There's no reason to send your kids down south for their schooling,' he told the audience. 'They'll get a good education right here in Broome.'

While the band was packing up its gear I talked to him. His name is Peter Ghouse and it turns out he's not from Broome at all. He's Malaysian and his mother was Chinese. He first came here in the early eighties and in Broome has found his true home. He teaches music and Indonesian at the high school.

'Music here is very strong,' he said. 'There's a lot of players, lots of energy and people wanting to play. In a town like Broome, there are less distractions. Kids make their own music. It's always been like that. Broome has produced a lot of good musicians—look at Jimmy Chi, look at the Pigrams.

'Broome's a great leveller of people. In Broome, even Lord McAlpine gets around in slippers with his shirt undone.'

Attitudes towards Alistair McAlpine, the eccentric English lord who's credited with putting Broome on the map, are sharply divided. People still talk about him all the time, although he's rarely seen in town these days. When he first came here nearly twenty years ago he fell in love with the ramshackle air of the place: the sprawling, open-sided houses in their gardens shaded by mango trees; the pawpaws falling from the trees; the violently coloured bougainvillea. He started buying the town up—twenty, thirty houses. He could see the potential. Then he built the Cable Beach Club resort, and the zoo, now defunct. He is almost solely responsible for preserving the look of the town, a look that is now replicated in any new building. But many people resent McAlpine for the rapid growth of the town and the influx of visitors who overtook Broome.

When the zoo closed (McAlpine blamed its failure on the pilots' strike of 1989), the land was subdivided. It is now covered with expensive homes and holiday apartments, way beyond the reach of the local people.

In that regard, McAlpine was just the last straw. The Native Welfare Act of WA had already done the real damage. It's instructive to hear Donny talk about the Native Welfare Act, the way it prevented Aboriginal people from getting on, stopped them from buying land, the curfews it imposed on them—things that were still happening in the 1960s.

There are all sorts of anachronistic laws still on the WA statutes. Among them the Crimes Act, which according to Bruce's friend Angela, who works for Legal Aid, dates from 1913 and outlaws, amongst other things, the riding of camels on a main street.

Sorry Day

Sorry Day in Broome was not a big affair. 'Reconciliation goes on here every day,' the principal of Broome primary school told me. The school decided against a general assembly. Instead, each teacher discussed reconciliation in their classroom in a way appropriate for the age of the students. About a third of the school's students are indigenous.

In the afternoon we went to a ceremony on the site of the former Catholic 'orphanage'. Chairs were arranged in a semicircle on a scrappy piece of open ground. When everyone was assembled—there were maybe a hundred and fifty people—the dull religious music that had been playing changed to Archie Roach's 'Taking the Children Away' and everyone stood up. Three figures began to walk towards us from the gates: an Aboriginal woman carrying the Aboriginal flag, a white woman with the Australian flag, and a Torres Strait Island man carrying the blue, green and white Torres Strait Island flag. As the music played, a few Aboriginal women in the audience wept.

There were short speeches—from the woman minister of the Uniting Church (on behalf of all the churches), from the acting commander of police, a big man in khaki and long socks—'the Aboriginal and Torres Strait Islander flags fly outside our police station, alongside the Australian flag'—and from the Shire President, Angus Murray, also in shorts and long socks. Murray didn't say 'Sorry' but he spoke of the Shire's commitment to reconciliation and the formal agreement with the traditional owners of Broome.

At the end a young priest, Brother Shane Wood, launched the Kimberley Sorry Book and people queued up to sign it.

*

I've decided to do a little work for the local rag, as a good way of getting to know what's going on in the town. Returning to a previous existence, and quite a strange feeling it is, too. Very familiar in some respects but totally out of kilter in others: Why here? Now? It's more than ten years since I worked regularly as a journalist. Spending time in the tiny office of *The Broome Advertiser*—total staff five—reminds me of how much I loathe offices. Much nicer here, in the garden with the lizards, even though it will soon be too hot to work.

 To help forget our housing dramas I went with Annie to Derby, two hours north-east of here, on her assignment for the *Advertiser*. A group of traditional owners was signing an historic agreement which will allow mining giant Rio Tinto to explore for minerals on their country, a remote stretch of land north of Derby, accessible only by boat or helicopter.

There were perhaps twenty people sitting under the trees outside the hostel when we arrived—a handful of elderly Aborigines, a few younger men, a couple of white lawyers and advisers from the Kimberley Land Council (KLC), and the men from Rio Tinto to one side. A striking white woman in a flamboyant red hat walked towards the group, a very old, frail Aboriginal lady leaning on her arm.

I sat down next to an elderly man, Ken Oobagooma. He and his wife. They both had the indefinable air of leaders.

'Are you pleased with the agreement?' I asked.

'Only thing important,' he said, 'that it come from the heart. Both sides.'

His wife gave me a penetrating look and put the fingertips of her hands together. 'We have to meet like this, you understand?' she said.

Inside, in the hostel's recreation room, the director of the KLC, Peter Yu, began the formalities. He is smallish and trim in slim-fitting corduroys, sports a Chinese-style goatee. His speech was aimed equally at the press, the company and the traditional owners. He's very experienced, very smooth, very likeable.

The atmosphere was polite, wary but hopeful. The KLC's chairman— hugely fat, youngish, wearing a sloppy joe, thongs and the Aboriginal colours on his big black hat—recalled the politicising effect of his early days at Noonkambah. A couple of older Aboriginal men also spoke, their soft, accented voices hard for me to understand, expressing fears that this agreement will have to be renegotiated constantly, that Rio Tinto's intentions may not be 'from the heart'. They wanted reassurance that the company will assist them in getting to and from their land. The company spokesman addressed then respectfully, talking of co-operation jobs, and so on.

With this agreement, if minerals are eventually found, the traditional owners will be able to say, 'You can't mine here because it's important to us, but a kilometre along, or past that point, yes, you can.' And there'll be some jobs and training for Aboriginal youth, in exchange for huge profits for the company. This is exactly what the Howard Government wants to get rid of—countrymen negotiating with miners about the use of their traditional land.

Wednesday

The computer's back in storage under the bed (there's no way to lock the Rat Palazzo), so I'm forced back to the journal. God knows where the last few days have gone. We're both increasingly disoriented from a combination of too much happening and our continuing homelessness. Everything seems either too fast or impossibly slow. Is this what they mean by Broometime?

We're packed, the phone is about to go off, and we still can't get hold of the key to our new house. It's pushing my buttons—fear and homelessness. I have to remind myself that it's not Hungary during the war, it's just a little glitch in accommodation in hot, lazy Broome.

Visiting Bob Noble

Bob lives in a shabby tin cottage on the best piece of waterfront in town, right next door to the ghastly half-finished development called The Catalinas. He's been offered $500 000, then $700 000 to sell up, but he's sitting tight. Says he's waiting until the developers offer him a full million.

Bob's in his late seventies, ruddy, silver-haired, still handsome in a raffish way, keen eyes, aware of his own charm. When I arrive with the tape recorder he's on the verandah with a coterie of blokes. He seems to love to have people around him but takes little notice of them.

We have to go inside to talk because the noise from the building site next door drowns everything out. His living room is a mishmash of broken-down furniture and mysterious paraphernalia: a photograph of his wife in World War II army uniform, a couple of kitsch paintings of semi-nude women, papers and general litter. It's not depressing, just a bit grimy and scattered, like a larger version of a bloke's shed. A few yards away is his real shed, where he's restoring an antique sideboard. In front of the shed is an old boat he's fixing up.

'I bought myself a yacht yesterday,' he says gleefully. 'I'm repairing it already . . . I bought it cheap. Guess how much I bought it for, go on!'

I can't guess

'Fifteen hundred! People say it must have cost five, six thousand.'

It's a broken-down old thing, splintered and paint-peeling. Near it sits an old rusty caravan, of which he's also very proud.

Bob's wife lives in the old family home a couple of blocks away. They've lived separately for many years. 'We're good mates,' he says.

He's straight off on his 'life story'—an often-told tale of strung-together exploits: cattle rustling, crocodile shooting, gaol, fights and feuds, big money.

Bob came to Broome after World War II, newly married, disillusioned with army life and eager for something different. He took up the trade he'd first learned, butchering, with a spot of cattle rustling on the side.

'I knew every part of butchering. I'd go out to the bush, knock a few beasts off. Bring 'em back, cut it all up, tray it, and my partner [who owned the iceworks] would sell it. I supplied all the pubs, restaurants, serveries I was even sending meat to Derby, by plane.'

Soon he was regularly supplementing his earnings from the butcher shop with cattle rustling. 'I wouldn't go to the same property two or three times—I'd move around. There's a plain out here called Buckley's Plain, just north of Broome. And I used to call it Buckley's Bank, because nobody looked after it, nobody attended to it. I could go out and get beef any time I wanted. Beasts would come right into the middle of town and drink water, right to the Shire's bloody back door. I'm not kidding you. The money was unreal. Unreal. Everything I touched was cash.

'I mustered wild horses, too, from Buckley's Plain. Mustered them, sold them. From the cash I made from the muster I bought property at the back of Cable Beach—five acres. I put a tank on it, a windmill, cultivated it and I turned it into abattoirs. That was about '54. All this land around me, it was vacant, all the Japanese market gardens had been abandoned, and I bought one of them; that was another three acres.

'I had a piggery there, too. This fella from Derby caught these wild pigs for me for five pound a head. Some were enormous—300 pounds. Some were little ones, but they grow. I had this utility going around the town for me, all the scraps from the pubs feeding 'em, plus all my scraps from the butcher shop.'

Bob's probably worth a lot of money. From the way he talks, he's got a nose for it. I thinks that's the story of Broome, to some extent, even now. Adventurers of all kinds, and all nationalities, with a dream of making money.

When I get home, Annie brandishes the key to our house. Tomorrow we can move in!

Film night

The image of film nights at the CWA hall may stay with us when much else about Broome has faded. The small wooden hall is almost on the waterfront, a short stroll from Town Beach. It's like all CWA country halls—homespun curtains, motto on the wall ('Through country women, for country women, by country women', or some such). There's a dozen of us at best, mostly scruffy, clutching our bottles of water under the ceiling fans, not saying much.

The film club is Bruce's contribution to Broome's cultural life. He is in charge of getting the movies sent up, and also of manning the projector. He fiddles with it with slightly trembling fingers (there is always a problem) and finally out rolls some old classic or worthy documentary into the humid night air.

At the end, Bruce goes out for a relieved cigarette. A couple of comments are exchanged, and we move off, some walking, others climbing into beat-up kombis, one man in his little motorised wheelchair with jaunty flags attached—a trademark around town.

Last night was *Monsieur Hulot's Holiday*, a period piece even when I last saw it thirty years ago. Still wonderful.

Thursday

We've moved, thank God, and we're almost through the first bout of cleaning, rearranging and shopping.

Now we're finally in our pleasant, renovated (and more suburban) little house I think we're happier because we can control it, put our own personality on it. The Rat Palazzo had its own history and personality, one that came close to menacing us.

Yet paradoxically, homesickness is hitting us badly for the first time. I miss the dogs, I long to be in our cool wild garden or slogging up the hill past the cows in the cold and wet in my gumboots. Instead I'm wandering around here on these flat hot streets in my shorts and sandals, feeling lost and alienated.

At least this house has a fenced yard, which has activated the idea of asking our friend Margie to bring the dogs with her when she flies up next month. The mere thought of having them to fuss over again makes me feel a bit better.

June 1

Today we've taken our cue from the outside world. It's a public holiday (WA's Foundation Day) and we've taken the whole day off. It was delicious getting up late, sensuous to lie in bed lazily stroking each other. Then we wandered down to Matso's to drink coffee on the verandah. The sun was fierce by 11 a.m. We walked home slowly.

How tempting to turn this into a nine-month holiday. In bed this morning we discussed trying a middle course—between 'sinking in' and seeing what comes to us, and the pro-active approach that feels so uncomfortable.

*

Now that we're organised, there are no more excuses to put off work. I've set up a table in the spare room as my desk and you're using the covered terrace as your office. I wonder how long you'll last out there, even if it is relatively cool at the moment—just under 30 degrees Celsius.

We're beginning to realise that there's no such thing here as cold weather. The midday temperature rarely drops below 30 degrees, even in June. The nights can be cool, but it's the level of humidity that marks the real difference between the Wet and the Dry.

Most people think we're here to write about Broome's exotic history. They're puzzled when we say we want to write about contemporary Broome, as if their present lives could not possibly hold interest or validity. But that's exactly what interests us: the minutiae of what's happening now.

But I'm still having difficulty approaching new people. I had to force myself to speak to Wendy and Sue at the bookshop yesterday. It was a start, a small achievement to come home to you with.

Wendy, who owns the shop, is a small, chunky white woman, wispy blond hair, permanently quizzical eyes. She was Baamba Albert's first wife. She was a nun before she married Baamba and had two kids with him.

Wendy caught on quickly to the kind of book we want to write. She seems very quick off the mark generally. She talked about the gradings of interracial mixing in Broome: the whites who never mix with the blacks, the blacks who never mix with the whites, and the whole range in between; the complex social strata in the town; the hierarchies, even among the drop-outs.

The Catholic Bishop of Broome

On that fateful holiday in Broome last year, I was already intrigued by the bishop. We were out on a Sunday morning stroll. Turning a corner we saw a sea of cars. We thought there must be a football match on. But it was the roll-up for the Catholic Church. We went inside. My notes from that time read:

'The church is packed. A young Asian man stands at the door; Aborigines, serious, neat and silent, sitting towards the back. An old dog lying quietly at the door while the humans just walk around him.

Inside, little girls of all colours decked out in white finery for their confirmation. A simple triptych behind the altar. The priest (the bishop I think), a burly, olive-skinned man with a shiny pate and a certain command about him, refers to 'these difficult times', meaning Hanson times. He talks about unemployment—how it would be 33 per cent or higher if it weren't for the work-for-the-dole scheme which most Aboriginal people are on.

I think I want to do a book on this place. I start planning it in my head.'

Annie had the same thought at the same time.

Last Sunday I went to mass again at the same church, Our Lady Queen of Peace, just across the road from the Rat Palazzo. Again a packed church, an interesting sermon by the bishop, and around me little pictures of Broome life: a young married couple, she blonde, he huge and dark, and their two gorgeous brown children; an older woman, part-Aboriginal, part-Filipino perhaps, crying into the hem of her skirt at the end of the *Missa Kimberley* mass.

But how to reach this Broome?

I want to get an introduction to the bishop.

Seeing and not knowing

I often see the true inhabitants of Broome walking up and down the street outside our house. They stroll along, talking, pushing a pram, laughing, sometimes fighting. Most of the people one sees walking are black—those various shades of black or brown or honey that one sees everywhere on the streets. This is about as close as we have come to seeing the everyday life of the mixed races of Broome.

And it's becoming frustrating, this seeing and not knowing. In the few weeks we've been here we have met dozens of white people. At meetings and community events I strike up conversations, am introduced to people. We exchange information, know when to smile and laugh, slide easily into familiar conversational mode. We have not met before, we live on different sides of a vast continent, yet we know how to behave with each other. Centuries of Europeanness buffers us.

But so far it is only at Mass or some church event that I've seen a truly mixed Broome group. Here, too, we are introduced. But the people are shy, not sure what they are expected to say to us, and conversation falters. If I show an interest in them, they look puzzled. Why do you want to know about me? The old men are different: dignified and assured. Then language becomes the problem. They talk but I cannot follow them; I understand maybe three words in ten. They talk on, calmly, and I could scream in frustration. Then someone arrives to take them home, a delicate shy-smiled niece, or a surly teenage boy, and they rise painfully, lean on their sticks and shuffle off.

Tuesday

A somewhat better day today. Not a huge amount achieved, mind you. The Shire meeting (everyone calls the council 'the Shire') was even drearier than most council meetings. Anything interesting was in camera. Most recommendations were passed without comment or debate. Lyn Page had three motions about the preservation of historic buildings. They were passed unanimously, if unenthusiastically, as if there was an undercurrent of resentment about having to preserve things.

A proposal to get SBS television up here got the go-ahead. The Shire only has to put up half the money—$25 000. The Kimberley Development Corp and Western Metals are contributing the rest. One cute thing—there was a petition from forty-three inmates of Broome Prison who are keen to get SBS!

There are three Aboriginal people on the council and six whites. 'All real estate agents,' Bruce said when I met him at Town Beach afterwards, (alluding to the ethos of the white councillors, if not their actual occupations.)

Bill Reed

I've already seen him around town several times, sometimes in company with Perpetua: a shortish, ruddy man, probably in his sixties, well-preserved and neat, with an immaculately parted short-back-and-sides haircut. Always with a genial air (although word is that he's not always as kindly as he looks). Bill Reed is a major player in the pearling business, but he tries to keep a lowish profile. He came to Broome in the early seventies on a year's consultancy at Kuri Bay. Now he runs Linney's, the most elegant and upmarket of the pearl shops.

'When I first arrived in Broome I saw this collection of white iron buildings and thought, "My God, is this it?" But somehow the place had tremendous charm about it. It intrigued me because it had scarcely changed—it was still a colonial outpost. The member for the Upper House dressed in a white suit and a pith helmet. I just couldn't believe it. She was a pretty wild-west town. At the Roebuck Hotel there'd be wild sprees—black-fellas, whitefellas, dogs, women, men...

'The pearling was pretty moribund. There was just the one big company. Streeter and Male were the Australian partners in it, based at Kuri Bay. There was one plane a week back then, on Fridays,' Bill says. 'People used to come out to the airstrip just to see the plane land. Just to see it! They introduced a second plane on Tuesday. I remember talking to an old Aboriginal chap one day; the plane went over and he said, "Gawd, I must've been drunk. A bad week. It's Friday already."

'I said, "No, Mickey, it's not Friday, it's Tuesday. Now we have two planes a week." "Aw, that's very bad," he said. I said, "what's bad about that?" "Now you don't know what day of the week it is."'

Bill had worked overseas for twenty years, doing research and development into pearling for the United Nations and the Food and Agriculture Organisation before coming to Broome.

In the 1970s they were still 'swinging the lead', that is, dropping a piece of lead with tallow on it to see what the sea floor was like. 'My God, I couldn't believe it. Even in Africa we didn't do that.'

But times have changed. Broome is now the world leader in pearl farming, with the most advanced technology. Exports have gone from about $25 million a year when he arrived to about $250 million a year. Most of Broome's pearls—about 95 per cent—are exported. Until fifteen years ago all the pearls were packed up and sent away. It was Bill who set up the first pearl shop in the town.

'People said I was crazy, that Australians wouldn't buy Broome pearls because they were too expensive. Now there are half a dozen shops with a range of pearl jewellery greater than you would see in any city in the world—and a lot of it sells. There are some people who come to Broome specifically to buy pearls.'

Bill says, 'When I left Australia in the 50s it was the most racist place you could possibly imagine. We were the good fellows. Even the Poms weren't much good, but as for the rest of the wogs, frogs, wops, dagos and fry-pan faces...Well I came back and found all my friends working for the wogs, wops and dagos and Australia was a much better place as a result.'

People still travelled up to Broome by boat. The boats went through to Singapore. 'A lot of the pearling industry was still indentured labourers. Malays, Filipinos. Recruited through Squire and Butterworth in Singapore. How colonial can you get! At Streeter and Male they still had ink wells and wrote with pen and ink, the clerks standing up behind the desk.'

'You almost expect to see that even now!' I say.

'That's true. Everything used to close for two hours in the middle of the day—perhaps that's not such a bad idea. But the one restaurant in town, Wings, used to put a sign up: "Closed for Lunch". If you wanted lunch you had to go before 12 or after 2, because Mrs Wing wanted her sleep.

'The main employer in those days was probably the abattoir, which only worked for about six months of the year. Soon after that, Woodside Petroleum came in exploring here, and we thought that was a boom because it brought a hundred people into town. A few years later, Woodside left and people said, "Broome's finished. It's the end of Broome." Now businesses come and go and there's scarcely a hiccup.

'Back then the roads were all dirt. Once we got the bitumen road from here south, the tourists started coming. It's a much easier place to live now. You can get fifty-five varieties of cheese or bread or yoghurt. Before, there was one truck a week and it wasn't refrigerated. Most people had a vegie patch. You had to.'

Bill says the social stratification in the town has been breaking down for a number of years. When he first came to town, the Male family were on the top. Being invited there for dinner meant you had made it. 'If you were the bank manager you might be invited for afternoon tea.'

What's interesting about Bill Reed is that he is very much part of the business world; sophisticated, wealthy, but also a great supporter of the Catholic Church, and of Aboriginal organisations and causes. He turns up at community events, and puts his money where his heart is.

According to Bill, recognition of native title has in general improved relations in the town. There's now respect for Aboriginal people that wasn't there before, helped by the success of creative artists like Baamba Albert, Jimmy Chi and Queenie McKenzie.

Bill says the whites who grumble about native title holding up development are 'just a small minority'. 'The white-shoe brigade want to come in and make a quick buck and get out. But a bit of delay could result in a better development. All they need to do is budget in an extra year to negotiate with the local people. If you don't want to do that, go to Queensland.'

Bearings

Three

Meeting Fongie—An extraordinary trajectory—Tea after Mass on Sunday

A The Queensland elections yesterday and One Nation may have as many as ten seats. The Coalition bore the brunt of it—an 18 per cent swing against them. Labor may just win a majority of seats; otherwise it will be a three-way right-wing coalition.

We're shocked. Race has been the issue in this election, no matter how much Pauline Hanson denies it. Beneath her appeals to 'ordinary Australians'—simply by making appeals to 'ordinary Australians'—is the message that it is 'us' versus 'them'.

∫ Neither of us is doing well at the moment. You're in bed doing one of your escapist sleeps and I'm in a foul mood, not knowing what to do with myself. I feel as if this whole enterprise is unravelling, and possibly us along with it.

It's not just homesickness. It's probably more to do with One Nation's success in Queensland. You're probably right when you say that the Hansonites' triumph merely serves to carve up the conservative vote and brings the right wing out of its National Party closet. But I still have this hateful, stomach-churning feeling that Australia is changing fundamentally for the worse.

Over twenty years ago when I heard that Whitlam was sacked I instinctively rushed out onto the street, but I was in outer-suburban Blacktown and the streets were empty. A similar feeling now—do something, contribute to the debate, don't reproach yourself later as people did in Europe in the late thirties *for not having taken notice of the signs.*

Here in Broome it isn't, of course, at all as we hoped. It's far more complex, and more depressing. Three streets or less from the elegant, renovated pearling-master homes hidden in their deeply shaded gardens are the pockets of Aboriginal housing. This is where the roads gets stragglier, the dust deeper. Many of the yards are scattered with junk and the houses are unkempt. Every night drunken Aborigines gather around the bottle-strewn vacant block opposite the Conti's bottle shop. The squalor is half-hidden in Broome, but it's still there.

It seems, after just a month here, that those who are most part of Broome's fabric, who are comfortable or who have 'made it', are of mixed race. Their ethnicity is so embedded in the town's history that it's no longer an issue. But many of the town's Aborigines still live in an underworld. An underworld I'm scared of and don't even know if I want to enter.

The Hanson debate takes on an extra dimension here. 'Multiculturalism' is part of people's day-to-day lives. I like that, yet strangely, instead of feeling more implicated in Broome, closer to Asia, closer to Aboriginal culture, I'm feeling more European than ever, more aware of my difference. That my family has been on this continent for five generations seems hardly to count.

Maybe this is the reason for my continuing sense of alienation. Ten times a day I say to myself, 'I don't want to be here.' Then I look around at the blue sky, the gorgeous weather, the leisurely pace, and I think, 'Are you mad!?'

Sometimes this place feels both totally artificial—a European outpost on the edge of nowhere—and boringly familiar—just another Australian suburb full of people obsessed with their cars, their booze and their holidays. On ABC radio yesterday, the enthusiastic morning presenter attempted to have a talkback session on 'Your hopes and dreams for the Kimberley'. She got one caller.

Maybe you're surprised by feeling that you don't quite belong 'in your own country', despite your Irish Catholic roots going back five generations. Whereas I quite enjoy the not-quite-belongingness. The part of me that's still a migrant kid is used to that outsider-ness. And there's an edge to Broome that I like. I like its raffishness, the mixed currents of anarchy and order. The history of Broome is still alive. In most other small places the past feels long gone, hidden under the weight of the torpid present—just a few old photos and bits of junk in the local museum, a yarn or two in the pub. Broome is not like that.

Meeting Fongie

At last! And just when I needed it. Last night I got my first glimpse of Broome's emerging young leadership. They are Broome-born, in their thirties, mainly mixed race, working in all sorts of government and ATSIC-funded organisations. One of them is Kevin Fong. He is a suave, charming, lively sort of guy with short black hair that points upwards and black, steel-framed glasses. He's known as Fongie to his friends.

The name of Fong is everywhere in Broome. 'Fong's Store' is just a street back from where we live and is a local institution, even though it has been there only since the sixties. There are several businesses in Chinatown owned by the Fongs.

Kevin is a real powerhouse. He's the managing director of Goolarri Media, the Aboriginal radio and soon-to-be-launched television station. He is also the president of Shinju Matsuri, the 'Festival of the Pearl', held each year in August. Until last year Shinju had been deteriorating into a tacky affair, run by white business people and aimed at tourists. It had lost its uniquely Broome character. But eighteen months ago Shinju was 'taken back' by the locals—that's how everyone puts it.

I met Kevin at a planning meeting for Shinju held one evening at Goolarri Media. Going in cold, knowing nothing of Shinju's history, I was expecting a committee dominated by ponderous white blokes. I couldn't have been more wrong—and to think I almost hadn't bothered going! I found a group of people virtually all under thirty-five, more women than men and hardly a white face among them. The atmosphere was comfortably familiar—most of them have known each other all their lives. Kevin is clearly the boss, but everyone, even the two girls who are the youth members (a delightful pair of young go-getters) felt free to participate.

Kevin was immediately welcoming and friendly towards me, but I could sense a calculating glint behind his eyes. At one point the thought occurred to me, 'I bet this guy runs just about everything in town.'

There was an impressive woman there called Vanessa Poelina. She was so lithe and lively that at first I thought she was one of the youth members, but she's actually the girls' aunt! She is dark-skinned, thin and agile, with short black curls and a friendly, engaging face. She was wearing a gorgeous pearlshell pendant and carrying a Filofax. Vanessa works for one of the health services.

Afterwards, outside the demountable that serves as a radio studio, I ran into Maxine Chi, who I met the other day at the Kimberley Land Council. She introduced me to her brother, Jimmy Chi, the songwriter and musician. Jimmy was about to go on air as part of the 'Mary Geddardyu Show'. 'Mary Geddardyu' is really Mark Bin Bakar. He's another of the up-and-coming generation. Standing on the verandah, I could see him inside the studio on the other side of the glass: a big man with a mop of springy dark hair, working the controls while a stream of high-pitched talk and jokes poured from his mouth. It sounded like a cross between the Goons, Edna Everage, Aunty Jack and Broome humour, all mixed up in the local creole (known as Kriol). What with the Kriol and all the in-jokes, I had trouble following it, but Maxine and Jimmy rocked with laughter. 'Mary Gedarrdyu' has a huge following among Aboriginal communities across the Kimberley. Apparently when Mary is on air there's less drinking and less trouble in the communities—everyone's at home listening to the radio.

In his day job, Mark Bin Bakar is artistic director of Goolarri Media. Clearly a mob to watch.

*

Goolarri is the sort of organisation we thought we might find in Broome. Modern, professional and run by Aboriginal people. Its front foyer could almost be that of any radio or television station anywhere. Smart couches, a coffee table with magazines scattered on it, a tall reception desk and, behind it, two receptionists, a young woman with dark hair, fair skin and suspicious eyes, and a plump, round-faced Aboriginal boy with a jolly, efficient manner.

When I went back there this morning, for the first time in Broome I felt underdressed. In the offices upstairs, most of the women were wearing suits or smart trousers and high-heeled shoes. The place was buzzing. Goolarri is the official organiser for NAIDOC (National Aboriginal and Islander Day of Celebration), which this year will be happening here in Broome. NAIDOC is now a week-long festival of indigenous culture. Hundreds of the country's indigenous heavyweights will be descending on the town. As well, Goolarri is getting ready to officially launch its television station on July 6, during NAIDOC Week.

Kevin Fong showed me around. He's obviously proud of the place. And he introduced me to Mary Tarran, a striking black woman—again, in her thirties. She's organising the hundreds of traditional performers who will be coming to Broome from across the Kimberley for NAIDOC Week. Mary is the coordinator of a proposed Aboriginal culture centre.

June 18

Today you went out to do an interview and you came back energised with gossip, stories, people; a peek into the complexities of Broome's political life. Now it's my turn to feel out of it, reluctant to go out there and do it. Instead I'm reading *The Drowning Dream*, by Peter Burke, about Broome in the 'romantic' days early last century. I like this bit, from the diary of the narrator:

> Five things the Romance books (*Pearlers of the South Seas* and ilk) don't tell you about pearling luggers:
> 1) They stink (bilge, rotting oyster flesh, Asiatic cooking), and you do not become accustomed.
> 2) Cockroaches, which are everywhere and nibble your toes at night.
> 3) Food is evil.
> 4) Every small wound turns septic. I am a mass of sea boils.
> 5) It is dangerous.

Not only were the first Aboriginal divers paid nothing for this dangerous and dirty work, but pregnant Aboriginal women were forced to dive to depths that killed them. Later, imported Malay and Japanese divers were paid, but only a fraction of white wages. They worked horrendous hours and dozens were crippled or killed year after year.

I've also been reading *Port of Pearls* by Hugh Edwards, an account of Broome's first hundred years. An unpretentious, well-researched book. Broome has had its periods of boredom, isolation and parochialism, but nonetheless, what a history this little town has! Its beginnings as a mosquito-ridden outpost, its boom years when it was the world's leading exporter of pearlshell and four hundred luggers lined Roebuck Bay. The last-outpost-of-Empire enclave of the pearling masters in their white suits, drinking French champagne on their verandahs, a household of native servants at the bottom of their gardens. The slumps in mother-of-pearl prices, the revivals. The Japanese air attack on Broome in World War II. Then postwar decline, followed by the combined advent of cultured pearls and tourism, which saved the town from extinction.

Some of that risk-taking, hard-drinking feel is still here, underneath the surface of civic pride and propriety. Bob Noble fits rather well with the swashbuckling, racist, money-minded men of old Broome (even though I can't help liking him.)

An extraordinary trajectory

Wendy Albert came around in the evening after she'd finished work at the bookshop. We sat on our front verandah with a drink. It was just cool at dusk; a light breeze had sprung up.

Wendy's has been an extraordinary trajectory. Into the convent at sixteen to become a nun, out again eight years later, when she went to work as an administrator for the Aboriginal Legal Service in Alice Springs. It was a very political time. As an ALS employee she was ostracised by the white community, so she veered to the black. Baamba (whom she always calls Stephen) was living in Alice at the time; they moved in the same circles. By the time she arrived in Broome in 1974, she was married to him.

Wendy's years with Baamba were before he became famous, but even then he was always in demand as a singer and raconteur at parties. I get the impression the marriage finished because Baamba preferred partying to the responsibilities of a family.

In the early eighties, when she was still a Catholic of sorts, Wendy became involved in a little bookshop run by the nuns. Back then, *The Thornbirds* and *Fear of Flying* were forbidden books, burnt in the convent incinerator. There were still three glass cases full of holy pictures when Wendy bought the shop in 1990. She transformed it into a quality bookshop, a Broome landmark.

Wendy's brown eyes are perpetually amused, as if almost everything intrigues her. Only very occasionally do you see the ex-nun peeping through. She's a sophisticated, sceptical woman, with wide-ranging interests and opinions.

Wendy's advice to us is to get to know the builders, as another way of looking at power and influence in the town. If we get to know a builder we get to know the architects, the tradesmen, the developers, and where the money is. My head aches with the possibilities and how many of them we will fail to pursue.

Talking of possibilities, we've twice seen an intriguing man around town. First at the Lugger Bar, drinking with the town's businessmen. He stood out because he certainly didn't look one of them, although he seemed at ease. Long fine blonde hair to his shoulders, a ruddy, alert face, jeans, pointy black boots. A few days later at the court house we saw him again, a black lawyer's gown thrown carelessly over his jeans and open shirt. It turns out he's the Aboriginal Legal Services barrister. Rumours abound around him. We've arranged to have a drink with him next week.

Tea after Mass on Sunday

The bishop was there in his white robes, purple sash and jewels, smoking a cigarette. He's fairly tall, strong, pleasant looking. He seems very approachable. Susan cadged a cigarette from him and said, 'First time I've cadged from a bishop.' He laughed.

'Here's a couple of women you should meet,' he said, and beckoned over two lively older women. Pearl Hamaguchi and Sally Demin. Sisters, although they don't look alike. Pearl must be about sixty. Dark hair, an expressive face that can change from serious to quizzical to full-blown laughter within moments. Smartly dressed and feisty. Sally is a little heavier in build than Pearl; a calm, down-to-earth woman. She lets her older sister make the running.

'Tell them about your mother and Aunty Bella,' suggested the bishop.

Pearl and Sally told us Aunty Bella and their mother had been put into the Catholic mission at Beagle Bay when they were little girls. Aunty Bella is ninety-six now and still devoted to the Church that raised her.

'Can we come and visit you?' we asked Pearl.

She agreed, probably only because the bishop was there.

*

Pearl and her husband, Hiroshi Hamaguchi (whom everyone calls 'Hama') have a lovely new house built in traditional pearling-master style, but with a slightly Japanese feel—all gleaming polished floorboards and partition walls. Hama came from Japan in 1955 and worked as a captain on the pearling boats until eventually he and Pearl set up their own pearl farm. They sold the business last year.

Pearl's voice is unusual; careful, singsong, sometimes it almost sounds as if she has a foreign accent, perhaps from living for more than forty years with a man who even now does not speak very good English. We sat with her under the covered porch outside the house, built to catch the east-west breeze, and she took up the story of her mother and Aunty Bella's childhood.

The sisters were born on Ruby Downs Station in the east Kimberley to an Aboriginal mother and a white father. He was a partner in the station. When they were small, the girls were separated from their mother and taken by camel train to Wyndham, where they were put on a boat bound for Broome. They arrived in Broome almost starving because the older girls on the boat hadn't let them eat the food they were given—white men put poison in flour.

'When they arrived in Broome at the jetty they couldn't even walk,' Pearl says. 'They were so weak. They were registered, then they were shipped to Beagle Bay, by lugger. This was in 1909, when my mother was four and my aunt (who tells me all these stories) was seven.

'When they got to Beagle Bay—to see these nuns in their great big white habits! They thought they were birds. Their first introduction to Christianity was the old benediction—this is after they've been processed and washed and dressed and deloused. They put them in what they called bag dresses—just made out of cotton flour bags. So they're sitting in the sand there for their first benediction and the priest turns around and he holds this shining, monstrous thing up in the air. And one of the little boys, he shouts out in their language "Hit the dirt! This is a weapon he's got. He's going to shoot us!" The nuns and priests didn't know what was happening—all these little kids throwing themselves down.

'And this other business—the liturgy, where the priest calls out and every-one responds, "Saint Catherine…pray for us, Mother of God…pray for us." The kids thought, "Hey, I can relate to this, like a corroboree, the chanting." So they started clapping their hands and saying, "Pray for us, pray for us."

'It's not just Mother and Aunty Bella who had these experiences. It's all the girls they grew up with. I've got fifty women that I call "Aunty", what they call orphanage kids. Well they weren't orphans—they were just insti-tutionalised girls.'

But Pearl insists Beagle Bay was a good place, and that the station owner, a friend of the girls' father, sent them there for their own good. She has no time for 'all this saying "sorry". Why should anyone be sorry? Most had good memories of that time.'

Pearl's mother left Beagle Bay when she was about fifteen. She was sent here to the convent in Broome.

'It was a sort of finishing school; they taught them how to iron and starch and make scones and polish floors, polish silver. Then they billeted them out to be servants to white families. My mother got a good family—Mr and Mrs Carrick. He was the Bank of NSW. Just a young couple on their first assignment in Broome. The nuns would pile all the girls in the horse and cart and take them around and drop them off—at the pearling master's, the bank manager's, prominent people—then pick them up at night. They lived at the convent until they found their husbands. They were very closely supervised.

'There was this other very strict policy; my poor mother and hundreds of other girls like her, who were called half-castes, that word which you're not supposed to say now. Which is ridiculous! The worst thing you could ever do was to get involved with Asiatics or white men. But laws were meant to be broken!' Pearl laughs. 'On Sundays they'd get their five shillings and go off to Chinatown. And Chinatown was nothing like it is today. Can you imagine what it was like when the luggers were in? Three hundred luggers, eight men on each one. So here were all these Asiatics. The nuns said, 'You mustn't attract attention. Don't make eye contact.' And here we are, we've all got Asian fathers!' She laughs uproariously. 'They managed to attract attention all right!'

'They couldn't have gone for Aboriginal men, not after being educated and expected to live up to white standards. And they couldn't really marry half-caste boys. They all grew up like sisters and brothers.'

Pearl's mother fell in love with a man called Jimmy Chi, who had a Chinese father and a Japanese mother.

'Jimmy Chi?' I ask. 'The father of Jimmy Chi the songwriter?'

'Yes. He's my half brother...From my mother's side I've got a Scottish grandfather and a full-blood Aboriginal grandmother, and from my father's side I've got a Chinese grandfather and a Japanese grandmother. That's Broome! All my generation are like this. Some have even more, maybe two more, say Filipino and Malay. A lot of us say 'Please don't ask me what I am, please don't ask me..."

'We were identified as quadroons. There was the full-blood native, then there was the half native, the half-caste, then the next generation...I would ask my mother, "Why am I quadroon?". Well, because you're a quarter black. And I compared it with some of my friends. Their half-caste mothers married white men, so they were quarter-*cast*, instead of quadroon. Then, there were octoroons...Well, it was colonial times.'

She showed us some photos of her mother, who was very beautiful. 'Right in Chinatown was this photographic shop, run by Mr Mirikami. He was a Japanese photographer. My mother had a beautiful girlfriend, we used to call her Aunty Eva. He'd call to them, "Barbara, Eva, come and sit for me". Because they were in their Sunday best. "But Mr Mirikami, we haven't got any money." And he used to do it for free, they were such good models. Look at their Sunday best!'

We oohed and aaahed over Barbara, over her smile.

'So it makes me angry when people come up here and think we're still coming out of the bush,' Pearl said, suddenly fierce.

Then she brought out a photo of her father, Jimmy Chi, standing in front of his taxi which had the number plate 'BM1'. Before the war he had operated Broome's first taxi. But the family had lost touch with him. 'He found someone else,' Pearl explained simply.

'Broome families! Don't ask me to explain. It was circumstances. We were so multicultural. The lifestyle we led, we weren't so conservative. You couldn't be. Not like the English—all under the carpet, hush, hush, don't talk about it. You couldn't live that way, because circumstances made everything…more natural.'

Pearl and Sally don't share the same father. 'You get it?' she laughs. 'I've got six sons but they've all got the same father. I was more fortunate.'

Another photo: 'This is my husband when he first came out. Elvis eat your heart out! He told his mother, "Oh, I'll just do this for a year." Forty-two years and he's still here, and he blames me, of course. I say, "I didn't do the chasing." I was sixteen. He was my first boyfriend. It was lovely in those days, growing up in Broome. Imagine being a teenage girl…'

Monday 11 p.m.

We've just arrived home after four hours and at least eight scotches with Gordon Bauman, the Aboriginal Legal Service lawyer. What can one write about Gordon? As you said, sent by God. When he went off to the loo we looked at each other and said, 'If only we had a tape recorder!'.

When first I talked to him on the verandah of the courthouse the other day, he said he had to cope with Aboriginal people and their problems at home as well as at work, so I assumed his partner was an Aboriginal woman. Tonight he said his family comprised an Aboriginal mother and her son. Then it turns out that it's the son who is his partner; the woman is his mother-in-law!

Would anyone believe it if it weren't true? Beefy blokey ALS lawyer with long bleached hair, whose partner, it seems, is a beautiful Aboriginal boy of twenty-six?

We'd heard a rumour that he was a transvestite. But there's nothing effeminate or 'gay' about Gordon, until you notice the long nails with their chipped, colourless varnish. True, his long blond hair is fetching, and perhaps more carefully washed than a 'normal' bloke's would be. But he's ruddy-faced, big-featured, ocker-voiced, and he has a hearty laugh and an easygoing manner.

He talked about Damien without self-consciousness. He told us that his life wasn't always like this, far from it. He was married for many years and has three kids. His oldest girl is at university doing law. He hasn't seen his family in a long time, although he seems to know what they're doing. He was always bisexually inclined but thought nothing of it, didn't even particularly like gays. Full gayness, Damien and becoming so involved with the Aboriginal community, have all only happened in the last ten years. He is slightly bemused by it all, but he looks, feels, talks like a man who has come home.

It seems as if Gordon's 'mother-in-law', Peggy, is almost as important to him as Damien. Peggy is ill with kidney disease. She adores Gordon. He loves to sit by her and have his long blond hair stroked. His life has become totally entwined with hers and Damien's. He keeps referring to the caring, the love and the tolerance he's found in the Aboriginal community. If he's on a bender, everyone looks out for him. He likes and needs that feeling of being embraced. Says he gets lonely without it.

He thinks you have to take sides eventually in the race divide and his 'side' is definitely the Aboriginal. 'The great love they give you, you can't describe it, it's never-ending.' He took a $30 000 drop in salary to take on the Aboriginal Legal Service job in Broome.

Because he is a white lawyer, Gordon is a 'catch'. But he's also aware that in other respects he's no catch at all for young, gorgeous, queeny Damien. They are very jealous of one another. Damien bashes him up a bit—when he's been drinking—but Gordon says there's an underlying compatibility. They've been together nearly six years.

Gordon's just moved out of Peggy and Damien's house after a fight with Damien. But he says cheerfully that he'll be moving back in, maybe even tonight, if Damien will have him. Every few days he moves out, stays away a night or two, then it's back home.

Gordon is both wonderfully bizarre and so—well, normal. He talks about this extraordinary life of his with utter frankness. And he seems to enjoy his identity as a heavy drinker. As the drinks piled up on the table he was totally sober. And he probably stayed that way till three in the morning.

A lot of the time his stories sound outrageous, but there's an underlying seriousness to much of what he says. And no matter how drunk he gets the night before—he might not even get home— he always performs in court. Says a hangover focuses him.

He suffers a lot from depression. But he's solved the problem of wanting to kill himself: 'I always tell myself, "I'll do it in the morning". But by morning I no longer want to do it.'

Four

Baamba Albert—The telling of stories—Gordon in the Tote Bar—Bob's salon—Dirty feet—The Durack Gallery— Vanessa's heritage—The last of the pearling luggers

I love the lack of adornment in the churches here, their openness to the elements. The Uniting Church is particularly plain, almost puritan. There are no pews, just plastic portable chairs arranged across the length of the church, so that the pulpit backs onto the side verandah and the congregation looks out to the garden beyond the minister's figure. There are no stained-glass windows; just a few notices, a Sorry Day poster, and the high ceiling fans, immobile on this coolish Sunday.

At the Uniting Church I find the religiosity more naked and confronting than at the Catholic Church. I'm used to the mediation of ritual, its distancing effect—something Jews and Catholics have in common. At the Uniting Church it's more sincere and personal, and I feel more of an imposter. Although just about everyone else is also a stranger, if not an imposter. Two-thirds of the congregation are tourists—neat short-back-and-sides retired couples here to see the winter out in one of the several caravan parks. I have the feeling that many of them are at church more for a temporary sense of community than for religion.

I'm getting an unusual amount of religion—the Catholics last week, the Uniting this week. There's a little flood of longing amidst the boredom and alienation. I can see the attractions of religion more clearly than I used to: organised quiet time, a reminder of the constant, simple values, a renewal of the sense of awe. I look at the lady minister, Glenys Gill, whose patent sincerity and faith literally shine out of her, and I think of the high price she must pay for belief—her tiny congregation, the threat to the survival of her very profession, the constant intellectual rearranging she must have to do. She is a brave woman.

The Moderator of the Northern Synod is the guest preacher today. She's been staying with Glenys and her mild-faced husband who plays the organ, in the manse just behind the church. It seems that Glenys has confessed to her that even though she's not much of a homemaker, she's decided to open the manse up as a B&B. An example, the Moderator says, of how we are called upon by God to do things that are not easy for us.

Now I'm intrigued! I would have thought the B&B was born more of financial necessity, or boredom due to insufficient congregants, rather than God's call. Will it be perhaps the only *operating* manse in Australia also functioning as a B&B?

Baamba Albert

Baamba will soon be leaving town to star in the national tour of Jimmy Chi's *Corrugation Road,* so I went around to see him. On the walls of the neat small house he shares with his second wife, Pam, are posters of Baamba in *Bran Nue Dae*, and of the Modern Dreamtime Dancers, a troupe of Aboriginal kids that Pam has just taken on a successful tour to Korea.

Baamba seemed a little surly, even suspicious, at first. But tape rolling, he was in fine form. When he's telling stories of his Broome childhood, the actor in him comes out. His face becomes mobile, the grin impish, the eyes shining and mischievous.

'When I was a kid we'd always watch the pearling luggers coming in. They came in every six weeks to two months. It was always something to look forward to. And of course it was sad to see them going out, but it was beautiful, too, watching them going out in the evening, people up on the hill waving goodbye, singing farewell songs. And when they were coming in, we'd be having bets on top of the hill on which would go faster. You'd see them racing to get in first, because after being on the ocean a while they'd be looking to getting to the Roebuck [Hotel]. You'd know when they were coming in because of the full moon. When it's high tide it's too deep to go diving. So every big spring tide they used to come home. The whole town changed when they came in. They'd spend their money on the three G's—gambling, girls and grog.'

I asked Baamba about his mother, whom he intensely admired. She was born in 1922, one of fourteen children, in Lombadina, a mission on the peninsula north of Broome.

'When the missionaries came to Lombadina, they took all the kids away and put them into dormitories. From an early age my mother was conditioned by the Catholic system. In her teens she was one of the first native nuns. But she didn't go through the whole vows. Auntie Lizzie Puertollano, I think, was the first one that left, then everyone else followed.

'The missions taught our people to become domesticated: to sew and to be butchers and bakers and candlestick makers. A lot of our parents became nannies for the pearling masters here in Broome. Mum was one of them. She worked for Mary Durack and Horrie Miller. Then at one stage she was working at the Roebuck Hotel as an assistant cook, and during those years she met my stepfather. They met before the war but they didn't get together till after the war because my old man got interned. He was Japanese, my stepfather.'

Baamba didn't know who his real father was until he was a young man. 'I saw him sometimes, but we didn't get together till I was eighteen. That's when I found out he was my father. In those days it was taboo to talk about those sorts of things.

'I've got an older sister, Claire, and she was put in the orphanage—a lot of girls were put in the orphanage because their mums couldn't afford to have kids. Being single parents, some of them were barely surviving, like my mum. Our grandparents looked after us in a shack up on Kennedy Hill. Then mum started in the Church. They used to call her Mother General because she'd look after the church and the garden. She was always concerned about other people. She was a remarkable woman.

'Even while we were up on the Hill, we used to share our food. Like when Dad used to come back from the luggers, he'd save the tinned food for a rainy day, for people in the community. And he used to bring turtle and dugong and the old people used to come and they'd feed all the people on the Hill. That was the good thing about the luggers—they'd feed the community.'

'When did the music start?' I ask.

'When I came back from Perth. My brother was playing in a band called the Broome Beats. They were the first electrical band in town. They were all in their teens; they had to have a special licence from the cops to play in the pubs. My brother taught me guitar—I was seventeen, eighteen. After the band played on Wednesday you'd kick on and end up on Cable Beach at six in the morning. Seven o'clock you'd have to be at work! I'd do the same thing on Friday...It was full on in the seventies, a big party on most nights. Hippies were already here; free love everywhere...'

Baamba's mobile rings. He answers: 'Baamba's Chinatown Tours' and takes a booking, then rummages for some photos to show me.

'These are photos from when we were practising for our thirty-year reunion...the original Broome Beats. When Jimmy [Chi] came home from Perth I was already here and singing in the band. Jimmy bought himself a guitar and a chord book and taught himself how to play, and that's when he started writing songs.'

As soon as I turn the tape off, Baamba's indifference, his lack of interest in communicating, comes back. Possibly because he is more aware than most of the interviewing process, of what I'm 'up to'. It's as if he's spent all his energy on performance and can't be bothered giving me any more. I drive him to the Tourist Bureau so that he can pick up a fax, then to the Conti so that he can catch up with a couple of mates in from Darwin. He sits in the car, silent and withdrawn.

The Telling of Stories

Perpetua is being very kind to us, taking us to various events around town. Today she's taking me to the Catholic Education Office for the launch of *The Telling of Stories*. Subtitled *A Spiritual Journey by Kimberley Aboriginal People*. It's a kind of local version of the Stolen Children's stories, except that it's really about the effect of the Catholic Church on Aboriginal people's lives, as told by them.

A marquee has been set up in the grounds. Lugubrious religious music is playing on the loudspeakers, a few plain-clothes nuns and priests mix about and there's a little buzz of excitement in the air. The MC is a serious-looking man of Chinese–Aboriginal or maybe Malay descent and clearly a community stalwart. The choir is made up of that already familiar but still exciting Broome mix. A big-boned full-blood Aboriginal woman stands next to a frail little woman called Juanita, who looks Filipino but may have Caucasian and Aboriginal in her genes as well, and next to her stands a lone white male—small, white-haired Peter Bibby, local identity, editor of the book, convinced Catholic, and a stolen child himself, being one of the kids sent out from England to institutions here.

An elderly priest, Father McKelson, is one of the speakers. He is a linguist skilled in several Aboriginal languages, and he makes a few sophisticated references, mentioning Derrida in passing.

'The history of the Aboriginal people is written in blood,' he says.

'There is much for the white man to be ashamed of.' But then, 'This suffering of Aboriginal people has been given meaning by the suffering of Jesus Christ.'

Now he's lost me.

Some of the storytellers in the book are called up to speak, all women, of varying ages and skill in English. Engaging, forthright women. Emily Charlie says, 'Everything I know, about cooking, cleaning, reading, the nuns taught me. Thank you!' Another old lady recalls the mission's pet cockatoo who cawed 'pray for us, pray for us, pray for us' the live-long day.

On the lawns we eat a huge and varied lunch of sandwiches, cakes and hot Asian dishes. Next to the tea urn, there's still-warm buttered damper with golden syrup. Damper and tea from the cattle station days, Asian dishes from Broome's mixed-race history, a touch of white gentility in the no-crust sandwiches.

I meet Maria Mann—large, bright, sophisticated, of Finnish origin, smokes a lot. She's secretary of Environs Kimberley. The hot environmental issue up here is a huge dam planned for the Fitzroy River to feed water to the cotton growers south-east of Broome.

Bruce introduces me to Phillipa Cook, who is on the board of Magabala Books and is a domestic violence coordinator. Phillipa is a light-skinned Aboriginal woman who was once married to Labor Senator Peter Cook. A bit of a powerhouse. There seem to be quite a few female powerhouses around Broome.

Gordon in the Tote Bar

Our second night with Gordon. We are both very much at our ease. We like Gordon. He is very engaging, but it's also the casual frankness about his sexuality and the devil-may-care mix of anarchy, world-weariness and idealism that makes him feel familiar.

'Apart from the transvestism, which makes him a bit unusual,' I say to Annie as we walk home, 'he'd be right at home in the Sydney Push!'

The back 'black' bar is Gordon's usual drinking place at the Conti. We are the only whites in the place. Almost as soon as we walk in, the bouncer asks if we know there's another (white) bar. The back bar—the Tote as its known because it's next to the TAB—has vinyl floor tiles and harsh fluorescent lighting. It's large, dreary and filled with pool tables. Nearly everyone is playing pool.

In the back bar Gordon becomes very calm. Drunken people come up to him all the time. He smiles, doesn't say much, listens, touches them reassuringly from time to time, and remains imperturbable. He says he can't explain his affinity with Aboriginal people, except possibly by the Gypsy blood on his mother's side.

Gordon was in the Army for a while, and went to Vietnam. Then came a stint as a patrol officer to the Northern Territory, rounding up Aborigines needing 'help'. With the election of Whitlam his job was changed to that of 'adviser'. That was the beginning of his involvement with indigenous people.

He married quite young. His ex-wife is a Baptist. 'I liked her better in her hippy days,' he says wistfully. He didn't drink as much in those days but she still criticised him for it. He was a womaniser back then, too. 'Not literally while she was in hospital giving birth, but close! You wouldn't have liked me in those days, girls,' he says. 'I was terribly hard. All my softness, all this caring for kids and the downtrodden, has come since Damien. I'm a different person.'

Gordon was a station manager in the Northern Territory when one of his mates bet him a carton of beer that he couldn't get through a law degree. At his graduation from Melbourne University four years later, the Dean shook his hand. 'Gordon, it's been a pleasure to have you,' he said. 'But I can't say we've succeeded in being a civilising influence on you.'

He worked in commercial law for a while but it soon dawned on him that criminal work was the only 'high', and that winning a murder trial was the best high of all. He went back to the Territory as a criminal lawyer. His second trial in Darwin was a murder case. He won.

'Before a jury, Mr Bauman,' the judge said to him, 'you're like a fox in front of a dozen chickens.'

Bob's salon

Bob Noble was busy planing down a sideboard outside his shed while his 'salon' waited for him on the verandah. The young blond god who runs the outboard motor place next door was there, along with a new addition, an alarmingly skinny old man, barefoot and dressed only in skimpy shorts and a felt hat with a long feather and shells stuck all over it. Wispy little beard, long concave face. He was so thin that he looked like a walking rib cage.

'Who's he?' I asked Bob, trying not to stare.

'Him?' said Bob, barely glancing his way. 'Old Doug. Been around the last few years. He's just a con man.'

Later I learn from Wendy Albert that old Doug is actually an artist and an ex-clergyman who lives on an old blue floating caravan among the mangroves.

I ask Bob if I can meet his wife. His eyes light up every time he talks of her. Yet he doesn't spend much time with her—her choice, I suspect.

'Yes, I'll take you around to meet the wife but I'm a bit busy today, love. You'll like her. She's a lovely person. Do you mind coming back, love?'

He speaks to me with an old-fashioned courtesy, a fatherly hand on my back.

I stay sitting on Bob's verandah for a while, drinking a milky coffee, chatting with the blokes and taking in the outdoor decor. Two toilet bowls, one silver, one white, acting as pot plant containers, two wicker washing baskets also filled with plants, an old washing machine which seems to be in constant use, and some daggy orange kitchen chairs.

*

On the way home I went into the museum, just across the road from Bob's. It's an unprepossessing low-lying building, half swathed in a scrappy scarlet bougainvillea. It stands next to a vacant piece of red-earthed land on the edge of Roebuck Bay. Inside it's a ramshackle Broomeish sort of place, the important and the unimportant jostling each other for room— pearling masters, Japanese divers, Aborigines, wrecks of boats and planes, photos of the old town and its polyglot inhabitants.

On the front verandah there's a tumble of old gravestones engraved with Japanese characters and what looks like Portuguese Creole. I also notice a display stand that houses leg irons and chains used for transporting Aboriginal prisoners. On the glass case is stuck a small printed notice:

**The Broome Historical Society presents the past as it is,
without comment. It is apolitical.**

Imagine the bunfight over that among the worthies of the Historical Society!

I came across an oral history by a man called Secombe who worked as a shell opener on the luggers in the years 1919–1920. Secombe's was a lazy life. Everything on board was done for him by the Malays and Koepangers— his washing, his meals, his coffee brought to him in the morning when he woke up.

He describes Carnarvon Street, the main street of Chinatown as 'like

Hay Street [in Perth] on a Friday night. Coloureds were just cluttering up the footpath, but as soon as a white person came along you could hear someone say in Malay, "Orang puti datung", which is "white man coming", and they'd get off the footpath and let the white man pass through.'

Dirty feet

Everyone in Broome has dirty feet. The fine red pindan creeps between sandal and sole and gives the bottom of one's feet a dark reddish tinge. Outside every front door is a pile of thongs and sandals. People take off their shoes before entering a house but it doesn't help much. The tiled, wood or slate floors are permanently gritty and grimy. Walking around inside all day, even in the cleanest house, turns the soles of your feet black.

Our new house has a bidet, which seems a bit over the top in such a modest house. When we first saw it we laughed about using it to wash our feet. But now I'm convinced that's what it's for. Every night before going to bed I have to wash my feet in the bidet so as not to dirty the sheets. Then I smother them in moisturiser to stop the skin cracking. The heat and dust and constant exposure can dry the skin on your feet so badly that the cracks bleed.

Maybe that is why Lyn Page usually wears closed shoes, smart canvas or silver or gold slip-ons. But I've seen her barefoot at home. Smartly dressed, curled up on her elegant sofa, even she still has dusty soles.

We called in on Lyn on Sunday and sat around her big dining table drinking champagne. Her friend Chi, the local fortune-teller and new-age seer, was there. I'm not sure about Chi's background. In times past she probably would have been called Eurasian. She's not a local. She speaks with a 'cultured' hybrid accent and has almost unnaturally yellow-brown skin, as though she spends a lot of time under a sun lamp. She was wearing a striking, off-beat dress and was made up as though she were on her way to some special occasion. But there apparently was no occasion as she seemed in no hurry to leave.

The talk was of past lives and hidden spirits and guiding hands. Chi is all earnestness; Lyn, thank God, leavens her 'spiritualism' with gales of hearty laughter. Lyn was in her usual Sunday garb: a threadbare pale grey jumpsuit that's an old favourite. A cat-suit—there's definitely something feline about Lyn.

The champagne was to cheer herself up after failing to get Liberal preselection for the seat of Kalgoorlie. It went to a bloke from down there who has his own plane. Candidates need their own planes to get around an electorate like Kalgoorlie—the largest in the world. The Labor bloke has one, too.

Lyn's persona of businesswoman, president of the Chamber of Commerce, councillor and prominent Liberal sits a little oddly with this other Lyn of seances and 'channelling' and inner voices. But the relaxed and irreverent, anything-goes Lyn of Sunday evenings can quickly change to a sharp-tongued, flashing-eyed political plotter, if the subject warrants it.

Monday

On a good day, Broome promises so much. But on a bad day I walk these wide untidy streets, the sun beating mercilessly on my back, and I am reminded of nothing so much as the backblocks of Port Stephens—middle Australia preoccupied with fishing and family barbecues, the laid-back weekend suburbia of the 1960s.

The climate is relentlessly unvarying. You get sick of the blue sky. And the constant traffic noise—not as noisy or busy as in the city, but continual and somehow pointless—where is everyone going? To the supermarket? Fishing? There's not much else to do. Yesterday, Sunday, was for once overcast and threatening rain, so we cancelled plans to go to the beach. For the first time I understood why people go to the supermarket for an outing! They were doing a roaring trade down at The Boulevard, one of two big shopping malls that have opened in the past couple of years.

It makes me fear that we may be too late, that whatever was once unique about Broome is too far gone, erased here like everywhere else by suburbs and supermarkets.

Thursday

I've never before been lazy or undisciplined, but here I cannot make myself *write*. I wonder if it's the lack of 'a room of my own', nowhere to settle, nowhere to close myself away. My 'room' is a trestle table on the side terrace, with a roof and ceiling fan that make it a sort of outdoor room—but no door.

I haven't worked out a modus operandi for being here. I can't seem to relax into the place as I know we must. To give in to 'Broometime', as people call it.

I might not even show you this. You've gone off for a coffee at Town Beach. I didn't want to go with you. At the moment I need the space to be miserable. I try to be better when you're around, but it's tiring.

∫ You say you just don't want to write any more. Then you give me a quick look—not hostile, more complicated than that—and say you don't want to write with *me*.

'Write for yourself then,' I say. 'I don't have to see it.'

I don't mind doing more of the writing until you get out of this low, but this is our first joint effort, our *collaboration*. I can feel you pulling back from it and that scares me.

Friday

Λ What I said yesterday about not wanting to write with you is true and not true. This journal writing is about all I can handle at the moment. What I'm finding hard is handing over my writing self to a collaboration. You were pleased that I didn't feel threatened when a few years ago you shyly told me that you, too, wanted to become a writer. It never occurred to me because a writing self is a private and separate thing from the everyday self. Normally these different selves don't trespass on one another. But now we're trespassing on one another all the time. We've decided to forego the space, the individuality, the privacy. And I'm finding that hard. It's like handing over the last bastion of my life to someone who has already taken over every other corner of it.

It's not making me love you any less (as it has a bit in the past). If anything I love you more—I admire the way you are adapting so well to being here, now the weather is getting cooler. The climate suits you. You're looking cute. And you're getting lots of work done. Good thing one of us is.

∫ How do we manage each other through this? Buggered if I know. We predicted boundary difficulties and border clashes between us, and now here they are. But I love you, and it's going to pass. It always does. And then suddenly it will be my turn to go down.

*

Λ The dogs arrived today! Margie brought them with her as 'baggage'. We were ridiculously anxious and excited when we heard they were in the air, but they survived their arduous journey admirably. As soon as he got inside, Scruffy sniffed around for a few minutes then plonked himself on a familiar mat that we'd brought from home. It's lovely to have them with us again. We're spoiling them both to death.

The Durack Gallery

Perpetua had to go out this morning so I'm minding her gallery for a couple of hours. There's a beautiful atmosphere in this old building next

door to the Rat Palazzo. The big front room has high ceilings and is lined with timber boards. On the verandah Perpetua has suspended a large leather water pouch, with a tin mug dangling nearby. I can imagine something similar hanging on the verandah at the old Durack homesteads at Argyle or Ivanhoe.

Perpetua is thinking about using the name Durack again and dropping her married name. People up here think of her as a Durack anyway and the marriage is long over. Being a Durack is a demanding business. It seems to consume much of Perpetua's energy. I think I would run away from such a burden but she has consciously taken it up—coming back to Broome and setting up the Durack Gallery, selling her mother Elizabeth Durack's work, and now, reclaiming the name as her own.

We first met Perpetua not long after the Eddie Burrup scandal broke. But it wasn't till after we arrived back here that we discovered just how implicated she is in the whole Burrup business. It was at her suggestion that Elizabeth Durack started showing work under the Eddie Burrup name, and it was Perpetua's idea that Elizabeth submit the work in the National Aboriginal and Torres Strait Islander Aboriginal Award.

There are three Burrups on the wall opposite me. I like them. I like the rich but subtle merging of colours, their swirling atmosphere. They are by far the most interesting of Elizabeth's works. They don't look particularly Aboriginal, although Aboriginal artists are now painting in such a variety of styles that I might have believed they were if I'd seen them before the scandal broke. They are so different from Elizabeth Durack's better-known earlier work—her sketches and paintings of everyday Aboriginal life in the Kimberley—that I can understand why she might have felt the need to use a 'nom de brush'. And that after a lifetime of involvement with Aboriginal people there were strong currents in her psyche wanting to break through.

But she should never have entered the Aboriginal art award. That's where I'd draw the line.

The Eddie Burrup persona has upset people here, black and white. Bruce remains friendly with Perpetua but will no longer come to the gallery and is angry that she continues to show the Burrup paintings. His friend Peter Walsh, who was fostered out by the church and lost touch with his Aboriginal family, won't have anything to do with her any more.

Perpetua says no-one has come out and condemned her to her face, that she wishes they would. Bruce says people in Broome are too polite.

There are long associations here. People have known the Duracks a very

long time, from the very beginning of white settlement in the Kimberley. When Perpetua came back to Broome she was returning to the comforting embrace of dozens of local people who have known the Duracks all their lives. The Duracks might once have been colonial appropriators but they are also 'family'. Local Aboriginal people may not approve of Elizabeth's and Perpetua's actions over the Burrup business but they are not about to condemn them out loud.

Perpetua took us to a graduation at Notre Dame, the Catholic University. Bruce likes to gobsmack visitors by telling them that Broome, with a permanent population of just 10,000, has four universities! And indeed, apart from the TAFE college and the Notre Dame campus, there are agencies for both the Curtin and Edith Cowan Universities, and an offshoot of James Cook's School of Tropical Medicine. The Notre Dame campus is fairly new in town and it was the first graduation of Aboriginal students.

The ceremony was a quiet but intensely theatrical event, staged out in the open at dusk. Flaring torches were set up on either side of the audience. At first, all that could be heard was the soft insistent sound of the didgeridoo and the low voices of women chanting. Heads craned as the music slowly got louder, coming upon the audience by stealth. The peacock colours of the academic procession emerged from the dusk—purples, scarlet and ermine for the professors, royal blue sashes for graduands.

Two Aboriginal women came down the aisles, performing a smoking ceremony. The smoke smelt like incense—a nice touch for a Roman Catholic event. Esther Bevan, a member of the university board, an impressive white-haired Aboriginal woman, explained the significance of the ceremony. As the graduands received their diplomas, she read out a little potted biography for each—what tribal group they came from, what they had done so far in their lives. A mother and daughter were graduating together. Many were teachers' assistants in remote communities on their way to a full teaching degree. Their families, who had come long distances to be there, listened intently.

One sour note: the presence of the Federal Education Minister, David Kemp, the man who abolished the Aboriginal training allowance and has cut swathes through Aboriginal education. After the ceremony Bruce had a go at Kemp, much to the annoyance of Sister Pat Rhatigan, the head of the Broome campus. Her ire wouldn't worry Bruce a bit; he's cheerfully bigoted about Catholics. 'Did you notice,' he said, 'how all the Aboriginal graduates got diplomas while the white graduates—all three of them—got degrees?'

Vanessa's heritage

I went to see Vanessa Poelina today, the woman Annie met recently at the Shinju meeting. Slim, lively, dark curly hair. Plenty of guts and heart. Thirty-four years old but looks younger. We talked in the airy office behind the Sun Picture Gardens where she and a young white woman run the Health Promotions Unit.

Vanessa is increasingly fascinated by her mixed heritage. Her mother was a clever Aboriginal girl from Derby who never took up a scholarship because she was married off at fourteen to her promised husband. She had six children, then one day she upped and left, taking the kids with her. She moved to Broome and met and married Simon Poelina, a Timorese diver who came over from Koepang for seasonal work each year. She had another six kids with Simon, the second last of them Vanessa.

Marrying non-Aboriginals ran in Vanessa's family. 'My mother's older sister married into Chinese,' she said. 'See, if you did that you were exempt from being recognised as an Aborigine. A lot of families that were married to Filipinos were also exempt from the Aborigines Act.'

'So some of the marriages were deliberate?'

'Probably. There was a method in the madness...The old women were very secretive. It's not till they pass on that you know that so-and-so was really that person's son. There's a lot of discrepancies. There was a lot of sleeping around with the women—it was open to the white men to do that. This is a town with a torrid little history.

'As a little kid you didn't take much notice of the old people's stories. I wish I'd listened better. Up the Hill we'd say, "Tell us more story, tell us more story", and we'd lay down and listen to all the stories, but we didn't really listen properly. And now it's like a big jigsaw.

'Our family had a kind of fish shop, with our nets across the creek. I used to get some big swordfish and manta rays and everything. We spent weekend after weekend patching the nets, too. Dad was a doer; you don't wait for someone to tell you to do it, you just do it. We're quite like that too, us kids. Use your initiative. We're not frightened of work.'

Vanessa was largely brought up by her father after her mother became a Jehovah's Witness and came to regard Aboriginal lore as 'black magic'.

'My dad used to come over here as a seasonal worker only, then suddenly he never went back. We'd say to him, "You don't want us kids to learn Koepang?" "Oh, hard enough time learning English," he'd say. It was a battle for him just to learn English. It was like that with all the community. You'd see Japanese, Chinese, Koepang, Malay, all sitting at the table and all just relating. They developed a kind of common pidgin language on the luggers.'

How do you identify, I asked her, as Aboriginal, Koepanger, mixed race?

Vanessa shook her head. 'I'm a Broome-ite. We just say we're Broome-ites. You accommodate and respect all the different cultures—it's the beauty of being a Broome-ite. It's not like, "I'll be a Japanese today and I think I'll be Chinese tomorrow." You've grown up with all those different cultures, so you respect what each one has to offer. You take bits and pieces, you just sort of blend it in.'

Vanessa is full of information, opinions and ideas, delivered in a cheerfully scatter-gun fashion. She doesn't go in much for the Stolen Generation rhetoric. 'The Stolen Generation!' she says scornfully. 'What about the Lost Generation? Bringing them home! To where?

'The bureaucrats who took kids away—they were just as cruel to their own mob.' She cites the treatment of poor Irish women, and of the children brought out from England. She sees it more as a case of the poor and the rich.

'More a matter of class than race?' I ask.

'Oh yes,' she says, eyes blazing.

The last of the pearling luggers

For the last few years the *Cornelius*, the last of the old wooden lugger boats, has been used to take tourists on sunset cruises. Last night a freak storm—in the 'dry' season!—tore it from its moorings and smashed it to pieces.

We set out early to see the wreck. The pindan road to Gantheaume Point was closed due to the unseasonal rain, so we had to slog four or five kilometres down Cable Beach to get there. It was a splendid, mono-chrome, brooding walk—endless grey sand, grey-green sea, grey-blue sky. There were hundreds of jelly fish strewn along the tide line, also in sub-dued colours—browns and greys with patches of pale purple.

The *Cornelius* was literally in a thousand pieces. One longish section of the hull was half-buried in sand. The rest—wooden drawers, engine parts, bits of plastic and metal, a sodden visitor's book—was scattered along the beach. A strangely awesome sight. It felt like a death.

*

This morning I went around to see Bishop Saunders, armed with the tape recorder. We sat in his lounge room. From my small experience of ecclesiastical living rooms, the last in Romania, they are much of a muchness: slightly gloomy, not big on aesthetics or decor, but comfortable. There were a couple of holy pictures, a not-very-good Aboriginal painting (Perpetua tells me the Bishop is a sucker for people coming to his door to sell stuff), a photo of his ordination and a cute photo of him with three other bishops in various bits of headgear, he sporting a rakish baseball cap. In the adjoining dining room there was a print of the famous Elizabeth Durack painting of Aborigines converging on an outback church.

I asked questions but didn't direct him too much. I sensed he was enjoying the chance to reflect on things.

The Church, he said, was moving back to a more pastoral role. 'We no longer hold economic positions here, thanks be to God, and our priests can be priests. We still give support through schools—a lot of those schools would have closed without us...The Church here was never meant to be in a governing role. I keep saying to my priests, identify issues of importance. If it's substance abuse, or native title, then stand with them in solidarity. You can't avoid a "political" role. Of course, some disagree with this stand. One of the Shire councillors, a friend of mine, said, "I don't believe in the Church becoming political. You're taking a political stand on native title."

'"No," I said, "I'm taking a moral stand, you're just seeing it that way. I might be using political tools, but if there were no moral stake in this native title thing, I wouldn't be interested in it."'

Was he referring to Lyn Page? He wouldn't commit himself. But on Lyn he said: 'She's a friend. I keep it open, I always go back. I don't alienate. I had dinner the other night with Lloyd [the diocesan architect and our landlord] and his wife at Lyn's, and the conversation turned to Gantheaume Point and whether it will be developed. Lyn believes in this trickle-down effect as all Liberals do, which is piffle. It doesn't work. We exchanged words, but I ring her up the next day, make sure the avenues are open. It doesn't mean I'll change my views. Hope she does!' He laughs. 'But having said that, Lyn's the only one who turns up to the Notre Dame things to see the kids graduate. She's always there. If there's a youth thing on, she's there... As long as you're consistent, people know where you stand.'

I sussed him out on our perception that the term 'mixed race' has become too loaded for general use, has even become unacceptable. He said, 'These days few people would call themselves "mixed race" or "coloured" or "half-caste", officially at least. Mostly they call themselves Aboriginal, or maybe "indigenous", or "countrymen". But amongst themselves they'll say, "those blackies who came into town this morning" or "the coloureds who . . ." Out in the bush the older full-blood people still refer to "half-castes" without any self-consciousness.'

The bishop told me a little story about his early days as a priest at the Lombadina mission north of Broome. 'When I was in India I acquired a painting of Our Lady that depicted the Virgin as an Indian woman. I thought I'd hang it in the church. One day I was kneeling in prayer in front of it when an old Aboriginal man walked in. He took no notice of me, only the painting. He stared at it, then shook his head, very disapproving, and muttered, "a half-caste, hummpf!" and walked off in disgust.

I took the picture down.'

Five

Love of country—Twenty-one cases in a morning—
Rubibi—Vanessa's family—On Matso's verandah—Peter Yu
of the KLC—Sunday with Lyn—Choosing sides

At last, a decent work space! I've moved the trestle table inside and given the top of it a couple of fresh coats of paint, bought myself a twenty-dollar desk lamp, and finally I'm set up. And it's made all the difference. I liked the idea of working outside but, in reality, without a proper desk to go to every day I felt adrift.

It was encouraging, too, to go into town on Friday afternoon and run into lots of different people we've already met, including Vanessa Poelina and Mary Tarran, who's the coordinator of the proposed culture centre. Vanessa and Mary are both part of the rising, younger elite of old Broome. Most of them work in government or ATSIC-funded organisations—the new power bases.

These new power bases have their own complexities. Maxine Chi (Jimmy Chi's sister) told me the other night that she's thinking of abandoning her university thesis because of the difficult dynamics within indigenous organisations. Documenting internecine Aboriginal politics creates bad blood and may not give a true picture anyway. 'You've got to respect people's privacy,' she said.

I've just read about Jimmy Chi Snr in *Port of Pearls*. During the war he was interned because his mother was Japanese. When he was released, his house had been burnt down and his taxi stripped. The RSL opposed his return to Broome. Now his children are among the town's leading citizens.

I hadn't realised that almost all the Japanese divers and crewmen who came to work in the pearling industry were from a single twenty-mile strip of coastline in the Wakayama prefecture, along the east coast of Shingu. In particular, from the village of Taiji. There's now a Taiji Street at Cable Beach.

Love of country

Mary Tarran's skin glows as no white skin glows, however healthy. Everything about her has a shining quality. Her bright friendly eyes, the thick black hair pulled back in its bun, her teeth against the bruised colour of her lips.

Mary spent a lot of her childhood on Kennedy Hill. She is a Broome girl, through and through. She has an easy manner, a swinging gait that invites one to follow. And so I did. An incredible, confusing couple of hours. My way of looking at the world is so different from hers. It is not so much a matter of colour, but of experience. She has been forced to make some accommodation with my world; I am in total ignorance of hers.

Listening to Mary, I could relate to her smile, her humour. Language was no problem (she is a convent-educated girl). But when she started to tell me about her work with the culture centre, and to touch on Aboriginal politics, I was aware that she was deeply resentful and conflicted. And I was equally aware that I had none of the knowledge that I would need to understand what was upsetting her. It wasn't just that I couldn't get her to start at the beginning and tell me in a logical fashion what was going on. It was that her mind had been trained in a certain way and it wasn't a way that I could hook into. Every now and then she would slip into a path that I could follow; would say, 'This is going to happen' or 'We are having a meeting with so-and-so' and I would latch on to these snippets and try to build up a scenario. And yet in her restless movements, the moving of papers from side to side on the desk, her agitated eyes, which kept throwing me quick glances—expecting me to understand more than I could understand—I could see a whole sea of events and conflicting interests and complicated relationships that I am not privy to.

But despite this, I have a feeling we can be friends. And I want to keep going back, keep trying. Is the incomprehension mutual, I wonder? I doubt it. She has had thirty-eight years of sussing what it is that whitefellas want and expect of her. I didn't get any sense that she finds Europeans problematic. The problems that are bedevilling Mary at present are to do with her own people. They are the source of her frustration. Although as yet I don't know why.

When Susan and I first decided to come to Broome, I expected that one of the most challenging things would be confronting my fear and ignorance of Aboriginal Australia. We live in a part of the country where one almost never sees a black face; where the closest I, at least, have come to issues of aboriginality is the distance between the lounge chair and the television set. I have been comfortably, if not unselfconsciously, an armchair liberal.

A few days after we arrived, I was at the drive-in bottleshop one night and an old Aboriginal woman, the worse for drink, came up to the car and hung on the door and said 'Can you give me a lift home, luv? Can you?' and my first reaction was fear, and my second, guilt. I didn't want to give her a lift home. She was unsteady on her feet and bedraggled and she reeked. I was saved by the attendant who said to me, 'Take no notice, the bus will be here for her soon.' And I was relieved. But still the guilt. 'Will she be all right?' I asked. He nodded, 'The bus'll be here soon.'

That old woman could have been Mary's mother, although I know it was not. Her mother is the much respected Cissy Djiagween, one of the elders of this area. Mary's is an important family. Her grandfather, Paddy Djiagween, was also Mick and Pat Dodson's grandfather. Paddy Djiagween grew up at Beagle Bay, became a tailor and lived to be 106–111, according to his tombstone. The inscription on his headstone reads:

> The sun rises, wind blows, grass grows
> The tide comes and goes
> No-one can ever take your land.

*

Many of the Aboriginal people one sees around town do not live in Broome. Often they come into town for a day or two from outlying communities, to visit the hospital or a friend in gaol, or to shop. They travel many hours in small white minibuses, or on the back of utilities. During the day they sit in the park to rest and refresh themselves. Isn't that what parks are for?

But tourists see black people sitting in a park and you can see them avert their eyes. They mutter, 'lazy', 'layabouts', 'drinking'. Even if there is not a bottle in sight, even if the people are just sitting there under a tree out of the heat of the sun, talking to each other, enjoying the day. The sight of black people sitting in a public place offends. 'Don't they have homes to go to?'

As late as the 1960s there was still a curfew to stop blacks from coming into town at night. Yet who was considered 'black' at that time? Chinatown must have been full of people of mixed Aboriginal and Asian blood. I wonder how the mixed race people were identifying then? And to what extent that has changed. All the talk I hear now is of 'indigenous' and 'non-indigenous'. What of all those in between?

There is a small Aboriginal settlement on a sandhill above Chinatown, called Kennedy Hill after one of the early pearling masters. In the late seventies the Shire Council tried to wrest it from the people who lived there because they wanted it for tourist development. It is one of the few elevated spots overlooking Roebuck Bay. I've been told there are ancient middens on that hill—it has always been a camping place for countrymen. These days most of the residents are Thursday Islanders. They originally came over to work in the pearling industry.

The Shire didn't get Kennedy Hill, but a bit further along a big hotel was built—The Mangrove, a sprawling two-storey place in off-white brick, with a wide, grassed terrace at the back that overlooks the bay. Tourists walking into Chinatown from The Mangrove pass by the middens on the top of the dune, then the dusty unpaved streets of the Kennedy Hill settlement, before descending into the commercial hub of the town.

Twenty-one cases in a morning

On Monday I went down to the court early. I could see Gordon inside in his shirt and waistcoat, organising his mountain of files. Later he came out in his barrister's gear to have a fag on the verandah. He looked hot in all that black. Black jeans and boots and his silk over the top. He didn't look happy.

'I've got twenty-one cases today,' he said. 'If I was in private practice I'd be getting a thousand bucks for each one of them. Instead of six hundred a week.'

The paddy wagon pulled up beside the courthouse and four Aboriginal prisoners climbed out in a leisurely fashion. With them were three police officers. The senior one was George Dann, member of an old local family. There's a certain proud-warrior look that the Dann men have.

Police and prisoners hung about on the verandah in a relaxed way. A

constable walked purposefully across the verandah towards a prisoner—
then held out his cigarette lighter to light the man's fag.

Sitting in the court, waiting to begin, two black girls approached
Gordy. While one asked him a question, the other stroked his wig. The
two little pigtails on the back of his wig matched his hair so well that for
a moment I thought he had braided up his own hair.

The judge was from the Supreme Court in Perth and had a toffy
accent. He was wearing scarlet, purple and black robes. In this setting the
effect was bizarre.

There were a lot of people in for mentions, remanded till next month.
One of Gordon's cases was a middle-aged dark wiry man from Kalumburu,
way up in the north-east Kimberley, who was arrested six months ago and
had been in the remand section ever since. Six months! The Department
of Public Prosecutions still had no brief from the police. Gordon asked that
the man be given bail and be allowed to reside in Kalumburu. It was granted.

Gordy was well-organised, prepared, polite and considerate of his clients.
Each time one came in he would show them where to sit and reassure
them. It's easy to see why the local people are devoted to him.

There was a Douglas Victor D'Antoine up for defrauding the
Commonwealth. He's an ATSIC Commissioner who runs his own fishing
business in Derby, some sort of relation to Donny, our former landlord.
He wasn't in court because he was out fishing. He was remanded till next
sitting.

All of the cases heard this morning are people pleading guilty and
whose case has been fast-tracked because of it. As each of his clients takes
the stand, Gordon tells the judge that 'Section 49 has been met', which means
that the defendants understand the charge and the process. This is a special provision for Aboriginal people.

In each case, Gordy knows the story. A man from Hall's Creek assaulted
his wife twice. Gordy described it as 'A tragic case. He has suffered by
who he is and where he has come from...Drink, that's what it is, sir.' The
defendant had shown remorse because he had slashed himself after he slashed
his wife.

A young boy of nineteen has got a bad report from the psychologist,
who doesn't think community-based care will work for him. He's committed
a couple of thefts.

'He's not easy to relate to,' Gordon tells the judge. 'You can't blame a
19-year-old for that. He's not friendly. He feels that life has dealt him a
harsh deal.'

After Gordy's eloquence, the boy gets a twelve-month sentence, suspended for eighteen months.

There is something heartbreaking about Gordon and the work he does. He sees so much misery and dysfunction and he's touched by it. Is it any wonder he drinks? He drinks and goes on rampages, just like his clients. They empathise with one another.

A white man who has married into an Aboriginal family is next. The guy has been going through a rough patch, getting depressed. He committed some robberies to get some money 'so he could get out of Broome'. This is a common defence. Gordon uses it quite a bit and it seems to work—as if Broome is a source of temptation.

At the mid-morning break, Gordon's face is almost as pale as his hair. Hypoglycaemia, he says. He's had nothing to eat.

I offer to go get him a sandwich.

'Nah,' he says, 'we'll be breaking at one.'

At 1 p.m. there's no sign of him going to get food. He stands on the verandah talking patiently to a young black girl who has been waiting for him. Then says he's going back to the office to grab a coffee.

*

June 30

Heavy rain overnight—the second in as many weeks. Most unusual for this time of year. But it cleared this morning so I could take the dogs for their usual walk. It has become a new routine since they arrived. We head towards the bay. When the tide is high, the bay is like a hill of blue at the end of the street; when it's low, it's faded milky green with patches of pale brown mud flats rimmed by mangroves. Back in the pearling days there were no mangroves here. They were all cleared away so the luggers could beach with ease.

I cross the road to the foreshore just before the old tin pearling shed. It's owned by Paspaley Pearls. It is now derelict and has a sign forbidding drinking, but the concrete verandah is littered with broken beer bottles. Once across the road I let the dogs off. They race from tree to tree, sniffing. Jacko rushes down to the sand, to the high-tide mark, and sniffs at the fishy detritus that's been washed up, then rolls in it. Scruffy is busy pissing on bushes and defiantly kicking up clouds of red dust with his back feet.

There's lots of traffic on the roads, people heading for work. Trucks and utes and four-wheel-drives, many of them driven by countrymen. We're not far from the old Anne Street reserve, which still had a fence around it until twenty years ago. A lot of the local people still live in that area, in

HomesWest houses. Very few indigenous people own freehold. I begin to see why the D'Antoine house is so special, to Donny and to others.

It's extraordinary the resentment that whites here feel over some of these old Broome families getting title to the land they're living on 'without having to pay for it'.

Going past the Conti bottle shop, I keep an eye out for broken glass. There are often people hanging around outside the bottle shop at night; sometimes there's shouting and the occasional fight. Gordon says the shouting means nothing, but it takes some getting used to.

It's after 8 a.m. when I get to the Seaview newsagency and the *Australian* has just come in, on time for once. The assistant cuts the binding, rips off the 'Ansett Air Express' sheet and I get the first copy.

Rubibi

Rubibi is said to be an Aboriginal word for the 'soak' that existed near where the prison now is, although there's another theory that it's really Kriol for Roebuck Bay. The name has been taken by an organisation of local Aboriginal people set up with the help of the Kimberley Land Council. The idea is that various traditional owners in the Broome area come together to negotiate with the Shire, and to prevent competing native title claims. It's a way for different Aboriginal groups to settle between themselves who belongs to what country.

Rubibi is made up of representatives of three local tribes, the Yawuru, the Djugan and the Goolarabooloo. It's still in its infancy and I gather there are teething problems, but Rubibi already has its place in history. The famous 'right to negotiate' clause of the Native Title Act first became a warning bell for the conservatives when Rubibi insisted on being consulted on local developments.

At the moment Rubibi is waiting for the State Government to sign the Broome Framework Agreement, which would give Rubibi similar rights to those they now have under the Act—a safeguard in case the Federal Act goes.

∫ Was Virginia even more right than we thought? Does having a 'room of one's own', a shuttable door and privacy, really make an enormous difference? Certainly you look and feel completely different since we sorted out your work room. We finally moved an unwieldy cupboard out of the bedroom and brought the long trestle table in from outside and voila! you have a decent work space and we each have a room of our own. About bloody time! We should have twigged earlier to the absolute necessity of this.

Yesterday was rather a good day. We set off with Scruffy and Jack for the Saturday markets which are held in the grounds of the courthouse. We were all hot and thirsty by the time we got there. The tourist season is really taking off, and every conceivable stallholder is out there cashing in. Some of the long-stay winter visitors—retirees and young backpackers—make a bit of money selling jewellery or watercolour sketches or candles. There are makeshift massage tables with a sarong or two looped around them for privacy, and mangoes prepared a dozen different ways—ice-cream, smoothies, jam, chutney. We shopped for fresh vegies (one has to be there by 10 a.m. or they're gone), then sat for a while on the outskirts under a big boab, eating frozen mango ice and giving the last spoonfuls to the dogs.

We bought a large flat pearl shell from Roy, the lantern man. We first met Roy at Perpetua's gallery where he was exhibiting some rather lovely cane 'vessels'. He is an engaging, curly-haired Pom, a laid-back adventurer, attractive to women but not conceited about it. His little business in wicker lanterns, pearl shells and pearl buttons has suddenly taken off, and his lanterns are selling as fast as he can make them.

At any outdoor event in Broome there are lots of food stalls—Indonesian, Malay, Thai, occasionally even Dutch or Japanese. Stallholders set up at the courthouse markets on Saturdays and at the Thursday night markets in Chinatown. They will also go to Town Beach if there's a community event or a 'Staircase to the Moon' (a magical Broome phenomenon when a rising full moon coincides with a very low tide so that the moonlight creates a 'staircase' across the mudflats).

Some of the stallholders do really good business. Peter Ghouse, the music teacher from the high school, has a mobile kitchen at the courthouse markets every Saturday. There are not too many restaurants in Broome—just three Chinese, the Thai Garden, and a few others offering multi-ethnic cuisine. The stalls with their satay sticks, lumpias and curries, are the cheapest and most popular way to eat. That's how we are eating, more and more. Broome doesn't suit the sort of cooking we're used to, and the kitchen at Guy Street gets unbearably hot. Here all we want to eat is salads, curries, laksas and fish.

In the afternoon we went out along the red pindan road to the races. We arrived late so we only saw the post-race two-up. The raucous energy of it! A ring of yelling, sweating men and women on a dusty stretch of ground behind the grandstand. We met Hungarian Magda, who married into the Broome aristocracy when she married Kim Male. She was too engrossed in the game to talk to us. Magda was a barmaid at the Roebuck when she got Kim by the short and curlies. You see Magdas on the Budapest streets pretty frequently: savvy, pert and sexy—bright, but totally uninterested in things of the mind. Very different from Kim (short for Kimberley), with his ponderous manner and white shorts and long socks.

*

When we were here last year we admired the narrow wooden Anglican church with its pretty French doors opening all down one side. I remember thinking how incongruous the elderly minister and his small all-white flock looked, genteelly taking morning tea after the service. And how utterly different and vital the scene was at the Catholic church around the corner.

I wanted to visit the Anglicans this morning but I couldn't get myself up in time for the eight o'clock service. Later, we went past the church while walking the dogs. It was packed with tourists, mostly elderly retirees. Through the open French doors we heard the minister refer wistfully to all the winter visitors who will be going home once the cooler months are over, leaving the church with near-empty pews.

It's quite a social phenomenon, the number of retirees perpetually wandering the country in their caravans. I can see how endless touring might be preferable to mouldering in the suburbs playing bowls or putting money down the pokies. So why does it make me feel vaguely sad? The rootlessness of it? Or maybe because there is nothing to really miss in the towns or suburbs these elderly people have left behind.

Here in Broome there are four caravan parks, all full during the winter, the majority of the inhabitants retirees. They stay for three, four months. You see them all the time in the Seaview supermarket: grey-haired couples, hand in hand, wandering the aisles. The tourist industry doesn't like them much. They don't spend enough money.

Vanessa's family

I'm intrigued by Vanessa's siblings, all eleven of them—six half siblings from her mother's first marriage to a Hunter, then the Poelina tribe. Since her younger brother's suicide, Vanessa is the youngest. They are a bit unusual—not Catholics, for one, in this intensely Catholic part of the world, and perhaps with a wider-than-usual range of careers and interests. Yet the Poelina family has not escaped the decimation caused by frequent premature death and suicide. All in all, they strike me as a paradigm of how a Kimberley mixed-race family with a bit of ambition might fare.

Over lunch at our place, Vanessa ran through the Hunter clan first. The Hunter children's dad was mostly Aboriginal, although the 'founding father' of the Hunter clan was a white beachcomber from the early days.

'There's Ernie,' Vanessa began, 'just turned sixty. He spent over thirty-five years in the Water Authority till he became redundant. He's become the chairperson out at Pandanus [an Aboriginal community outside Broome]. Then Mervyn; he's a bit of an all-rounder, right into mechanical things. Always been a person who can get a job because of his skills, you know. He speaks many languages fluently. He used to be a pearl diver. He went out as a young fella with my dad, that's how he managed to pick up all the different lingos. He's putting a book together about those days—he's given it over to his son to research...

'Then Victor—he's the ATSIC chairperson in the Derby region. Then there's Eric; he's been in road maintenance, so he travels. His family live in Derby and he drives a grader. Terry, deceased. Glenys; she was an ATSIC commissioner, a regional commissioner. She's now the commissioner for social justice. She lives not far from me in Broome, but she travels quite often. She goes into all the prisons around the country...I keep saying to her, 'It's not about that, it's about keeping 'em out of there, you know?

'That's the Hunters. Then there's the six Poelinas. There's Petrus, he's the eldest. He's a male nurse. His wife is from New Zealand so he's currently over there, doing aged-care stuff. He's really good at that. So we're just waiting for him to come back; that will be his job on the river.'

What job on the river? Vanessa has a dream, she says, to move herself and her family out of Broome onto her mother's country on the Lower Liveringa and set up a self-sufficient community there, teaching the kids life skills, maybe even attracting the tourists. With Vanessa's energy it's probably not just a dream. She might just pull it off.

'Then my sister Anne; she's always been into Aboriginal health. She's highly qualified, but at the moment she can't get a job in her own community... Then there's Sue. She's just a home person at the moment. She's got a little boy. Then there's Neville. He's always been in the pearl industry. He's now a lecturer at TAFE with small boat proficiencies. He goes to the communities. They've got to do the course now because the communities are going to be doing boat tours.

'Then there's me in health promotions, and my youngest brother is deceased as well. My mother ended up having eight boys and four girls.'

Vanessa's father, Simon Poelina, the Timorese Muslim who used to ritually kill goats, much to his wife's disgust, later became a stalwart of the Anglican church. When he died not long ago, two Anglican bishops—not one, Vanessa told me proudly—presided over his funeral in Perth. But his ashes were brought back to Broome, to be scattered over Roebuck Bay.

Simon's kids were the only non-whites in the Anglican congregation, although the Poelina tribe used to tour the other churches, too, getting a taste of them all. The Catholics looked askance at such eclecticism.

Vanessa remains scornful of the Catholics to this day. She sends her own kids to St Mary's but only because all their friends go there and she doesn't want the kids to be isolated. She tells them to take all religion with a grain of salt. To make up their own minds.

On Matso's verandah

Matso's is one of Broome's oldest buildings. It was originally a Japanese-run store but has seen various manifestations since—the latest as café, art gallery and boutique brewery. The main building has a big central room with dark oiled floorboards and verandahs on three sides, set up with tables and canvas director's chairs. There is a paved garden, old trees. Elegant and cool in an understated last-days-of-the-empire way.

We went to Matso's to meet Dave Lavery who works for the KLC. Dave is a young Canadian lawyer; earnest round blue eyes; fluent and serious in that slightly overwhelming Canadian way; thoroughly nice. He seems at once impressed, fascinated and frustrated by his contact with the Aboriginal world.

He is, if anything, over-respectful of the culture but is also at his wit's end because of the amount of internal conflict he encounters between tribal and family groups.

He talked freely, almost as if he found it therapeutic to talk to us, because no doubt he has to be careful what he says to his Aboriginal colleagues, whom he clearly admires. His stories ranged widely. He began by telling us about the infamous house on Gantheaume Point. A lone house—a large showy number—sits amid the isolated splendour of Gantheaume and, in the usual complicated Broome way, it's not some rich white man ruining this important spot, it's Corrie Fong, from one of Broome's oldest mixed-race families. The story goes that the piece of land has been in the family for years. Corrie was happy not to build on it, as long as the government compensated her by giving her a larger piece of land elsewhere. But the government never came through, and Corrie said 'stuff the lot of them' and built her house there anyway.

Now the house is unpopular with black and white alike, and stories and gossip about it abound. Dave's story: five or six of Corrie Fong's relatives have died in the last year, clearly demonstrating in the eyes of the locals that Corrie is living in a place she is not meant to be living in. She is not there much (she's got business interests in Perth), so if someone goes past there at night, the lights, the TV, the video are all activated and there is a sudden electronic maelstrom in the darkness.

According to Dave, 90 per cent of the destructive infighting in the Aboriginal community is among the men. The women are far more cohesive. He puts it down to the effects of stolen children, poverty, grog and dispossession. With notable exceptions, this current generation—men between thirty and sixty—have been too fucked over to function effectively.

Despite the Census figures, which put the figure at much less, the Aboriginal population of Broome is actually 35 per cent to 40 per cent. And if you take out those people who have lived in Broome less than five years, then the Aboriginal population is as much as 85 per cent. A large number of the whites in Broome are only here for short periods, on two- or three-year contracts.

Dave and his KLC colleagues are concerned about plans for a new airport. The developers and the State Government want it near Coconut Wells, about twenty kilometres north of the town, right over Aboriginal law grounds. 'It would mean the end of traditional life in this area,' Dave says. Even having the flight path over law grounds would be a problem because secret ceremonies could be seen from the air. Two important song cycles cross in Broome. One runs from Gantheaume Point to One Arm Point, the second from Gantheaume Point down the coast and across towards Alice.

Peter Yu of the KLC

Peter Yu has been the public face of the Kimberley Land Council for twenty years. These days his horizons are international but he's enmeshed in this place, very much part of multi-racial Broome. We went to see him yesterday at the KLC offices.

He has an intense liveliness about him. Eyes that fix you. He speaks with great clarity. When we first saw him at the Derby meeting between Rio Tinto and the traditional owners, I was struck by the ease and verve with which he moved between Aboriginal elders, activists, miners and PR people.

We had been warned that Peter would not want to talk much about himself, but he was actually at his liveliest when talking about his early life in Broome. Like most Catholic kids, he went to St Mary's, a virtually all-black school. Then suddenly, in early adolescence, he was sent to school in Perth. He was the only non-white kid in his class. The few other coloured kids in the school were also isolated in white classrooms. 'We used to joke among ourselves that they were trying to make a "super-nigger" race out of us. We went to the best private schools, we had elocution lessons...'

So being sent down to Perth worked for him?

'Yes and no. I came back with skills, yet that sense of dislocation stays with you. The kids who didn't go away have a stronger sense of belonging. The kids who were sent away at twelve or thirteen on bursaries and scholarships always have a sense of something missing.'

In Perth they were not allowed to mix with other Aboriginal people. Once a month, white families came on a Sunday to take them home for the day. 'It was a very nervous relationship. We hadn't had much to do with whites, and they didn't know what to do with us.'

'How long ago was this?' I ask. (It's hard to imagine a Peter Yu uneasy in white society, so perfectly does he seem a part of it now.)

'1968 to 1970.'

These days Yu sends his own daughter to boarding school in Perth. 'I don't even know why myself sometimes.'

Education in the Kimberley is a thorny issue, given the dilemmas surrounding language and communication. Peter thinks that the present uneasy divide between Kriol and English in schools is part of the historical legacy of the master/servant relationship. Even Kriol is complicated. Broome Kriol is Malay-based, while in the rest of the Kimberley it's English-based. 'If I started talking Broome Kriol now, you wouldn't have a hope of understanding me, but you'd pick up a lot more if you were listening to Kriol at Derby or Fitzroy.'

Peter wants to see a regional Kimberley body established which would take charge of education and make it culturally appropriate. If indigenous people had a grasp of their own languages, he says, then their English skills would be likely to get better as well. 'People learn better in their own languages. Our kids are in the system now but they're not achieving. Why? They are getting the education meant for middle-class white suburbia. But we are distinct. There is no getting away from that, and different educational forms must be found.'

He refuses to be drawn on the question of tension between full-blood Aborigines and mixed-race people. For him, the only game in town is the relationship of indigenous to non-indigenous. But later, when we return to it indirectly, he talks about the tension between 'those who had their dog ticket and those who didn't'—that is, those who played up their Asian blood and had citizenship rights, and those who didn't or couldn't. It was common wisdom that the only way to get on was to 'marry white'.

Anne says, 'Well you not only married white, you married a girl from my old school, Newcastle High!'

Peter grins. Shortly afterwards he suggests we meet again over a dinner with Sarah.

Sundays with Lyn

We called in to see Lyn Page—it's becoming a bit of a Sunday habit. She's always casual on Sundays—no make-up, no shoes, just shorts or maybe only a T-shirt and knickers. We were sticky with sweat from just being outdoors, but she was in her front yard, pulling out weeds with gusto. Lyn's so taut and terrific that she looks at least ten years younger than her age, more on a good day. She must be in her mid-fifties.

We're gradually piecing together her story from her stream of anecdotes and gossip. She came to Broome in 1986. Lord Alistair McAlpine brought her over from Sydney to run Sun Pictures, the open-air movie theatre in the main street. Only half of Sun Pictures is actually in the open air; the back half is a tall timber structure, enclosed on three sides, with old movie posters on the walls and relics from the early days of cinema in the foyer.

Lyn arrived one February to 40-degree heat and appalling humidity. But she stuck it out. Now she loves the heat, luxuriates in it; says she resents it if she ever has to leave town during the Wet.

After running Sun Pictures for a few years, she took over a takeway food place called Mango Jack's that was and still is a bit of a Broome institution. She worked behind the counter night and day, seven days a week, selling fish and chips, and gained some street cred as a result. It was a long way from Double Bay.

From there to the Chamber of Commerce, to the Shire. Lyn is firmly aligned with the pro-development faction on the council, although she's also keen on preserving Broome's heritage—the McAlpine legacy. Unsurprisingly, she is a fan of McAlpine—of what he saw in the place, and wanted to preserve. She's adamant that heritage and development can coexist.

At the moment there's a fight over the location of the new airport. The present airport is virtually in the middle of town. When you're sitting in your deckchair at Sun Pictures, the planes fly so low overhead that their headlights are reflected on the screen. Whenever the 8.30 p.m. Ansett flight thunders over there's always a nervous gasp from the tourists in the audience. With the number of flights increasing, there's a feeling that the airport can't stay where it is much longer. And being so close to the town makes the old airport ripe for redevelopment. Part of it has already been sold off for housing, in fact—the sort of housing that few of Broome's original inhabitants can afford.

Lyn mentioned the stalemate over the airport the other night. She blames 'native title'.

At the mention of Rubibi, her manner is guarded, as though part of her knows that Rubibi is a good development—remarkable, ground-breaking even—a way for white and black to meet and talk and make accommodations with one another. Yet she is also suspicious and resentful of its potential influence.

Lyn is a bunch of contradictions on so many issues. She has the same schizophrenic attitude towards Aborigines that we've come across time and again here. Because she's so interested in matters spiritual, she professes to be envious and in awe of Aboriginal people. So she praises their spirituality (which is bound up with their connection to the land), but in the next breath she slams land rights.

Choosing sides

There was a large photo of Kevin Fong in the *Broome Advertiser* last week, a list of the activities of Goolarri Media Enterprises on a large board behind him. The photo captures his public persona—confident, articulate, his easy charm. But I'm beginning to see that behind that smooth exterior there's a lot of tension. He is the classic go-between, the person who is everywhere and belongs nowhere. Broome is the perfect—perhaps the only—place for him. Broome is full of people who don't quite fit anywhere else but fit easily here.

There are two Fong families in Broome, the William Fongs and the Percy Fongs, descendants of two Chinese brothers who married into local families. Kevin's father was William Fong. His mother was descended from Septimus Roe, a European surveyor who helped carve up the north-west. A descen-  dant of Septimus's married a local girl, Kevin's great grandmother, who they believe was of Torres Strait Islander descent, although there may also have been a Scandinavian connection. The next generation, Kevin's grandmother, married a Malay.

Kevin calls it 'a modern-day multicultural mix,' which, he says, has its downside.

'If I walk into a room, which table do I sit at? The answer to myself is, where I feel comfortable. I'm proud of all those skins, or cultures, but it is a very hard thing to come to terms with if you're not balanced or you don't accept who you are. It sounds romantic to be multicultural...but I think the reality of Broome is that there are actually very few people who practise and identify with all their cultural groups. They'll pick one.

'Then you've got a class system within that multicultural world...my mum and dad had nothing, my mum and dad used to live in the sandhills behind the meatworks, and every day there'd be watermelon stew. My mum raised seventeen of us—I'll get into that later. The fact is that Mum and Dad worked so hard, and had a vision and a goal. They bought this land thirty years ago and Dad had the vision that all of this would one day be housing. This was all bush here, we used to catch things with shang- hais. This is where we used to cook a feed, right here.'

We're sitting in Kevin and Alison's pretty, recently completed house, on a parcel of land behind Fong's Store. Willie Fong set up his store on the edge of town, but it's no longer the edge of town. Some of Kevin's siblings live in adjacent houses.

'With us having the shop, for example, we became—within the multi-cultural thing—rich. We experienced that all our lives: "Aw, but he's a Fong-shop boy." It was like you were being judged by your peers. I always resented that, and still do. I'll go to the pub, for example. The same person that I grew up with and went to school with will just assume that because my last name is Fong I've got money in my pocket and that I'll shout him a beer. If I asked the same thing of them, their answer would be, "But you've got Fong shop".'

A couple of years ago Kevin had a kind of breakdown. And he thinks it was tied up with the whole question of identity.

'I spent four years in Perth. Donned the suit and tie, played the protocols. Managed to maintain my identity behind that. But at the end of the day, it's where you really see the stark arrogance and the racism and the ignorance. When you associate in that society, among the bean counters and the lawyers, in those sorts of pubs. And you know, and you feel it, that you're either indigenous, or you're not.'

If you're neither black nor white, you have to choose—'you have to put yourself to one or other side of the ledger'. Kevin thinks this is the reason so many of his generation have returned to Broome. In Broome, so many of them are in the same boat that the whole question of identity can be pushed to one side.

The next generation of Fongs is even more mixed. Kevin's wife Alison is white. She came to Broome as a girl and she and Kevin have known each other since their schooldays. When their six-year-old daughter Rachel came home from St Mary's recently and said she had to choose what 'nationality' to dress up as for the Shinju float, she was overwhelmed by her choices. Kevin explained her different parts to her by showing her flags.

'That's the positive side of multiculturalism. The downside is those people who haven't had the opportunity or the support to be able to deal with that... I think personally that that is why a lot of people commit suicide and go off the edge. They can't cope. It comes back to that analogy: If I had to walk into a room one day with all my family, of all my different cultural make-ups, where would I sit? That's never happened to me yet. I've never yet experienced having to choose, and that's going to happen one day. At a wedding or at a conference. My answer is, you grab your own table and see who sits with you.'

Sojourn

Six

*Bob in prison—Minding the gallery—Bible stories—
Jimmy and Pat—What to call the Bishop—Conflicts
of interest—Land and story*

SWe visited Gordon at his new home, the flat above the Aboriginal
Legal Service office in Napier Terrace. It could be a nice flat
except there's no furniture—just two plastic chairs and two swags
on the floor in front of the television.

There was no sign of Damien. We're dying to lay eyes on him. I liked
the story of how he and Gordon met. When Gordy was doing his first
stint in Broome as a Legal Aid lawyer, he was living with an Aboriginal
woman whom he refers to as his second wife. She was a relative of
Damien's and introduced them in a bar. It was instant attraction. Damien
followed them home. He and Gordy had it off that night once the wife
had gone to bed. Then Damien stayed on—just sat in the living room for
a week, refusing to budge. Eventually Gordy's wife gave up. She said she
could and would fight any woman for Gordon, but not this man.

When Gordy was transferred to Kalgoorlie, Damien's mother, Peggy,
went with him. She lived with him there for three years. Damien just
came down for occasional visits, but he'd ring up every second day from
Broome and ask for money. Gordon always sent it. 'The post office at both
ends came to know us well.'

Gordy hasn't been long back in Broome and he's not sure how long
he's staying. The ALS job isn't confirmed as permanent yet; it started as a
four-month locum.

'Broome looks all right on the surface,' he says, 'but under the surface it's a very racist town. Whites don't want much to do with you once they realise how involved you are with blacks.'

Afterwards we went for a meal at our favourite Chinese restaurant, Son Ming's. You enter from the street through French doors, into a clean, spare room. Green walls, dark oiled floorboards, orange vinyl chairs around the tables. There are two sets of red and black Chinese characters on the walls. No other titivation, except a few modest red lanterns hanging from the ceiling.

Son Ming's is always the same: a scattering of beefy white couples, a family or two with young kids, and Harvey the Painter in his corner. Harvey is thin, scrunched and sombre. He only shows animation when drunk. He eats reading the paper and drinking a glass of red wine, then he smokes three or four cigarettes with another glass or two of red, his bottle sitting in a chilled bucket in front of him. He rarely looks up, except for a quick surly sweep of the room as he eats.

Harvey is just one of Broome's large cast of itinerants, eccentrics and hippies, young and old. Word is he sleeps under an old house, once the home of the defunct *Broome News*, at the top of Dampier Terrace. You see his paintings around the town's galleries—strong colours, flat 'primitivist' perspectives, much more cheerful than him. They're good.

Bob in prison

At Bob's I sat in a different spot, the better to view the wonderful junk shop that is his living room. The large model of a sailing ship, the gingerbread clock (or is it a tea-pot?), the two grinning pink and blue dogs with what looks like a china egg in the middle, the bits of electronics lying about, the crappy books and magazines. Bob sits placidly in the midst of it, receiving his visitors, ignoring the floating in-house population who silently make cups of instant coffee at his overflowing sink.

This time Bob told me about his stint in gaol during the fifties, for rustling. For two years he'd eluded suspicious local cops but they finally caught up with him when his offsider drove to the pub in the getaway vehicle without changing its tyres.

'They put me through the court. I pleaded not guilty. I defended myself, but I just didn't know how to defend myself; I was an idiot. I sat in the box, and they're all talking, this and that, and I says, "Excuse me, when do I get a turn?" and the prosecutor says, "You've had your chance".'

He got twelve months in Broome prison.

After a few days of watching the warder's habits, Bob managed to escape. 'I went out one night, got over the fence and come back the next day. I went home, of course. My wife got a surprise! So they put me in another cell which had a cement floor that high off the ground. There was no way out of there...'

Bob appealed his sentence and he was out in six months. But he was forbidden to go near his old butcher shop. To make matters worse, his partner had cheated him and cleaned up all the money. Bob caught up with him in the Roebuck Hotel. 'I said to him, "You be out of town tomorrow. You'd better be gone, because you won't live. What you've done to me, you've robbed me, my family..."'

'He went. He went, love. I was a bit of a killer in those days—a wild fella. Until then, I'd had money, a lot of money. I'm not bragging.'

While he was inside his wife had worked at Topsy's café to make ends meet, although she hadn't breathed a word to him at the time. 'My wife's a beautiful person. She lives in a house about three or four hundred yards down there...I go down there quite often. We're good mates. Bubbles is her nickname. She's one of the Pembrokes; the Earl of Pembroke. Goes back in the stud books as far as Lady Gladys Constance Pembroke. She was lady-in-waiting to the Empress Eugénie. The two daughters and the wife, they've got their books. I call them stud books.

'One girl is married to a Kennedy. They've got the internment camp at Willies Creek. They intern the illegal Indonesian fishermen there. The other one's in Perth. I bought her a house in Perth. They're all set up. I'm still working. I don't mind working...'

I like Bob, despite myself. He's tough and rough and as cunning as a shithouse rat, but he has a streak of irreverence, and another streak of kindness and courtliness that somehow sits easily with his unabashed ruthlessness.

Minding the gallery

I rather enjoy the occasional stint at Perpetua's gallery. I like the quiet beauty of the space, the wide floorboards, the glimpses of verandah, the ceiling fans turning, the mozzie coil drifting its sweetish smell.

Interesting, the power of the Durack name amongst many of the older tourists. Some want to pay, thinking it's a public gallery, some ask if it is the Durack home. Many go away with an Elizabeth Durack print if nothing else. Today a couple of older ladies wanted to see the Duracks that Perpetua keeps in the centre room. I also pointed out 'the ones she has done as Eddie Burrup'. Now would that be enough to satisfy Bruce?

It was fairly quiet so I could keep on reading Ernestine Hill's *The Great Australian Loneliness*. The book's prose is often purple, but wonderfully so. Hill was an intrepid woman and a talented writer, but page after page is littered with the unquestioned prejudices of her times: 'wild blacks', 'niggers', 'lubras', 'savages', 'little brown Japs'.

Perpetua remembers Ernestine well; she was a friend of the Duracks, and Ernestine's son lived for some years with Mary Durack's family.

Times change, although too slowly. In 1940 Hill devoted one sentence to the story of Pidgeon: 'a police black-boy "gone bad", who shot a trooper, ran away with his rifle, and murdered four white men before they caught and killed him in a tunnel of the Winjana [sic] gorge.' Today there's a whole book written about Pidgeon, under his Aboriginal name of Jandamarra. Eventually, once the full story of the Kimberley is written, Jandamarra and the Bunuba people's heroic battle may well be seen as analogous to stories of the French Resistance in World War II.

But that's a long way off. For many whites around here, Pidgeon is still just a blackfella gone bad who shot some policemen.

Bible stories

Eirlys Richards is a grey-haired, direct woman with an inexplicable shyness to her. She is neither pretty nor plain until she smiles into your eyes; then her eyes are the clearest blue, and she is dazzling. She must be at least sixty but when she goes into the house to get milk, she runs as easily as a girl. She lives in a modest house planted with trees and shrubs to screen it from the road.

An ex-missionary and linguist, Eirlys semi-retired to live in Broome after seventeen years at Fitzroy Crossing. As a devout young schoolteacher, she enrolled with the Summer Institute of Linguistics, a curious outfit that amalgamated serious linguistic work with 'bringing the Bible to the natives'. The Institute specialised in unwritten languages, eventually translating the Bible into the chosen language.

Eirlys and her colleague Joyce Hudson went to Fitzroy to learn Walmajarri. They arrived in 1967, the year when Aborigines got what are often referred to here as their 'drinking rights'. Initially Eirlys and Joyce worked with pictures on cards to build up a vocabulary, then with a couple of Walmajarri men who taught them grammar. 'One of the men caught on so quickly that he was giving us the answers before we could ask the questions.'

Meanwhile, the Walmajarri learned to read their own language—the men first, then the women. 'It's a man's world, even more than ours,' Eirlys says.

After seventeen years, with a furlough every five years, the two women had translated a small portion of both the Old and New Testaments into Walmajarri. Even that achievement was incredibly laborious; they would test their own translation by getting the local people to tell the story back to them.

Eirlys regrets that they didn't get it all done. But she is realistic, too. Walmajarri is a dying language, she says. It started to die when kids from different language groups were thrown together in hostels away from their parents and were forbidden to speak their own language. Kriol evolved as the common tongue among the under-forties. It has become a rich language in its own right, better for expressing emotions and better adapted to modern life, whereas Walmajarri is richest in naming, with hundreds of words for plants, animals, weather and every kind of physical detail.

Eirlys now teaches Walmajarri to Aboriginal kids in schools, just as you would teach Greek to Greek-descent kids.

She explained one thing that's puzzled me—why many Aborigines who've lived all or most of their lives in Broome, and have gone to school here, still speak indifferent English. 'The schools regard Kriol as an inferior form of English and not a separate language, even though it has its own grammatical structures. So the kids have to speak High English at school, then revert to Kriol at home, but they never really tell the difference between the two.'

Eirlys shows me her illustrated Bible translation. She says it's still used by a few people. On her last visit to Fitzroy Crossing, an old woman begged her for another copy 'because hers was falling apart with so much use'.

For a moment, pride in her achievement fires in Eirlys's blue eyes, but I also sense a wistful acknowledgement of just how limited her work has been.

Jimmy and Pat

It was Eirlys and Joyce who first encouraged Pat Lowe to start writing down some of the stories she was learning from her Walmajarri husband, the artist Jimmy Pike. Pat has now written quite a few books, with Jimmy illustrating. The latest is *Jimmy and Pat Meet the Queen*, published by Wendy Albert who owns the bookshop. It's a delightful spoof on native title, done tongue-in-cheek like a kids' book. Jimmy invites the Queen out to see 'her' land—that is, vacant crown land—so that he can explain to her that it's really his land, Walmajarri land. How can the Queen 'own' his country, wonders Jimmy, if she doesn't even know where the waterholes are?

Pat and Jimmy met here in Broome when Jimmy was doing a stint in prison and Pat was working at the prison as a psychologist. Pat is English-born. We've seen her around town, a slight, sandy woman with a rather fierce expression. Jimmy is that rarity these days—an Aboriginal man from the desert whose contact with whites is relatively recent. His family didn't 'come in' from the desert until he was in his teens. He started painting when he was in prison. Now you can't even buy his paintings in Broome—they are shipped straight to his dealer in London.

When we arrive at Pat and Jimmy's they are on the verandah. The verandah looks a total mess, till you realise it is Jimmy's studio. Inside there's a pleasant, untidy living room full of books and some paintings, a small kitchen and another room or two beyond. Basic, lived-in and homey.

Jimmy is sitting on the ground, painting milky brown dots on an elegant sage background. There's another canvas nearby, finished yesterday, of a spirit man—all movement and muscles, very sprightly, done mostly in yellow on a white background. After a while he joins us at the table. We chat over tea and cake. Jimmy eats the cake delicately and thoughtfully.

A When Jimmy got parole, Pat went with him back to the desert and they lived there for three years—it was a condition of Jimmy's parole that he stay out of town. Pat loved it. I am filled with awe at her bravery and adaptability. But she doesn't make a big deal about it.

It was out in the desert that Pat started writing down Jimmy's stories. She writes the way she is—unpretentious and straightforward. She doesn't mystify Jimmy or his talents, and is not in awe of difference.

I ask Jimmy if Pat was a good student when they were out in the bush. 'Oh yeah,' he says.

'There's one thing I never learnt,' Pat says. 'I still get lost.'

Jimmy laughs. 'Oh yeah yeah. Always learning, walking bush.'

Pat says to us: 'You should see the children. They mightn't know left or right but they'll say, "This is east, this is west." You couldn't afford to have people who said, "I've got no sense of direction." But it's still a bit of a mystery to me how Jimmy finds his way.'

Jimmy 'hummps', a short laugh.

'I've understood it better since I've seen Jimmy in towns, because I realise that I use man-made cues all the time, whereas Jimmy uses bush cues. So he gets lost in the city because the buildings all look the same to him. Whereas to me all the trees look the same. To Jimmy, the individuality is in the sandhills and the trees.'

'Big sandhill will tell you where waterhole is, no problem,' Jimmy says. 'Or a tree, a big one. Not far from that tree, waterhole. Man got to know them trees.'

'It just depends where you were brought up,' Pat says. 'That is what is familiar. For him it's the bush, for me it's towns.'

Pat is careful never to exclude Jimmy; nor does she change what we're talking about because of him. But she is always aware of him, of his degree of comfort in or boredom with the white world.

'When we went to England we went to Portsmouth, where I grew up. You really liked the sea, didn't you?' she says to Jimmy. Then to us, 'But in London, Jimmy kept asking, "Where's the sea, where's the sea?" In London you must have felt really hemmed in.'

In Portsmouth, Jimmy went to sit on the beach. 'The beach like a river town,' he says. The stones. The relief of the horizon.

I ask about their relationship.

Pat looks suspicious. 'I hope you don't want some big romantic story.'

'No,' I say. 'But what about the cross-cultural differences, was that hard?'

'It was quite hard,' Pat admits.

'What you mean?' asks Jimmy.

'Because we're from different cultures...' Pat explains to him.

'Oh yeah,' says Jimmy. 'Pommy people come from overseas...take land. Some white men take black women. Half-caste people got going. Black man now gets white woman, to get back.'

'Turn it around, eh?' Susan says to Jimmy.

'Yeah, turn around,' echoes Jimmy.

'You mean a black man has to get a white woman now to make up?' Pat asks.

'Yeah. Now other way round,' says Jimmy. 'That's what everyone's saying. Young people.'

'They're all saying that?' asks Pat.

'Mmm.'

We all agree that there's a lot of it about, in Broome anyway.

'People must have resented it,' says Pat. 'A lot of the fights used to be over that. The white people who did get killed, it was often over women.'

She seems unconcerned that she has been drawn into the payback trade. She says, 'One interesting thing that I've noticed which I suppose I hadn't expected: When I took up with Jimmy I was interested in his culture and learning about it, looking to him to teach me, wanting to live more simply, in the bush etc. Whereas Jimmy, he looked to me for the other. He quite liked towns and likes being in town. I've never had a television, but Jimmy wanted one. So we got one.'

It has been a bit of a problem; she would often like to go bush but he wants to stay in town. 'At one point when we were in the desert, I remember it was Jimmy who kept on wanting to come back to town.'

They now spend more time apart than they used to, and do things independently.

'Jimmy has to be a blackfella and I have to be a gardiya. We can't become something else. I suppose I did have romantic notions of "becoming".'

*

Jimmy and Pat on their way to a garden party at Buckingham Palace

Gordon rang this morning. He's had the flu all week but has battled on at work because there's no-one else. He says he hasn't had a drink in six days— 'Must be a record.'

He is now living in the flat above his office, with a mattress out of his caravan and a TV and a fridge. Damien is sleeping there too, on and off. 'Very convenient for his night-time haunts.' That is, it's close to the Roebuck and the clubs.

Last weekend Gordon went fishing at Willie Creek and read my book *Sex and Anarchy*. He said he would have enjoyed the Push. 'I've always been in the wrong place at the wrong time.'

∫ Maybe that's why we feel sort of comfortable with him. He breaks conventions out of instinct—more as he gets older, not less, which he knows is unusual. I get the sense that his hold on the 'normal' world as a barrister, too, is precarious, that he courts being thrown out, and that if he stays on here as the ALS lawyer it will only be because the Aboriginal community insists on it.

It's extraordinary to think of the poverty in which Peggy and Damien lived until Peggy finally got her HomesWest home, and they met Gordy— on the edge of town, under trees, under bits of iron, scavenging for food. It went on like that for most of Peggy's adult life and much of Damien's youth. Gordy says she has no rancour or bitterness about it. She just points out a landmark tree or humpy when they go for a drive and tells him stories.

What to call the Bishop

Another session with Bishop Saunders, whom I'm now calling Bishop Chris. I'm almost ready to call him plain Chris, but I'm not sure how he'd take it. Our sessions are usually at about nine in the morning. The presbytery is only a block and a half away, and because of the relatively early hour it's possible to walk, slowly, in the gathering heat. At the back of the house (made of corrugated iron, like most houses in Broome) is a demountable office where Marie the pleasant secretary sits and where a priest or two in civvies wanders in and out. Marie rings through that I've arrived. Sometimes the bishop comes to get me, sometimes I'm told to find my own way in. (It's this relative formality, the need to make appointments with him, that a lot of the old Broome-ites dislike.)

He's always in an open shirt, sometimes in shorts and thongs, and the first thing is coffee. The housekeeper makes the first one. He makes the second. He gets out his cigarettes—he's a big smoker—and starts talking. After a while I cadge a fag. It's become a bit of a ritual.

We talk about the Community Development Employment Program (CDEP) as the Aboriginal work-for-the-dole scheme is called.

'It's a princely $165 a week. Yeah, the only thing you can say about it is that if it wasn't around you'd have forty per cent of the population unemployed. Politically it's useful for the Government, and it has bought us a bit of time. If it's about making people work for the dole for evermore, it's unjust. But if it's about buying time, passing on skills etc, then it can be useful.

'We should be producing enough plumbers in this town that we don't have to import them, enough electricians that we don't have to import them, enough carpenters that we don't have to import them. But they're still bringing all those people up from Perth.'

St Mary's high school is now offering a hospitality course and the bishop hopes the local hospitality industry will make use of it. 'But there's a lot of get-rich-quick types in town and they're not interested in training people.'

Bishop Chris dates his involvement with Aborigines back to his childhood. Although his parents were city people, they spent time in the bush when his father was a rep for Shell. 'I remember hanging around with Aboriginal kids and I could never work out why the difference in circumstances. They'd be invited to our place but I wasn't to theirs, or only rarely. It embarrassed me, the income difference.'

The family moved to Sydney, then London, where Chris was sent to a middle-class Catholic boarding school. Back in Australia he entered a seminary. That was around 1968 when the Church was in a state of flux.

'They were turbulent years. I had many fall-outs. At one stage I was virtually asked to leave. The place was run like a concentration camp.'

He got out for a while and went to university to do law, where he got involved in student politics. 'But I couldn't settle to uni. If I believed the Church to be corrupt—which had gone through my mind a few times—I thought the law was more so. I did an Aboriginal studies unit and that brought many issues to the forefront...That's where I got the idea to go to a parish with a large Aboriginal population. I couldn't see myself in Melbourne.'

His first posting was to Darwin, to a white middle-class parish. He hated it. Then he met the then Bishop of Broome, John Jobst.

'He was very Germanic, but better that than the Irish Columbans! He was keen on the rights of Aborigines. Looking back, he was a child of his times—a bit patronising but full of dedication, of love. He guaranteed that I'd be working with Aboriginal people.'

When Bishop Chris came here in 1975, 'Broome was a very different town—ninety per cent coloured, Catholic and poor, and 10 per cent white, Protestant and rich. The reserves were still going: Anne Street Reserve, One Mile Reserve and Kennedy Hill. The old town finished at Herbert Street. Until '67 or '68 there were town limits for Aboriginal people. They had to stay outside a certain grid, but the rule didn't apply to coloureds.

'There were very few industries apart from the meatworks and one pearling company. There were only two small caravan parks. But when the blacktop came, that changed everything.'

'What's the blacktop?' I ask.

He's amazed that I don't know.

'The bitumen!'

*

Archie Weller's reading at the Broome library seemed, superficially, much like a literary function anywhere. There was the usual assortment of genteel middle-aged women, a table set up with cheap wine and sandwiches, and a straggle of local intelligentsia: Bruce, Maria Mann, and a couple of familiar faces from film nights and art show openings.

So why not quite like elsewhere? Well, Archie, as the more-than-usually-dishevelled author, was no shock to anyone; Bruce in shorts, thongs and tattoos was right at home; the bluff, direct-eyed author from Derby who wanted to meet us over dinner to 'talk writing' was not quite your retiring Glebe poet. Nor was the cluey librarian, Valerie, who *loved* her last posting in Port Hedland—that end-of-the-earth mining town—quite typical.

Last night was the first time we felt 'at home' in Broome. I'm not sure why. I can't put my finger on it. Maybe because when I followed Bruce out onto the porch for a clandestine cigarette, I already knew most of the little knot of people gathered there. Or because as we were chatting companionably about the unseasonal rain, Wik and other matters, you came out to do your usual anti-cigarette chide, and half the company were already cheerily familiar with your nagging!

Maybe by now, just past our seventh week here, there are moments of simply being comfortable.

Friday, July 3

A Bruce has the launch of a book by a Torres Strait Islander coming up next week as part of the NAIDOC celebrations. The local islander people are planning a feast. Bruce went around to Kennedy Hill to get the shopping list and found 'the TIs' (as everyone calls them here) busy making clapping sticks and painting headdresses. Instead of using bamboo for the clapping sticks they were using PVC pipe. 'You can't tell the difference when it's painted,' Bruce said. They are going to dig a pit and roast a pig, which they insist on supplying. They also asked for three large pumpkins, a sack of spuds and a dozen chickens. 'Fresh or frozen?' he asked. 'Oh, dead ones,' they said. 'We don't want live ones.'

*

At the council meeting the other day an item came up about street drinking. Alcohol abuse is a vexed question in the north-west, and different communities have tried various schemes to control it.

Kununurra Shire was seeking support for a local law to stop all public drinking. There was silence for a moment, then Lyn said, eyes flashing: 'That's not fair! I'd like to propose that we NOT support moves to outlaw public drinking.'

Then they all started. The feeling was that it would be discriminatory and not fair on Aboriginal people. Kim Male seconded Lyn's motion, which must be a first (Lyn complains that he never supports her).

Angus Murray, the smooth-faced and serious Shire President, said he wasn't happy with the proposal either. A while back Rubibi had wanted drinking on Cable Beach outlawed—aimed at all those whites who take their cars down onto the beach for parties. 'We said we couldn't do that. Well, we can't now turn around and try to stop drinking in public places frequented by Aboriginal people.'

The councillors particularly didn't like the suggestion that police should have the authority to confiscate unopened cans.

Lyn said: 'They could stop you just walking across the park with a six-pack!'

Good one, Lyn.

Conflicts of interest

When not presiding over the Shire, Angus Murray is a real estate agent. He's in his late thirties, already a little on the heavy side. He's to be seen around town almost invariably dressed in shorts and long socks. His family is one of the 'establishment' families in town. But that just shows how young Broome is because the Murrays have been here only since the 1970s. Angus was ten when they arrived. But the times he describes sound colonial.

'Back then most of the Aboriginal people worked for white people so it was very much a boss/servant mentality, which has gone now. So while a lot of white people in Broome probably felt they were friends with Aboriginal people, it was probably just that they employed them and they were all nice people, so they got on.'

When he speaks, Angus sounds so reasonable, so genuine. Maybe he's trying hard to overcome that colonial upbringing. He's probably had to learn a whole new vocabulary. Little things give it away, such as the way he says 'the Aboriginal people' every time he refers to Aborigines, as though he has drummed this phrase into himself, to replace some less polite expression.

'A critical part of the reconciliation process has been giving them back some power. When I was here as a kid in the seventies there were probably no more than fifteen hundred white people and maybe two thousand Aboriginal people. If you wanted to get on council you had to go and see the main [mixed-race] families and get their support, because they had the numbers. But in the eighties that all changed. The town grew very rapidly, the balance of power shifted away from the coloured people of Broome and people no longer consulted them in the same way. What we're trying to do now is redress that balance a little bit, to redress the balance so they don't feel left out as Broome progresses.'

Angus says that one reason the Shire is pushing hard for diversification of Broome's industry is the recession of 1990–1991. The recession followed on the heels of the national pilot's strike of 1989, which devastated Broome's tourism industry.

'They were pretty shattering times. McAlpine sacked twenty-five gardeners one Friday afternoon. The building industry stopped completely. You don't realise until you go through something like that just how broad the effects are. That's why you can't just be dependent on tourism. You have to diversify, you have to look at things like the cotton industry, the oil industry, horticulture, all these things.'

But he says it is important to everyone that Broome's unique character be retained: no high-rise and no building on the dunes.

'Aboriginal people want the town to grow and be prosperous as much as any other group in the community. They want jobs for their kids, too. But they don't want to see the coastline destroyed.'

Only when I raise a criticism I've heard—that he and a couple of other people are involved in just about every major development and community organisation in the town—does Angus lose his cool at all.

'This makes me really angry. Every time I go to a meeting, it's the same people who show up, the same people who are prepared to get in there and have a go. I wish it wasn't so. As for the Shire, over the years it has been the business people who have shown leadership on council. That's life.'

*

Nolan Hunter is one of three Aboriginal councillors on the Shire and he is not so sanguine about the influence of certain white councillors. He says the permanent white population is such a small pond that they are constantly implicated in matters over which they are making decisions, constantly self-serving. Until 1985 the Shire Council was elected only by ratepayers. Most indigenous people (who live either on Aboriginal Lands Trust land or rent from HomesWest) were ineligible to vote. So the white community is accustomed to running the town.

Nolan is the director of the Mamabulanjin Resource Centre (called 'Mama' by people here). He is another impressive thirty-something with a future ahead of him, a big man with a squarish head and a fashionable haircut who looks more Torres Strait Islander than Aboriginal.

Nolan is very keen to try and get an Aboriginal-dominated council at the elections next year. But he says it is made difficult by the businesspeople in town having two votes—for residence and business—and a large part of the Aboriginal population living in the 'outer ward', up the peninsula, which has only two councillors.

As I'm leaving, I notice a plaque on the verandah of the resource centre announcing that it was opened by Paddy Roe, the senior man of the Goolarabooloo. Next door is some Goolarabooloo land, where I gather Paddy Roe lives. In his time, Paddy was one of the most high-profile Aboriginal men in the north-west. According to Dave Lavery, he gained his status in part because he was the first indigenous person in Broome to own a car.

There are quite a few cars outside Mama, white cars—an indicator of government money. One sees these cars a lot around Broome. Sometimes they are sedans, more often they are four-wheel drives: Toyota Landcruisers, those icons of the outback. And on the doors, the name or initials of whatever organisation they belong to. Broome is full of acronyms— BRAHMS, BAMA, KAMA, KALAC, KLC—and you have to learn them because people use them constantly. A 'B' usually stands for Broome, an 'A' for Aboriginal, an 'H' for Health, an 'M' for Medical, or maybe Media, a 'K' for Kimberley.

Cars are important in Aboriginal communities, indicators of status and power. Behind the wheel of the white Toyotas rides the new Aboriginal elite.

Land and story

I went over to Goolarri yesterday. It was busy, cars everywhere. I tried to get tickets to the NAIDOC Awards night on Monday but had to go on the waiting list. And the tickets are fifty dollars each!

I saw Mary Tarran while I was over there. She's worrying about how her fifteen hundred traditional dancers who are coming in for NAIDOC will fare if the rain keeps coming. 'Might have to let them camp in the shed,' she said. But rain before a big event, or before people travelling, was a good thing. 'Means everything is being washed clean.'

I love the way she drops these things into a conversation. Land and story and tradition are the substance of Mary's life. When she tells me a story her grandfather told her, her face lights up. It is why the culture centre is so important to her. 'This is a time when our culture is slipping away from us. And we have to have our culture. It is our identity.'

At present, the culture centre is nothing but a makeshift office in a corner of one of the old trucking sheds at Goolarri, with two desks, a leaking air-conditioner and a couple of chairs for visitors. But Mary has a vision for it. Plans have been drawn up but what is needed now is land on which to build. Mary is hoping for some land near Gantheaume Point, or Minyirr, as she calls it. But not too close: Minyirr is sacred and not to be interfered with. The presence of that solitary house of Connie Fong's pains her. She drops her eyes when it's mentioned.

Proudly, she unfurls the plans for the Bugarrigarra Nyurdany Culture Centre. It is in the shape of a gulil, or turtle. The turtle is associated with the area. Most of the structure will be achieved with landscaping. Concrete and glass will be kept to a minimum. There will be spaces for traditional and contemporary performance, an art gallery and archives, a multi-media centre. The most important thing for Mary is that it be a place where Aboriginal culture can be preserved and passed on to future generations. It is an ambitious project but achievable. The name means 'because of the Dreaming'.

The media routinely presents images of what is taken to be Aboriginal despair. Despair is hardly surprising, given the history. What is more surprising is the repeated evidence of hopefulness, hope that refuses to be quenched, a resilience that cannot be defeated. Here in Broome, there are many organisations, and many many people, who keep going out of hope. And sometimes not much more than hope. Mary's 'wage' as co-ordinator of the culture centre is a princely $167 a week, the standard CDEP (work-for-the-dole) figure. Her situation is not untypical. There are two thousand Aboriginal adults in Broome; seventeen hundred are on CDEP.

As well as running the culture centre, Mary spends a couple of days a week working with Rubibi. She's both a consultant to Rubibi and has an interest in it because her family are traditional owners.

'Doesn't that make life difficult for you?' I asked her. 'Wearing two hats? Wouldn't you be better off not working for Rubibi?'

'I have to,' she said. 'I have to be there to keep an eye on things, for my people.'

From a white perspective, it might be considered unethical to work as a consultant for an organisation that could benefit your family. But things are not so clear-cut here. It is impossible to draw boundaries cleanly. Even I am feeling that. I am being drawn in, my sympathies engaged.

There are problems between the three groups that make up Rubibi—the Yawuru, the Djugan and the Goolarabooloo. The Djugan are said to be a clan associated specifically with the land where the Broome townsite now is; the Goolarabooloo with land to the north of town; and the Yawuru with a wide area of territory around Roebuck Bay. There are a lot of Aboriginal people in Broome who do not belong to any of these tribes. There are many Bardi, whose territory is the northern part of the Dampier Peninsular, around One Arm Point. But also Karajarri, Nyulnyul, Walmajarri and others. Because this is not their country—even though they have lived here many years, may even have been born here—they are not involved in Rubibi. And there is some resentment about this.

However, the main problem with Rubibi at the moment is its lopsided structure. There are four representatives from each of the three groups, but this does not reflect the real numbers. There are seventeen hundred Yawuru, one hundred and eighty Djugan and only eighty Goolarabooloo. The Kimberley Land Council is trying to correct this skewed representation before Rubibi becomes a separate legal entity. Not surprisingly, there's resistance, particularly from the Goolarabooloo.

Mary and her family are Yawuru. She insists that all the people in Rubibi are Yawuru.

'The Djugan?' I ask

'We're all related,' she says.

'The Goolarabooloo?'

'We're all one people,' she insists. 'It's just about power. That's all they're interested in. Power.'

Seven

NAIDOC week—Conferencing—Return

A In those rare daylight moments when there's no traffic on Guy Street, a sudden silence falls and I can hear birds calling, then a truck engine starts up at the service station in Walcott Street and the peace is broken.

Over the weekend we were woken a couple of times by motorbikes roaring past in the middle of the night. I thought it was a plane coming in to land on the house, but it was just one of the bikey gangs, probably the Gypsy Jokers, who rolled into town last week and were rolled out of town on Sunday by the police. Apparently they have 'interests' up in Darwin and were on their way to an annual meeting. Keeping an eye on how the girls and the dealers are doing.

Our local gang, a branch of the Coffin Cheaters, was raided recently. A few guns were found but nothing really major. It is said they control the drug trade here.

*

Gordon came to dinner last night, still suffering from the flu, a bit more subdued than usual. He'd had a trying week. Last Sunday, feeling sick and sorry for himself, he went back to Peggy's house and moved his bed into the spare room. (The three of them seem to sleep in front of the TV most of the time.) He spent a couple of days feeling at death's door, and Damien hardly noticing. At last Damien became solicitous and moved his swag into Gordon's room.

Gordy had come to the conclusion that it really made no sense for the two of them to continue. As they were lying there, Gordy on the bed, Damien in his swag on the floor, Gordy told Damien that he really thought they should split up.

'I could only do it because neither of us had been drinking,' Gordon told us. 'Because of that I was able to be calm and reasonable and to tell him that I wasn't angry with him.'

'We've got nothing in common,' he told Damien. 'I'm too old for you, you don't treat me very well, you don't give me much affection. It really would be the best thing.'

Damien didn't say anything immediately. Gordy was feeling so crook he just wanted to go back to sleep. Then Damien said, 'I thank you from the bottom of my heart for the past six years.' Even that didn't melt Gordy's heart—'That's how crook I was feeling.' Instead, he thought, 'Good, he's accepted it. Now I can go to sleep.'

As he was drifting off, he heard Damien start to sob. 'These enormous sobs just went on and on. Next thing he was dashing to the bathroom to get some toilet paper to blow his nose—noisily.'

In the morning, Damien was up unusually early. Gordon saw him outside the window, standing in the garden with a blanket around his shoulders, watering the shrubs that Gordon had planted around his caravan—'something he would never normally do; indeed, has never done before.'

Nevertheless, that morning Gordy moved out and went back to the flat above the office. By evening, he was getting used to the idea, starting to think that he'd be quite comfortable there. 'I was actually starting to look forward to it.'

At about 9 p.m. there was a knock on the door.

'I just can't accept it,' Damien said.

And that was that.

NAIDOC Week

For the first time, NAIDOC Week is being celebrated outside a capital city and the chosen place is Broome. It's a huge coup, and the locals are determined to live up to the challenge. But there's an added undercurrent because of what is happening in Canberra. The Wik Bill is before Parliament and Howard and Harradine are about to do a deal that will cut the legs off the Native Title Act.

Sunday, July 5

NAIDOC mass at the Catholic Church today. The church was over-flowing. Thankfully it was a cool morning; the fans weren't even on. It was a *Missa Kimberley* mass. 'A rite for use in the diocese of Broome...best suited to celebrations in tribal communities...no permission to use the *Missa Kimberley* outside of the Broome diocese.'

I saw Kevin Fong arrive with his wife and little girl. There were a lot of children and teenagers. Two rows in front, a plump Aboriginal woman sat at the end of the pew. She had a very active little boy of six or seven with her, a slim, dark, quick-featured kid. He spent most of his time standing on the seat or hanging off the pew in front.

The bishop spoke of his disappointment with the week's events in Canberra. He fears that the opposite of 'one nation' is happening, that the nation is being divided.

Most people took communion while Peter Ghouse and his mob played— seven or eight musicians on various instruments, including guitar and didgeridoo. In the *Missa Kimberley* the liturgical is leavened with a lot of song.

Afterwards, cups of tea and a big spread were set up under a tree. Cakes, sandwiches, iced sweet bread. I talked briefly to Phyllis Bin Bakar, Mark's mother. During the service she was presented with the Sorry Book started on Sorry Day. It is to be sent with all the other sorry books to Canberra.

Phyllis grew up in the orphanage under Aunty Bella's care. Aunty Bella is a famous person in Broome. Her story is told in the Stolen Children report.

'Aunty Bella dedicated her life to looking after us,' Phyllis said. 'She never married, she never had a man.'

Monday

At the formal NAIDOC Awards tonight—Aboriginal of the Year and related awards—one of the winners was Aunty Bella. She couldn't collect her award in person as she's in hospital, so several of the women who were 'Aunty Bella's girls' at the orphanage received it on her behalf. Some of them are themselves frail by now. Phyllis Bin Bakar was pushed forward to make the speech.

She lifted her head and said 'I want to thank the nuns at St John of God for looking after us.'

A flash of rebellion against the orthodoxy of the younger generation! I suspect there are quite a few old ladies here who do not regret the life they had with the nuns. Mark Bin Bakar, who was the MC, came up to stand next to his mother. He is a big, bear-like man with a mop of unruly black hair and fair skin. He put his arm across her shoulders and said: 'My cheeky mother.'

Phyllis is small, with very short dark hair, dark eyes that seem mostly sad, and high cheekbones. She has a lovely way of speaking, an almost musical cadence.

'I'm still a Catholic,' she told me, 'and I've got my belief and I'll go on believing because that's the way I was brought up, and I'm not going to change. The St John of God nuns were lovely women, and were good to us. They were our mothers. As we were growing up we had happy times, we had sad times. Together we were like one big family. We played as sisters, shared with one another.'

I said, 'It seems to me that the younger generation—your son Mark and his peers—are much more critical of the Church.'

'That's true, that's true,' she said. 'But I'm strong. I always say to Mark, "Well, the white habits were our mothers." I'll remember them to the day I die. They grew us up.'

The Aboriginal women here always refer to the nuns as 'the white habits'.

Phyllis was taken from her mother when she was three and only saw her once again, many years later, when her mother said to her, 'You belong to white habits now.'

'I can understand that,' Phyllis said to me. 'She had a broken heart.'

*

At the opening of the Kimberley Art Exhibition, several of the women elders were brought forward to welcome everyone to their country. This looks like being a feature of every NAIDOC event. Mary Tarran was the MC. I saw Charles Perkins and several other familiar faces in the crowd.

Then over to Cable Beach for the Western Australia Symphony Orchestra. The temporary stage had been set up on what is called the Amphitheatre—really just a gentle slope between The Club and the beach. It was like something out of a Hollywood musical—the fading sun, the sea, a white marquee next to a palm tree, the musicians in white tuxedos.

Before the performance began, several 'Rubibi women', as they are being called—interesting that, a new tribe is born?—did the customary welcome. Cissy Djiagween, Mary's mother, spoke last: a simple heartfelt message in which she asked the visitors 'to please look after my country'.

The NAIDOC Awards dinner was held at the Civic Hall, a pagoda-like structure built in the seventies when Broome's oriental connections were becoming fashionable. At the entrance, semi-transparent white drapes etched with faint motifs touched us softly as we passed. The effect was powerful, as if you were walking through a dream-maze. Then back to normal in the main hall set up with round tables and white linen.

It was interesting to see the black middle class at play, renewing friendships and political contacts. In some ways it was like any other middle-class gathering, except that it felt warmer, and more purposeful. Despite the classy clothes and the up-beat atmosphere, there was also a strong undercurrent of anger. The politics of Howard's Australia was never far from anyone's mind or lips.

The usually mild-mannered Pat Dodson roused everyone in the room with the final speech:

'They can deal, they can legislate, it will make no difference. Whatever the gardiya does, the land belongs to us! ... These awards are made of boomerang, pearlshell and local wood. They come from this country. They don't come from the Queen and her Corgi dogs. We belong to this country. The gardiya will learn it one day. The Government is not dealing with us in a just and honourable way ... We the people must do our best to defend our rights!'

I saw no pulling of rank by the Dodson brothers or any other indigenous dignitaries. The only 'rank' pulled was in a subtle way with the white media—a 'don't touch me till I'm ready, don't push me' body language. Status seems to operate differently in the Aboriginal and mixed-race community. There are few formalities in their dealings with each other, and a lot of affection and kidding. The only overtly respectful behaviour is towards the old people. During the ceremony, a palpable love swept towards them from the audience as they were gently shepherded on and off the stage.

Old Paddy Roe received the award for Elder of the Year. He looked slight and frail, and rather elegant in a cream suit and hat.

A surprise emotional outburst came from Nolan Hunter, one of the three Aboriginal councillors, who was called on to accept a reconciliation award on behalf of the Shire. He didn't want to accept it, he said, when no white councillors had bothered to come to the Awards Night, and when the Shire proposed charging the NAIDOC committee $12 000 just for the use of the oval even though NAIDOC was bringing so much money and prestige to Broome.

There was indeed no official representation from the Shire. It was an extraordinary omission, given the impressive turn-up of Federal and State pollies.

Outside the hall, the smokers and talkers hung out on the verandah, catching up with each other. There were people from all over Australia. Many of them knew each other from around the bureaucratic and political traps. We talked to our friend Jackie Huggins, the Aboriginal historian and writer.

'Are you here to get an award?' I whispered.

'No, I'm one of the judges.'

Jackie was on the last leg of a week-long trip that had taken her to Sydney, Brisbane, Thursday Island, Broome. 'If I see one more TI dance...' she said and grinned conspiratorially.

*

I was supposed to fly to Perth this morning (I've been invited to a Jewish Literature conference), but I postponed my flight because I wanted to go to the open day at the Jarndu Yawuru Women's Resource Centre.

The open day was not what I expected. At this women's co-op there were probably more men than women! Everything was in that laid-back, slightly-out-of-focus Broome style. A troupe of Thursday Island dancers, with their bright skirts and deliberate movements and melodious melancholy singing, did quite a few numbers; in fact they were in danger of taking over the whole show. An old Aboriginal man who seemed to have just wandered in out of the desert rambled for a while in language and Kriol. Then a couple of dignitaries spoke, followed by a country-and-western singer—another Thursday Islander. And so it meandered on.

Jarndu Yawuru was founded, and is run, by a round little tyro of a woman called Theresa Barker. It acts as an art-and-craft co-op for women, not necessarily Aboriginal women. Business skills are taught, and there's a crèche. On display were painted plates, silkscreen materials, T-shirts and handmade clothes with Aboriginal designs, many by Theresa's more famous daughter, Pat Torres, Aboriginal writer, artist and activist. I bought a turquoise and orange vest (the colours of Broome), and a singlet for Annie with a parrot story on it.

I congratulated Phillipa Cook on her daughter Samantha winning one of the youth awards at the NAIDOC Awards last night. Sam is the lightest skinned of Phillipa's four kids, a 'you'd never guess she was'. She must be conscious of it because she thanked her family for making her culturally aware and proud of her Aboriginal heritage. I got the impression that, in her milieu, being light skinned is a disadvantage. You have a greater burden to prove you belong.

In the late afternoon we took the dogs, resplendent in their new leads—black for Scruffy, red for Jack—down to Town Beach for the Magabala launch of a children's book by a young Torres Strait Islander, Alex Tipoti. The microphone and the author's signing table were set up on the beach. Bruce, as the white editor in an Aboriginal publishing house, was standing very much to one side, officially invisible.

There was another lengthy round of TI dancing. I began to see what Jackie Huggins meant! Nearby the local TIs had dug an oven into the sand to cook their feast. Bruce told us exactly what was buried in there, slowly cooking on hot coals: 'Twelve chickens, four kilos of onions, two kilos of carrots.'

Peter Bibby, who seems to turn up almost everywhere like a small white wraith, came up behind us. He was, as always, full of useful information. Broome has a big community of Islanders, he told us, because in the old pearling days they were shipped in to be used as divers and deckhands.

Peter has blue eyes that fix you with an almost preternatural blueness. He is diffident and intense by turn, the intensity leavened by a quirky humour and a quickness of observation. He's one of Broome's perennials: writer, musician, intellectual, committed Catholic, involved in everything from the Fringe Festival to the church choir. He was Bruce's predecessor at Magabala. He's extremely well read, and his opinions are never predictable. The other night when we had dinner with him, the talk ranged from Greek ruins to Proust to local politics to Peter's experience as an English child migrant. He's not bitter at all. 'England at the time was a terrible place,' and the child migration program was 'entirely benign' as a policy. He benefited, on the whole, he thinks.

But I sense a dark, complicated side to Peter, that may have something to do with those early years.

We left Town Beach before the TI feast was ready because I had to catch my plane. My Jewish self—whatever that is—is to be dusted off for a day or two.

Wednesday, July 8

Howard's ten-point plan went through the Senate today. The Government has succeeded in winding back native title rights. For the first time tonight I really felt the shame: that this country, which has always been so ineptly proud of its 'fair go' tradition, should have harboured all along such ingrained unfairness and arrogance.

Tonight on the phone, Mum said: 'All those people who say they can't or won't say "sorry" because they weren't responsible for what happened in the past...well, now there's no excuse, now *we're* guilty. We're the ones who have done this—your generation and mine.'

But tomorrow the Kimberley Land Council conference begins—hopefully a new phase. It will be the first time that so many traditional owners, miners, pastoralists and industry groups have come together.

Sos Johnston is going to be one of the speakers at the conference. He's a former Broome Shire president, very entrepreneurial—too much so, some say. He told me that half the population of the Kimberley are Aboriginal and that most of them are unemployed. He wants to get them working, to harness this incredible asset. That's his vision—for Aborigines to be part of the development of the Kimberley, to be economically entitled.

It was Peter Yu who suggested I talk to Sos. According to Peter, 'No matter what happens with the native title legislation, it is the people on the ground who have to work out how to live and work together. That is what the conference is all about.' He expects negotiated regional agreements to continue, despite the removal of the 'right to negotiate' from the Native Title Act.

Conferencing

The Australian asked me to cover the KLC conference, which complicated my attitude towards it. Everyone else there clearly had a legitimate interest. But what was mine? Was I there as a journalist? A writer? A temporary resident? I found it impossible, at such an event, at such a time as this, to maintain the expected 'journalistic objectivity'—if that is ever possible.

Some people and quotes that stood out...

Gabriel Nodea from the Kimberley Aboriginal Law and Culture Centre said, 'Our elders stayed strong as everything changed around them. Our law, given to us by our people, never changed. Our culture is still strong and still practised.'

Peter McCumstie, an enormously fat man, chair of the Kimberley Development Commission, talked of the commission acting as a 'project brokerage facility'. He's keen to see more Aboriginal involvement—joint ventures, equity partners.

John Ah Kit, a Member of the Legislative Assembly from the Northern Territory: 'We are in danger of entering a period of despair and disunity. We can become victims or we can take a stand. If the former, history will not judge us kindly. Let this conference be the moment in history when we take a strong stand, and look after our lands for the future of our children.'

He criticised 'the conservative mantra that Land Councils are stopping development'.

Olive Knight, who is in charge of women and community affairs for the KLC:

'The past had a sheltered, settled feeling. Not as difficult or as complicated as today—when we have so many responsibilities and difficulties.'

Olive grew up at the Fitzroy Crossing Mission, then went as a maid to a station. 'The manager was a tough man but he was kind to me. I was paid four pounds a month.' In the 1970s, when award wages came in, she had to leave the station and go back to Fitzroy Crossing. She finished on a nice note: 'My life and my past is my own. My history I own.'

Keith Anderson, owner of Jubilee Downs Station and a man described as a 'pioneer in relations between indigenous and non-indigenous people', told of how he arrived in the Kimberley as a very young man and went to work for the Emmanuels on GO GO station:

'It didn't matter if you were white or black, you lived off bread and beef...the old men had dignity, humour and good health...Skin is exactly that. It's only skin, skin deep...It's important that the old mob have access to the land. I have an understanding of their right and need to come onto the land, always.'

Mick Dodson, former Social Justice Commissioner: 'Ten or fifteen years ago we wouldn't be sitting in a room like this talking about our collective futures. There's goodwill, a level of equality and a condition of relative strength that wasn't there before. The reconciliation movement of the past eighteen months is the closest thing this country has seen to a people's movement. People have left the Government behind.'

Ken Oobagooma, the old man we met at Derby who was a signatory to the Rio Tinto agreement, said, 'If we are Australians, if we are family, we should share this land together, brothers and sisters. Our blood is one. We must share this land. We are one land but two people; those on the right hand who are moving forward. And those on the left who are not moving.'

*

At unexpected moments I am confronted with my own racism. When I first heard that the KLC conference was going to be at the Cable Beach Club and was surprised at the upmarket venue; when I was talking to Ken Oobagooma and a KLC functionary came up and asked him for the key to his room and I got a small shock that this thin, elderly man in shabby trousers and jacket was staying at the Club. (Then in the next session who does Pat Dodson introduce as the first speaker? Ken Oobagooma.)

There was something surreal about the conference workshops. After the formal sessions, people broke up into groups and gathered in different parts of the lush Club gardens to discuss specific issues. Metres away tourists wandered past, towel and sunhat in hand. The 'communication' group was almost half made up of older Aboriginal women. I expected that the subject would be information technology. Not so. The older women were worried about the preservation of tribal languages. Most of them were from the language centre at Halls Creek.

The other major 'communication' concern was roads. With the home-land movement—Aboriginal people moving back to their country—tracks that might once have seen six cars a year are now seeing six a day. But there is no money allocated by ATSIC or the Government for making these into proper roads. Plus there are 290 000 visitors a year coming to the Kimberley, 85 per cent of them by road.

*

The Sydney Telegraph has run a story leaked from Senator Herron's office claiming that Pat Dodson is being paid $81 000 for organising the confer-ence—about four times what he is actually being paid. Herron said he would launch an inquiry into ATSIC's spending on conferences. All the KLC people are angry and depressed. So much effort has gone into this confer-ence; it is such a milestone. If people can't sit down and talk to each other, what hope is there?

To get away from it all, I took the dogs for an evening walk on the beach at sunset. There were bushfires out towards Gantheaume Point and

thick smoke across the racecourse. As I came off the boardwalk an easterly wind was blowing the smoke in a long stream across the dunes and out to sea. Thick pinky-grey smoke, changing the colours so that the vegetation on the dunes looked larger and bushier, almost forest-like, and the dunes became pinky-green hills. Out at sea the smoke was like a cloud, diffusing the sunset, then clearing to reveal an almost tangerine sky.

Saturday

A story has been leaked that Senator Herron spent more on private jet charter last week than was spent on the entire KLC conference. That might shut him up a bit.

Return

∫ I was only away three nights and two and a half days, yet it's taken us nearly a day to readjust. We've spent every day of the last ten weeks together since we left home. It was a shock at first, having to locate my 'alone' self. It always is. But after a day or so I almost start to enjoy it, while missing you. And then we're together again and the 'together' self has to be refound and retuned. Sometimes we're snappy with each other until the adjustment is made—as if we don't quite know what to do with the pleasure of being together again.

I left warm little Broome and landed in clean, prosperous, *cold* Perth three hours later. The thermometer had hit freezing. The first day of the Jewish Lit conference I felt alienated, unable to concentrate on all those (mainly male) egos spouting jargonised cultural theory in chilly lecture theatres. Broome seemed all light, informality and colour in comparison.

But as is the way of conferences, you get used to them. You burrow into the enclosed little world they offer, knowing it will be over soon. Then it's fun, exchanging views on books, getting a bit of gossip. But two days was plenty.

I haven't been among so many Jews in years. It struck me that we Jews have become so practised at expressing our alienation, our 'half-belong-ing', that we've entered the establishment through it. We're the professional 'other'; we write books about it. The Aborigines don't half-belong in this country. They belong fully, but they have also been fully dispossessed, so their marginalisation from the mainstream is the more extreme.

*

Sunday evening we went down to the oval to catch the last of Culture Day, reserved for traditional singing, dancing and artefacts. Perhaps four hundred people were there when we arrived, mostly Aboriginal families spread out on rugs and sleeping bags. On the periphery stood seven or eight dusty white mini-buses, the sort you soon recognise around Broome as belonging to outlying communities. Goolarri Media was set up beside the pindan dancing area, its cameras roving between the dancers, singers and audience, mikes arranged low to catch the groups of sitting singers.

Most of the performances made me feel sad. They seemed to be no more than scraps and fragments of half-remembered songs and dances, badly rehearsed. It depressed me, too, to see elderly Aboriginal women in those ludicrous bras—so old a concession to white prudery that they may have become part of the costume.

The men were half in ragged trousers, half in body paint. During one group dance, only one man seemed to know the steps, while the rest copied him half-heartedly. Another group of male dancers, with more fire and verve, did an extraordinary sequence of hunt and capture, but then they just repeated it over and over again, unless my untrained eye couldn't see the subtle progression. Peter Bibby, who materialised again, his slight frame and white hair emerging from the dark—you never actually hear Peter coming, but suddenly his pale blue eyes are smiling at you—said he'd first seen that dance here in Broome in 1962, and back then it was more complex, told an identifiable story.

I don't know. I can only record things I see and hear. I feel myself moving uneasily between the shoals of exaggerated respect for Aboriginal culture and the reefs of indifferent ignorance. You meet both phenomena among whites here.

It was actually cold on the wide expanse of the oval after the sun went down—a rare experience in Broome. We left early, not waiting for the final corroboree, feeling chilly and dispirited. And not a little guilty, because we were hurrying home to catch 'SeaChange' on the telly; a pleasant bit of fluff about white country-town Australia.

Eight

Shama of Blooms—Yawuru feminist—Lyn and Rubibi—
The flying bishop—Bush churches—The power
broker—Eirlys and Joyce—Vanessa at Guy Street

Some days there is such a flood of information, observations, impressions that there's no chance to absorb them before being ambushed by more. At the moment we are out and about, being our public selves almost constantly. 'Broometime' doesn't suit so much activity. The ALP last night, the bishop this morning, minding the gallery for Perpetua this afternoon, dinner tonight with the Broome Soroptimists. Sounds like a sorority of optometrists! Lyn is their president and she invited us along when we ran into her while cruising the dress shops. We were looking for some better clothes. It never occurred to us that we would need dressy clothes in Broome, but Broome people love dressing up. Lyn was trying on a pair of gold pumps.

July 16

I've been waking up in the middle of the night worrying about how to wade through the mass of material before us. The other morning we found our list of people ran to nearly eighty. I'm doing things I never normally do, like forgetting a name that I knew quite well last week. I map by names and rarely forget one. You're better with faces. For me, people's faces change as I get to know them—as though they literally come into focus.

Yesterday when we were walking the dogs in a different part of town, we ran into Mary. When I first met Mary at Goolarri I noticed only that she had a friendly face and was very dark—darker than most people one sees in Broome. Each time I've met her since, she has become better looking. After the NAIDOC Mass when she introduced me to her mother, she was looking so lovely that I complimented her on it. For once she had her long wavy hair hanging down her back. Yesterday you noticed it. 'Mary really is beautiful,' you said. 'I hadn't really seen it before.'

All the mini-worlds we're dipping into in just one small town! We're like bees with a myriad of blossoms—a quick nuzzle here and a hurried sip there. The Soptometrists, sorry, the SOROPTIMISTS will welcome you back with open arms, now that you've given them a theme for their float for the Shinju Festival. They were paddling around with a few weak ideas until you suggested 'Broome women through time' and they took it on. So we might be seeing the pioneer women in their long hot skirts and high-necked blouses, the Japanese prostitutes of Sheba Lane, the intrepid aviatrixes, the nurses and barmaids, and maybe Mary Dakas, the lone woman pearling master.

I always marvel at your ready stock of relevant ideas, even when the matter at hand has nothing to do with you. You put it forward calmly, without pushing, and invariably it becomes *the* idea, without other people actually noticing.

The Soroptimists are not quite the sisterhood we're used to; more your female equivalent of Rotary. All white, of course. They proved quite an interesting bunch once they dispensed with the faintly weird and antiquated formalities—grace, the 'Soroptimist's oath' etc.

Lyn, as this year's president, was very much at her ease, enjoying her prominence but not grandstanding. She is totally immersed in her life here. I think it's why the place suits her so well—she can give vent to all the different, sometimes eccentric, sides of herself, far more than she was ever able to as a Sydney socialite.

The Soroptimists, mostly professional and business women, raise funds for charity. When I think of all the work that went into a recent sausage sizzle, with all of $105 raised, I wonder why they don't just donate a couple of hundred a year each and save themselves the hassle.

The Labor Party meeting the night before was more familiar territory. There were a dozen of us, at best, in the Bucknall's pleasant middle-class Broome home. I'm always ambivalent about Labor Party activists. I like their no-nonsense practical approach, their world-weary analysis of politics that nonetheless still retains a touch of idealism. They are usually intelligent and well-informed people. But they're missing something—a spark, a new vision. They know Hanson's got that vision, in her own perverted way, and they're worried.

A visiting State pollie told me of his admiration for the new generation of black leaders: young, sophisticated, managing to channel their anger. He singled out Martin Sibosado, who's on the Shire. When he first met Marty in Perth, at university, his anger was threatening to pull him apart. Now, he says, he's a good operator on several fronts.

Shama of Blooms

Bob Noble often mentions 'young Shama' and how he helped her get a start in Broome when she was just eighteen, newly arrived in town and wanting to open a dress shop. He went guarantor for her on a bank loan.

Shama is tiny—a pocket Indian Venus, long curly black hair, big dancing eyes, energetic, all smiles. These days she is the driving engine behind the town's most popular café, Blooms, the place to see and be seen as you sip your latte. The old wooden building was once a gamblers' hall where men gambled with pearls while the local kids crouched in the dirt underneath the floorboards, waiting for tiny pearls to drop through.

When Bob helped her with the bank loan all those years ago, Shama was worried what else it might entail, he being a bit of a ladies' man, but he never tried anything, 'not even a little pinch. Do you notice how he never uses your name? Sometimes I wonder if he even knows it!' she says. 'When he rings me at the café, he's always asking for "ruby lips" or something like that. With all those young men who hang round him, he just calls them all "son".'

Shama meets Mrs Bob from time to time out shopping. She's a tiny lady, Shama says, very genteel, with a strong character.

Blooms was the first trendy café in Broome and at first the locals were very suspicious of it. Shama likes to keep it 'a bit bohemian, very relaxed'.

All the customers—locals, tourists, hippies, the famous—are treated the same. If the McAlpines go there (Lord Alistair's first act on arriving in town is to go to Blooms for a watermelon juice), or if Jimmy Barnes comes by after his gig at the Roey, as he did yesterday, Shama never tells her staff who they are until after they've gone. This is one of the secrets of her success. That and her passion for the place and her capacity to smile genuine smiles and still be hard-headed.

Shama has another story about McAlpine. After her first little dress shop on the waterfront, she moved her business to Matso's, which was then owned by McAlpine. While she was trying to negotiate the lease, he ignored her and kept talking to the only other man in the room. Finally she said, 'Excuse me, I'm Shama. I'm the one taking the lease.' And held out her hand.

*

Since I've been back from the Jewish Literature conference in I've been questioning the generalised affinity I've always felt with Aboriginal people. In Perth I was reminded of how different my own cultural roots are, how even in the most shut-off and inward Eastern European *shtetl* Jews were not as foreign to the dominant culture as indigenous people here were to the English conqueror. When I exchange remarks with a black bureaucrat or a member of the Aboriginal middle class in Broome I feel no gaps. But with someone from the remote communities, or the artists whose paintings I'm only just learning to appreciate but don't really understand, with the drunks in the park who buttonholed us the other day, what real links have I?

At my seminar in Perth I was asked a 'nuisance' question by a Jewish woman who wanted Jews to 'become nicer', as she put it, so that other people would stop wanting to kill them. Someone tried to answer her by saying that no-one (these days) asked the Aborigines to change themselves so they wouldn't be oppressed. 'Aborigines can't be asked to change themselves; they're too primitive,' she said. 'The Jews are more sophisticated; we should try to be different so that people won't hate us.'

There was a horrified PC reaction in the seminar room. But this woman's attitudes are not rare. My mother and many of her generation believe Aborigines to be a 'primitive' race. She is pleased but unbelieving when I tell her they are like everyone else—just people, with varying levels of intelligence, sophistication and morality. My generation no longer believes in the 'primitive' theory, but we do—guiltily or petulantly—want indigenous people to become more like ourselves, and quickly. When Noel Pearson or Aden Ridgway or Peter Yu come onto our television screens, many of us are relieved. We would like the whole indigenous world to be like them.

I catch myself despairing over the huge gaps that continue to exist. When I see, still, matted hair, unwashed bodies, poor English, the tattered remains of an old culture half-forgotten, it's momentarily easy to give up, generalise, retreat into an 'us-and-them' mentality. Real insight into a profoundly different Aboriginal view of the world is hard to acquire without spending time and having a flexible mind, an open heart. Otherwise all you get is the tiniest glimpses, before the door shuts again and you are again a puzzled, uncomfortable outsider.

It's still hard for me to accord proper respect to an oral culture, but I do begin to see. I begin to see when Eirlys tells me how rich Walmajarri is in naming. Phenomena to which we would accord just one word are divided into many sub-categories in language because the indigenous perception of the natural world is so much more detailed than ours. And I begin to see when I read Pat Lowe's *Jilji*, a fascinating account (based on her three years in the desert with Jimmy) of the knowledge and ingenuity required to make a life in harsh country.

I don't know how much of this I want to learn personally. I still feel queasy about the walkabout trips white people make—a week or two spent bush after which they come back starry-eyed about Aboriginal culture. But I do need some more tools for understanding, some more glimpses into that other universe.

Here in town, too, we learn things; small but important things. Not to make assumptions about a circle of countrymen sitting in the park; how Aboriginal families work; how to look differently at poverty. Getting to know Mary, how differently I see her dilapidated HomesWest house now I know something about the remarkable woman who lives in it.

Yawuru feminist

Kevin was nowhere to be seen at Goolarri this morning—he'd been called over to the ATSIC offices—so I went out the back to see if Mary was in.

Mary seemed distracted, shuffling papers, sorting things. She said she'd been at Rubibi all day yesterday and was going out with them again today. Again I got a sense of her frustration with the process she is caught up in. It is not that Rubibi is opposed to her culture centre as such, but it seems they are being obstructionist. I'm not sure why or in what way. She kept referring to people playing power games, about being dismissed because she is a woman, and a woman caught up in gardiya things, like paperwork.

I said, 'The difficulties of a Yawuru feminist,' and she smiled.

As a woman, Mary is not considered to have the Law. Yet she says she is Yawuru, it is her country, she has a grasp of the language. She had three Yawuru grandparents and a Bardi grandmother.

I told her that I'd like to have a more leisurely talk with her some time and she said she'd like that, that it would be good to talk. 'I feel so messed up inside sometimes.' She sometimes goes home at lunchtime and locks the door, pretends not to be home, and thinks and 'talks with' her grandparents. She almost became teary talking about them.

Mary said she wanted to go to the museum to see if there was anything there on Paddy Djiagween. I said I had looked for his grave in the cemetery but hadn't found it. She liked the idea that we should go there together and maybe also to the museum.

I went to the museum myself this afternoon to see what I could find on Paddy. I somehow felt it might be better to do an initial reccy on my own, in case some white colonial woman on the desk had never heard of Paddy Djiagween, even though he was a major Yawuru elder and lived to be more than 110.

I didn't find much to start with in the four red folders marked 'Local Aborigines'. But out the back, just before closing, I found two large yellow scrapbooks—Aborigines I and II—and in the first of these were several pieces on Paddy.

These folders on Aborigines are themselves an insult. There's mountains of material on the prominent white families, on pearling and the rest of it, but all there is on the local people are these six folders containing bits and pieces, scraps of stuff. And on the walls a smattering of photos of blacks.

Lyn and Rubibi

Lyn was complaining about the running of the coastal park management committee, which has Rubibi reps on it. 'It's a standing committee of Council and it's breaking every one of their damned rules,' she said.

Lyn refuses to see that the coastal parks committee operates differently *because* it has Rubibi reps on it, that it is part of the Shire's reconciliation measures and so of course is not like any other committee.

Whenever Lyn is uncertain of her ground, her speech becomes more pronounced, slower, more definite and 'proper'. I noticed it particularly on this occasion. She started being officious, going on about things not complying with standing orders. She's at her least attractive when she's being officious. She was saying that the two whitefella Rubibi reps on the committee, Dave Lavery and George Irving, both KLC lawyers, had a 'conflict of interest' because they were paid by Rubibi yet were on a Council committee. I said they were only on the committee because they worked for Rubibi, so it was hardly a conflict of interest. 'The Rubibi people don't feel confident to go on such a committee themselves and deal with the white man's world.'

'White-man's law,' Lyn corrected. But she agreed with my general point.

She started to relax after that, and her big grin reappeared, especially when Susan pulled out her papers and started to make a rollie.

Lyn and the Shire CEO, Greg Powell, are good friends, but their attitude towards the Shire could not be more different. Lyn is passionately implicated in the town, whereas Greg appears indifferent to it. To him it's just a job. Yet they're friends—I suspect because they are both outsiders. Although Lyn would like to be in with the Broome establishment, she never really makes it because she is just not conventional enough. She tries for a time, then she blows it.

We had a glass of wine on our verandah, then went to Sheba Lane for laksas. Lyn says Pat Dodson has been called in to mediate between the Shire and Goolarri over Nolan Hunter's comments at the NAIDOC dinner. According to Lyn, Nolan got it wrong about the Shire charging for use of the oval—it was a bond, not a fee, and it was reduced to $5000. She says the councillors were bitter because they weren't formally invited to any events. Goolarri says they were—that the Shire was given a list of the events.

The flying bishop

Tuesday, July 21

The bishop has agreed to take us with him on a trip north to Lombadina and Beagle Bay in his six-seater Cessna. The Kimberley has had a flying bishop as long as it has had a bishop—thirty-five years. Bishop Chris is the third bishop of Broome to hold a pilot's licence.

Lombadina and Beagle Bay were originally Catholic missions. The church used to run large adjoining cattle stations to provide food and income for the missions. When Bishop Chris was a priest at Lombadina, much of his time was spent running the station. These days the land has been handed back to the local people and the only role of the Church is educational and pastoral; there are no government schools in these parts.

We leave Broome shortly after 7.30 a.m. Once we are up high, Susan lets go of my hand. Bishop Chris, in his black windcheater and navy-and-white 'Sydney 2000' baseball cap, is businesslike at the controls. For the most part he ignores us. It takes about thirty-five minutes to get to Beagle Bay. We fly up the centre of the Dampier Peninsular over flat, unspectacular country—low trees, khaki scrub, an occasional ribbon of red pindan indicating a road or track. Off to the east, bushfires.

The famous Beagle Bay church, low and white, sits in the middle of a green expanse like a common. Around the edge of this common is the school, the convent, the community store, a few houses and a sickly green building that is the clinic. As the morning wears on, the little settlement becomes busier. There are nine tourist four-wheel drives outside the church at 11 a.m. (it's three hours on a rough road from Broome) and several outside the community store. Slowly a group of women and children gather outside the clinic.

The school has a high turnover among the mostly white teachers. A remote community like Beagle Bay is a steep learning curve for them and they rely heavily on the Aboriginal teacher aides. We watch one young Aboriginal woman teaching numbers to a small class of six- or seven-year-olds on a classroom verandah. 'What number that is?' she asks, not, 'What number is that?'

In the staffroom is a list of the Aboriginal teacher aides since 1974, and I notice some familiar names: Kerrianne Cox (surely the singer?) and lots of other Coxes—a Sahanna, a Dann, a Bin Sali and a Brigid Bin Mauris. Now there's an interesting cross-cultural combination!

By midday we're in the air again and on our way to Lombadina. At Lombadina, slim, delicate trees shade the grassy playground, which has been freshly mowed for the bishop's visit. The rustic church and associated church buildings are comfortably nestled amongst the trees. There is a sense of quiet and order.

Lombadina has a special place in the bishop's heart because he was parish priest here for four years. As soon as he arrives, he seems to relax. Someone has promised him some fish; at Beagle Bay he was given vegetables and honey. We tease him that the trip up the peninsula is really to get his supplies.

In the cemetery is a new grave, only two weeks old. An Aboriginal man, a friend of the bishop's, who hanged himself. Wherever you go there are stories of recent hangings. This man had probably been drinking. No drink is sold at Lombadina or Beagle Bay but people bring it in and sometimes take it out into the bush for a party.

On the flight back, Bishop Chris follows the coast. At Middle Lagoon (or Midlagon as it's also known) he flies a loop, dipping the wings to say 'Hi' to the Aboriginal family who run a simple tourist resort there. It is a stunning place: the curve of sand, the colour of the water, low cliffs behind. I immediately decide to try and get back there.

Bush churches

I was struck by the churches at Beagle Bay and Lombadina, both remarkable in totally different ways. The exterior of the Beagle Bay church is virtually a copy of a nineteenth-century Bavarian church. Inside it is luminous with mother-of-pearl shell—on the altar, around the windows, crushed into the floor. On the walls the stations of the Cross have been painted in flat medieval style—wistful echoes of Europe in this remote church glistening with white shell.

At Lombadina there is no harking back to a longed-for Europe. Here the church is tiny, built entirely of local wood and tin, and despite its lop-sided verandahs and crude structure, built to last. As the bishop said, it has a special atmosphere, 'quiet and prayerful'. Its thatched roof, made with mangrove boughs, is a feat of workmanship, and the dark floor polished with boot polish and vinegar is shiny with age and cleanliness.

The bishop told us that his years at Lombadina were the best of his life.

'Was it quiet'? I asked.

'Busy,' he said. 'My day began at six in the morning, finished at six at night.'

The community had a strong work ethic then, he said wistfully, with most people working on the mission station. Now there are no real jobs outside the mission environment. Almost all the people I saw working—a tradesman and the old lay missionary John Cox, who looks after the church and helps dig the graves—were white.

In both places there are rambling, cool old buildings for the nuns. Beagle Bay still has a couple of retired nuns. I saw one elderly woman going up the path of its wild garden with her shopping from the community store. There are no nuns left at Lombadina; John Cox has taken over the nunnery. The bishop has a lot of time for old Cox. 'A quiet, practical Christian,' he called him, and that's what he seemed to be, a down-to-earth man, ready to help anyone.

The bishop is more difficult to read the more you see of him. I suspect a harder man than I first thought. For all his surface civility to women, a man's man. In a low-key way he enjoys his power, but I think he is aware of not abusing it. He is rather brusque with children. As we were leaving, a delightful little girl came out of one of the houses, wanting to come in the car to the airstrip. 'Better check with the bishop,' old Cox said.

She climbed in with us, cheerfully chatty and chewing gum vigorously. 'I don't want you to go, Bishop' she said, 'When are you coming back?'

He didn't take much notice of her without being actually unkind.

'She just likes me for my chewing gum,' he said as we taxied down the runway.

The power broker

Greg Powell's reputation precedes him. He's the chief executive officer of the Shire. A lot of people respect him, and as many dislike him intensely. Everyone agrees he runs a very tight ship, letting nothing go past him, playing his cards close to his chest.

When we had lunch with him he was intent on disarming us. He's an engaging man with black hair beginning to grey, a salt-and-pepper moustache. He makes a big play of looking you in the eye, talking directly and freely of almost anything that comes up. But after two hours you have nothing of real interest out of him. And you realise he hasn't given a thing away.

About the only time I saw a spark of real irritation or anger was when he expressed a dislike of having to talk to the white advisers of Rubibi, rather than Rubibi members themselves. 'You get the white version of what they think the Aborigines want, rather than what the Aborigines themselves want. For instance, the fuss that was made about setting up barbecues at Town Beach, how that would offend Aboriginal sensitivities. Now it's the Aborigines who use the barbecues most.'

It's true, but I wondered whether Greg's annoyance was more to do with white advisers being tougher to get around.

Eirlys and Joyce

Eirlys Richards and her friend Joyce Hudson came to lunch on Sunday. Joyce is a rather taciturn woman in her early to mid sixties; it took a while for her face to soften. She and Eirlys worked together for seventeen years at Fitzroy Crossing on their Walmajarri Bible and dictionary.

Neither Joyce nor Eirlys took part in any activism while at Fitzroy Crossing, and even now their pro-Aboriginal views are only carefully brought out, after some testing of the waters.

'I've never been good at confrontation,' Eirlys says.

She doesn't seem like a woman who scares easily to me. She still thinks nothing of driving for hours down awful roads on her own to some remote community, then bunking down wherever is available. And she enjoyed the long arduous years on the mission in the time before there were better roads or telephones. 'The best years of my life,' she says, her face lighting up. But that's physical courage. Maybe there was spiritual courage, too. I'm more used to looking for intellectual or political courage. Women like Eirlys and Joyce are a mystery to me.

These days Joyce introduces Aboriginal languages into the schools. She told us an interesting story about the Aboriginal relationship to land. When she proposed the teaching of Bardi to kids here in Broome, who, if they spoke any Aboriginal language at all at home, might speak Bardi, she aroused the ire of the parents. This was Yawuru land, and only Yawuru was to be taught. This despite the fact that no-one in Broome except two or three old people can speak Yawuru any more.

Eirlys says kids around here might understand a good deal of what their parents say in language, but they won't speak it. It's not cool. Kriol is cool. When some Aboriginal children from down south came up for a school camp recently, the Broome kids were amazed to hear the southerners speaking language.

'When I was young,' I said, 'the last thing I wanted to do was speak Hungarian. It's part of being a kid from a minority culture.'

Tuesday

Joyce and Eirlys are conducting a five-day seminar for teachers of Aboriginal languages—part of a State-wide program to introduce each child in Western Australia to a language other than English by the year 2000.

It was the morning tea break by the time I got to the Tropicana Motel, or the Troppi as everyone calls it. Eirlys and Joyce didn't look too thrilled to see me—trespassing on their territory, maybe? But over tea they introduced me to two Aboriginal women: Dianne, who's teaching Yawuru in Broome, and Violet, teaching Bardi at One Arm Point.

Dianne is youngish, with a glowing skin and a bounce about her. Violet is older; skinny, quick and bird-like. Both were a little suspicious of me at first. Dianne was the first person to actually ask the long-expected question—how would I use what she told me?

Dianne's mother is one of three elders left in Broome still speaking Yawuru, so retrieval of the language is at a critical point. For one and a half hours each week she teaches Yawuru to kids at Cable Beach Primary, after which the kids go home to households where Kriol or English or another Aboriginal language is spoken. There are virtually no teaching resources, except those developed at a course like this. Over the five days of this seminar, story books, pictures and other teaching aides will be developed.

Violet is in a somewhat better position than Dianne. There are more Bardi speakers and the language is still more or less alive. Violet speaks Bardi to her mother, but she sometimes mixes in English words. Not unlike me and my mother Heddy communicating in Hungarian-English.

Violet is less interested in talking to me than in giving Dianne a scornful account of the new Aboriginal fashion in smoking ceremonies. She's never heard of smoking ceremonies in this area, she says, certainly not for women. 'But there's old Cissy [Djiagween] doing smoking everywhere, even around her house. I asked her about it, and she looked guilty'—indicating by her expression that she'd caught Cissy out. Dianne agrees that it's probably not part of Yawuru culture, although it's possible that there's something higher up in the men's culture that they're not privy to.

Understandably, there's a fair bit of confusion and debate among the younger ones as they try to relearn their cultures. In many cases their fathers and mothers were too dislocated or too mixed-race to know more than fragments, and the generation before that is dying rapidly. I was reminded of Vanessa telling me that there were distinctions between family and skin, but cheerfully admitting that she didn't really understand the skin classifications. And why would she, with her father born in

Timor and her mother fleeing her traditional origins in Derby to become a devoted Jehovah's Witness?

*

Mum and Dad flew in for a few days on their way back from Europe. Showing them around, we saw something of the commercial, tourist Broome that we've been more or less ignoring.

We'd decided on mother-of-pearl cufflinks for Dad's birthday present and asked Atelier Pindan, the newest jewellery shop in town, to make them up. Atelier Pindan is tiny and spare, painted burnt orange like a pindan cave. Linney's, in contrast, is large, long-established and very 'establishment': a custom-built showroom, all tasteful greens and greys, Indian-fans moving in slow rhythm from high ceilings. Linney's has six or seven designers. One splendid pair of earrings—winner of last year's Shinju Matsuri award for best design—would befit a Roman empress. Four-and-half-thousand bucks and far from the most expensive item in the shop! Broome's pearling industry is about serious money.

*

The hovercraft that takes tourists over Roebuck Bay glides into Dampier Creek—a monotonous mangrove ooze of twisted shapes, grey mud and scuttling crabs. Back out in the bay, we pass the new foreshore housing estate, perhaps the last such in Broome. The council, pushed by Rubibi, I think, has placed a ban on further private foreshore development. For a bit of turquoise sea and a distant view of the jetty lit up at night, you can pay $280 000 for a block of land—the price has gone up $60 000 in six months. New brash money is flooding into Broome.

Thursday

A delicious couple of hours on the almost deserted part of Cable Beach towards Gantheaume Point. It was warm and just a little windy. The beach was a long sweep of white sand, just one or two fishermen about. We had an impromptu picnic, then Dad sat on a folding chair gazing at the sea while we fossicked among the rocks.

Every tourist goes to see Broome's Japanese cemetery. It's an extraordinary, unexpected sight. Driving past you often see Japanese tourists wandering through it, young women in shorts and sneakers, clutching cameras to their chests.

There are over nine hundred graves—mostly those of pearl divers. Yet it's not a large place, just dense with tall, slender headstones. A few headstones are made of black marble, but most are long jagged pieces of local beach stone, carved with elegant Japanese script inked in black. Beautiful and elemental.

*

A farewell dinner for Heddy and Gyuszi, with Bruce and Perpetua in the posh dining room of the Cable Beach Club. Three huge atypical Nolans hang on the walls. Semi-abstract landscapes with wonderful use of the reds and blues of this area, but nil content. Perfect for a plush hotel. It seems Lord Mac personally commissioned his good friend Sir Sid to do them.

It's a curious place, the Club, as everyone calls McAlpine's five-star creation. It tries in certain ways to be part of the community, but I see no Aboriginal faces among the front-of-house staff. The young waitresses in the dining room are all English itinerants. In McAlpine's day there was a training workshop for indigenous locals, but it was never repeated. Coles Supermarket, on the other hand, has a policy of employing young Aborigines. Okay as check-out chicks but not on hotel reception?

Vanessa at Guy Street

Vanessa dropped by for a bite, saying she only had an hour, and stayed two. She ranges all over the place, her mind hopping, assuming that you know things, glancing off the topic when you ask her something. It's something I've noticed before with Broome-ites that I don't understand. Very rarely is a direct question directly answered, as if there is another agenda, or as if it's rude to ask a direct question. Sometimes the question you should have asked is the one being answered.

As a girl, Vanessa once lived in our Guy Street house when it was just a two-room tin shed. She lived here with her boyfriend's parents when she was fresh out of school and expecting a baby. Her daughter is now nineteen and in Perth studying sociology.

Vanessa has two other girls, eight and four. I saw her the other day in the shoe shop at Seaview with her two glorious kids dancing around her. She was more like a playful older sister with them than their mother. She said she'd pick me up one weekend and we'd all go to the beach together. She prefers the quiet red rock beach near the Port, not far from where Kimberley cattle are loaded for export, because not many people go there and she can fish in peace and the kids are safe.

She doesn't see much of the children's father, a white man who works at the isolated Cadgebut mine. 'He only comes in for a week each month, which is good, y'know. Because I'm the sort of person, if I want to move, I just want to be able to move. I don't want to go, "Can I have permission to to go over here?".' She imitates a girly voice. Her talk is full of miniature plays, acting out the parts.

'When he comes in, then it's, like, football and the pub. These white Aussies, they've got their own little subculture . . . The most important thing is him having his interaction with his daughters. He's from a family of Jehovah's Witnesses, so I understand where he's come from.'

As a young woman Vanessa got involved in theatre. She was in the first production of *Bran Nue Dae* and performed all round the country. 'Then I got employed to do AIDS education. When I travel to the communities I always talk first to the young ones, showing them pictures, answering questions they have. The old people look at you—"What's she doing with the kids?"—because all they ever see is government vehicles coming in and out of their community—they don't know who's the Water Authority, who's Social Security. They never know because the vehicles end up straight at the office.

'Once I finish with the kids I say, "Now I need to talk to the old people," so when the old people have seen me sitting with the little people, they come out. "Oh hello, girl. Where you come from?" Then my next step is to talk with them, get their input.'

From AIDS education, Vanessa moved to health promotions. 'It's something I've always been into—prevention rather than clinical treatment. Supporting them in their environment so they don't have to go to the clinic. But it's going to take twenty, thirty years anyway, getting away from the "I am sick" mentality.'

Vanessa is critical of many indigenous men in Aboriginal organisations. 'The Aboriginal medical services, for instance, they're just a big political game to the men. They're not the ones who have to look after the kids and the old people, it's up to the women.

'I went up to One Arm Point once to feed back some nutritional information, and I'm feeding it back to the menfolk because they happen to be on the council, and I said, "Oh youse all started cooking, have ya?". And they go, "Oh, I've got a wife". And I go, "Well, where is she? This is information that needs to go to *her*." They feel a bit more special because they can inform their wives. And next day it might be something more "important", like a new water pump.

'Even the KLC that represents the whole of the Kimberley, it's male dominated. The men sit over there and the women sit over here.'

It's typical of Vanessa, this starting off with something about herself, then moving full bore onto her ideas about life in the Kimberley. She's full of good-natured broadsides at institutions and individuals. Very much her own woman. Doesn't follow any line. She strikes me as someone at the junction of so many influences. Her language is full of localisms and dialect but also full of sophisticated references. It's colourful and idiosyncratic and takes huge leaps of logic and subject matter in its stride. It's almost a new language in itself, with lots of sub-languages crammed inside. There's plenty there for the white listener, but it doesn't quite hang together—you have to concentrate really hard. There's a language for the full bloods out in the communities, and there's another language for the kids in Broome, the hip ones hanging around the edges. And there's the shorthand language she uses with her contemporaries, the thirty-something Broome-ites with some knowledge of the wider world and some education behind them.

I wonder where she will eventually go? Right now she's getting a degree in health promotions, flying to Sydney for a few intensive days of study every couple of months. But there are a lot of possibilities for someone like her. There's the pull towards a self-sufficient innovative life in the bush, the attractions of community leadership and politics, the demands of her young children and extended family. I get the feeling she's weighing it all up.

Involvement

Nine

Time seems to have suddenly speeded up. The first period of total newness is gone, and with it the slowed-down pace of life. And the weather is better—hot dry days but cooler nights.

I walked the dogs in the fag-end of the day, the last light. The best thing about this weather is its intensity. It's unignorable. For five or six hours of each day it is hot hot *hot*, and then, about four o'clock, the first hint of cool, of an underlying breeze. By five o'clock you can walk the streets without sweating, and by six!—the delicious relaxation, the warmth still in the air but now as a caress.

Holy rollers

Despite all the religion in this town, it's not evident in ways you might first expect—wowserism or preachiness or respectability. Unexpected people still have strong loyalties. Perpetua's friend Alison, for example, who is a school librarian. Alison says yes, she has faith, waxing and waning a bit, but yes, she attends the Anglican church fairly regularly. And Perpetua herself goes to 7 a.m. Mass most Sundays.

I've been intrigued by strange ads in the *Broome Advertiser* for weeks:

The holy rollers meet on Sunday nights in the same room at the Conti where the Soroptimists congregate. As I walk in I'm confronted by a scruffy young man, beatific smile on his face, arms in crucifixion mode, seemingly in a trance. Later he moves to the front row, next to a tall meaty guy who trembles and shakes to the bland music being played by a small group in the corner. The young fellow pays adoring attention to everything Terri, the woman evangelist, says.

It's a mostly middle-class turnout: a few lone women, a pair of prosperous-looking visitors (she all in white) and a core of young marrieds seriously into their Bibles. The young couple in the row ahead of me are constantly fondling each other. (They are clearly regulars; she works the overhead for the songs.)

As the congregation sings, Terri encourages us to move our hands and bodies, to talk in tongues. No-one does, but Terri tells a story about being suddenly and unaccountably able to speak Chinese. Next to me is a young Japanese woman perusing her Japanese Bible. Terri and others pray over her, their hands on her head.

Through it all sits an old Aboriginal guy, totally impassive. No-one knows why he is there, and no-one seems to care.

Two caravaners speak. They don't really know why they've washed up in Broome except that God just told them to come here. It turns out that this is the central 'miracle' the whole outfit relies on; people arrive in Broome because they hear a call from God.

Terri preaches in a breathy, conversational, marvelling tone, with anecdotes in the 'My son won his grand final because I prayed!' mode, or 'The terrifying storm stopped because I asked God to stop it' mode. She says she has frequently had to do embarrassing things for God. '"Don't ask me to do this, God," I pleaded, "people will think I'm silly." But then I did it, and God was there.'

She does a lot of gentle smiling, inviting you to identify with her, as if she's saying, 'I'm just an ordinary mum touched by the divine.'

Terri and her husband Bruce came here three years ago from their 'perfectly comfortable life in Queensland' because God told them to. They believe there will be a revival here—they see Broome as a 'godless place'. (It's not the impression I've had.)

There were sandwiches after the service, but I left early to see if Gordy had turned up.

He hadn't. So we went around to find him.

Meeting Damien

We've met Damien at last! He looks both younger and older than his twenty-six years. He is quite dark, has the Aboriginal jaw and nose, the classic dignified flattened-out features that give him an air of timelessness—he could have been in the cast of *Jedda*. But he's also terribly hip: curly long hair tied girlishly at the nape of the neck; a quite lovely necklace. His accent and style are half Southern belle, half outback boy. He plays it sort of dumb and light, but every now and again there's a quick flash of intelligence and perception, plus some sly humour. He susses people out pretty quickly.

He told Annie that Gordon and he 'have a bond'. And they do, although it's quite indefinable. Indefinable but palpable. There's a kind of mutual respect and an enormous understated affection, definitely on both sides.

Gordon was looking rather seedy in shorts and singlet. But we noticed his shapely shaved legs. He told us that he shaves them every second day. It's an obsession to remain hairless. I asked him how he gets his women's gear. He has a friend in Perth who buys for him.

He was being upbeat about himself professionally. 'Oh, I'm a brilliant lawyer,' he said, and laughed. He keeps a pile of videos above the telly— the most gruesome 'records of interview' from his murderers and muggers. Says he watches them when he's depressed.

Mary in court

Despairing of writing, I went off to sit in the magistrate's court. Gordy was there on the verandah but only made one brief appearance before vanishing. I saw the names J. Tarran and M. Tarran on the court lists. Mary? I wondered, and then I saw her sitting on the benches, waiting her turn, looking serious. Instinctively I went over to the other side of the room, pretending not to have seen her. I didn't want to pry.

Mary looked weary, as if she'd done this more than once before. The magistrate obviously knew her and treated her with a matter-of-fact courtesy and sympathy. Her estranged husband was contesting a restraining order but he hadn't shown up. He'd broken a previous restraining order by smashing in both doors of her house while she was out, and dragged most of the furniture from the lounge room outside. Since then there have been disruptive phone calls. The magistrate granted her a further order for another twelve months. They discussed whether she could avoid seeing him. No, she said, because she regularly hands the kids over to him.

I gave her a minute to recover once she left the court, then went outside, but she was gone.

When I got home, I asked Anne about Mary's ex. I'd made a few assumptions: black, violent, probably a drinker.

'He's white,' Anne said. 'An anthropologist. I get the impression he's a bit feral. Mary says he's good with the kids. Do you know Mary's also got two grown-up children?'

Like half the women in Broome. They have a couple of kids when they're not much more than kids themselves, then another family much later.

The bishop and the GST

Bishop Chris was on the radio this morning, debating the GST with a Liberal pollie. He was trying not to sound too political; just a churchman voicing his concern over the GST's effect on the poor and marginalised. Nonetheless he would have made a good politician, and he knows it. He did quite well, but he forgot the most basic point that he'd made to me a few days ago—that the poor spend double the proportion of their incomes on food and so would be doubly disadvantaged if there were a GST on food.

I spent nearly three hours with the bishop the other day. He seemed tired and dispirited at first, and obviously feeling the heat—it was humid and oppressive that day, despite the 'dry' season. He relaxed visibly once he started to talk. At the end, he said he'd enjoyed it; he'd needed a talk that morning. That little bit of frankness endeared him to me. As did his telling me that he'd been to hear Jimmy Barnes when he was doing a gig at the Roebuck the other week.

Putting the bishop's tape onto the page, I have before me an image of him at our last session: in bare feet, old shirt and shorts, puffing on his fags, slouching off to get another coffee, so unbishoplike that I find him thoroughly engaging. It's not till I listen to the tape that I hear the evasions and rationalisations. His enlightened opinions and his willingness to acknowledge the bureaucracy and rigidities of the Church are disarming, but he's also very much a man of the Church. By definition then, he too has his share of hierarchical, orthodox and paternalistic thought. The trouble is, he'd probably be the first to admit it.

He is intrigued by me, too, I think. He actually told me he'd never met a Jew before! How did I feel about being in a Catholic church? Very comfortable, I said. Jews and Catholics have a lot in common; you can see the

Jewish origins still in some of the Catholic rituals. And there's further common ground in the weight placed on ritual, and a certain intensity.

He took all this in, then said, 'I wondered, after that Mass you attended, if any of the readings were anti-Semitic?'

I reassured him. But later he couldn't resist a reference to those who 'walked next to Christ but didn't recognise him', then said hurriedly that he wasn't just referring to Jews but all sorts of people, even in the present day.

I asked Bishop Chris if he'd ever had a crisis of faith. No, he said, but 'you have to see with the eyes of faith'. Then he gave me several examples of things which have moved him, manifestations of God, things hard to explain any other way. But no, he doesn't like the Lourdes stuff.

He's smart.

A night on the town

Damien was sitting on a kitchen chair in front of the TV, which was propped on another kitchen chair. He was watching the football—Fremantle Dockers versus the Adelaide Crows. Gordon was cooking spaghetti. He said he'd been out the night before and wasn't going out again that night.

'What are ya doin', girls? You ragin'? You wanna go dancin'?' Damien asked with his extraordinary Deep South accent.

Susan said she was going home to nurse her cold. She asked Damien about getting some dope.

'I don't want to hear this,' Gordy said, and went out on to the verandah.

Damien was delighted to hear Susan was an occasional smoker. He sat up in his chair and looked at us closely.

After a couple of scotches, Susan went home. Damien and I finished the champagne we'd brought. Gordon went across the street to the Roebuck bottleshop to get another bottle.

'I love him,' Damien said.

'One of the nice things about Gordon is he's non-judgemental,' I said.

Damien stared at me: 'You're *wrong*, girl!' He looked at me hard, then turned back to the game on the television. 'I gave up playing sport,' he said. I noticed how thin his legs were, like sticks. And, unlike Gordon's, his legs are hairy.

When the game finished, Damien stood up. He was wearing a rather nice self-patterned silk brocade shirt in a dull gold, with a waistcoat. Dressed for going out.

'I'm going to bed,' Gordy said.

'Okay, honey.'

As we were crossing the street, Damien said to me, 'Hey, you're walking like a bush girl!' I had one arm hanging by my side and the other crossed behind my back.

'You don't look much like a bush boy,' I said. 'Too sophisticated.'

'Why, thank you!' he said, delighted.

We went first to the Oasis beer garden at the Roebuck, where the Pigram Brothers, Broome's best-known band, were playing. Damien paid for me to get in. We wound our way to the dance floor. It was quite dark, a few lights around the beer garden but not enough to properly light the place. People milled through the darkness. The crowd was about 80 per cent Aboriginal, mainly women on the dance floor.

Damien loves to dance. When he's animated and with his hair pushed back, he has quite a beautiful face. Sloe-like eyes and very even features, a pouting sort of mouth.

'You are quite beautiful,' I told him.

'I am?'

'Yes, you are.'

He smiled and put his head on my shoulder.

After each number, we sat down briefly on the steps where we'd left our drinks. Then we'd be up again. I was beginning to wonder whether he intended to dance all night and whether I'd last the distance. But he soon suggested we move on to the Pearlers Bar.

You could barely move in the big bar so we went out to the courtyard. Damien said he didn't like noise. 'I prefer quiet places.'

'But you like music. That's loud,' I said.

'Music is different,' he said, 'that's something inside me. When I'm not dancing I like to sit quietly and watch. I don't say much.'

'Are you shy?'

'I'm impassive,' he said.

That impressed me. 'And what of Gordon? Is he just passive?'

'He's not passive. He does things eventually, when he's ready.'

Damien spotted his sister Glenys and some of her friends. They were down from Lombadina for a funeral. Other people joined us. No-one seemed drunk—I didn't see a troublesome drunk all night.

I told Glenys I had met her sister Milly at the Tote Bar. They both laughed. 'She's a mad woman!' Glenys said, and tapped her head.

Another relative turned up, a cousin, Jessica Djiagween, who turns out to also be Mary Tarran's cousin. 'I just left Mary at home watching videos,' she said.

'Is she okay?' I asked. 'I heard she had a bit of trouble with her ex.'

'She's okay now.'

We moved on to the Nippon Inn. The Oasis, the Pearlers, the Nippon are all within metres of each other. Crowds of people were streaming down Pearlers Row. It was busier at midnight than I've ever seen it during the day.

The Nippon is pretty much a standard nightclub: pretensions to smartness—a fairly stylish bar from what I could see of it in the dim lighting; dance floor with strobe lights; a DJ. We sat under a palm tree in the courtyard—again, away from the noise—and talked while Damien made comments about the men going into the loos. He told me that he and Gordon take it in turns to go out. He said they don't have sex much—once a month, maybe. He boasted that he has had it off 'with everyone in Broome' but has to be quiet about it because Gordy gets jealous.

'We've got this bond,' he said.

At 1 a.m. I told Damien I was going home. Mention was made of Susan's gunja.

'I'll be happy to get it, but I'll need some money,' he said.

I only had a fifty-dollar note, so I gave him that.

'The twenty I'll keep for myself,' he said, and pocketed it disarmingly. I kissed him on the cheek and left him to it.

Afternoon tea with Pearlie

When I went around to Pearl's this afternoon she was outside, on one of the reclining canvas chairs she likes. There were three little girls playing nearby, only one of them her grandchild, and several small dogs, none of them hers.

We went inside and Pearl made us afternoon tea—cheese and tomato on Saos, and Aunty Bella's leftover chocolate birthday cake.

'Bella likes the hospital,' Pearl says. 'She didn't even want to come home for her birthday.'

Pearl's husband was wandering about like a thin ghost. She ignored him, but not in a bad way. She told me he has emphysema from years of smoking.

In 1982 Hama was made redundant by Pearls Pty Ltd, Kim Males' company, after disease wiped out the pearls. He had been a captain on one of the ships taking live pearlshell to Kuri Bay. He talked Pearl into starting their own pearl farm. She didn't want to do it initially; said she was afraid of the risk. 'We'd always been just working people. That's all.

That's all I ever expected to be. "That's your bloody Binghi blood," he said to me. "You're so bloody negative."'

She laughs now as she recounts it.

They set up the farm at Gourdon Bay in 1984 with a licence for only 3 000 shell. They were disgusted that Fisheries only allowed them that much, when Hama had been in the business for years. Other people were given 20 000 or 30 000 straight off. The two eldest sons helped with the farm. They bought an old prawning boat to live on—they had no land base. And a friend who was a Japanese technician seeded the pearls.

Hama and Pearl had to borrow a lot of money to set up the farm. Their first harvest was in 1986. By 1990 they were out of debt.

The licence was increased to 5 000 shell then 10 000 then 15 000. They had sixteen employees by the end. After fourteen years they sold out to Paspaley for a good price. By then they had built two boats, one to gather shell, one to work the farm, and their house.

Four of their boys still work the farm for Paspaley. One of them, Dale, came in while I was there. I still can't tell Pearl's sons apart. They are all very definitely 'Hamaguchi boys'. Dale works off a pontoon in the bay, caring for the shell, cleaning nets. He prefers that because it means he can come home at night. One of the younger boys is a trainee cultured pearl technician on a Paspaley boat.

Pearl told me that another of her sons, Craig, had gone to see *Corrugation Road* the previous night with a white friend of his. They were both high after the show, loved it. As they were leaving, Craig's friend ran into a white couple he knows. They agreed it was a terrific show, then the husband added, 'even though they were all coons'.

'This is what it's like,' Pearl says. 'It never stops.'

I asked her what it was like growing up in a mixed-race family.

'We were the bottom of the heap,' she replied. 'Politically and racially. We were what they called polyglot, what Australia did its best to discourage. Because of World War II we were the most hated half-Asians. Because of the Japanese blood. At the post office when we went to get the mail, we'd get ridiculed because of our names. And at the butcher shop, you'd see these lovely cuts of meat. They wouldn't give it to you—they'd give you dog meat, the stinking meat off the carcass. We would never get served in the shop, they'd give us rubbish all the time. You knew if there were any whites in the shop that you would be served last. That lasted right up until the sixties. When I went to get married, I was abused.

'I discovered then, when I was twenty, that I had no birth register. I said, "Mother, how can you do this to me?" Because I knew she was a very intelligent woman. "Oh," she said, "I went to register..." We had to register through the Native Protectorate. We weren't hospital births, we were all home births in those days. "Mother, why didn't you register me?" "Oh, that silly Mr Neville or whoever," she said. (Mr Neville was for decades the WA Native Protector.) "I informed him about your birth..."

'She didn't, you know. She was afraid to. We were all secret children. A lot of my generation, never registered, because they were afraid to.

'Luckily my two midwives were still alive. Yeah! I had to get a stat dec. So I got registered in 1960, if you please!' She laughs. 'Never too late.

'Mother was worried that they could take me away, send me to Sister Kate's or those other institutions down south. These women were at the mercy, at the whim, of these so-called protectors. If you got a sadistic person, or someone with moods, they could do what they liked with you.

'We had two schools here,' Pearl said. 'The white school and the black school, and a lot of quadroons and octoroons went to the white school. The thinking was that if they went to the "white" school they would progress into white society.

'I went to the Catholic school, and my mother had her citizenship. Her friends would say, "Pearlie didn't enrol at the government school?" and Mum would say, "I'm sending her to be educated by the nuns." "Oh!" they'd say, "you're keeping her backwards, she'll have lots of black friends." Mummy said, "Well, I grew up with them people. What's good enough for them is good enough for me." Mum was a straightforward, down-to-earth woman. She was a good woman. She had no pretensions about status. She wasn't into that game. There was a lot of that in Broome.'

Dale was sitting at the table with us, having a snack. He is married and has a small daughter, Isabelle, who goes to St Mary's. Isabelle came home from school recently and said they were having a float for Shinju and all the kids had to choose which culture they wanted to dress up as. The family told her all the bits that make her up—Aboriginal, Chinese, Japanese, Malay, Filipino, Scottish. She could choose any of them. She chose Scottish. She is one-sixteenth Scottish. The family thinks this is a great joke.

Cultural gatekeepers

When I was over at Goolarri the other day, Kevin chased around to find a video of last year's new-look Shinju festival. We watched it in one of the editing suites out in the shed. The video opened with a man reciting, 'White man, yellow man, black man, brown...' and talked about Broome's cultural mix, the more than thirty nationalities represented in the town.

Pearl came on the screen, looking poised and confident, and said, 'Asiatics were not allowed to bring their wives, so what happened? They all got involved with local women.'

When the festival began more than twenty years ago, Kim Male was asked to choose a name for it. He had three to pick from—Chinese, Malay and Japanese. The Japanese was the easiest to get the tongue around. So that is how it came to be called Shinju Matsuri—Festival of the Pearl.

Kevin took on the job of organising Shinju last year because he had twelve months off before he started at Goolarri. He said: 'I'd just dealt with this whole identification thing—who am I, where do I belong. And I was getting peer group pressure stuff—"When are you coming home to help us?" Last year the old people asked me to do Shinju—all the cultural gate-keepers asked me to do it—and when I did it, with the team that I had, it really blew the other establishments away. Its inclusiveness.'

The 'cultural gatekeepers' are the bosses of the various ethnic communities, like Pearl's husband, Hiroshi Hamaguchi, for the Japanese, and Sally's partner, Ahmat Fidel, for the Malays. Ahmat will be this year's patron. Giving each Shinju a different racial theme is good for cultural tourism and for internal reconciliation. Kevin says it 'gives people with some of that bloodline the chance to explore that part of themselves'. That's what Kevin is trying to do, to explore his different bits.

'I know that I can never be at the true Chinese table, in decision-making terms. That has to be full-blood people. I can't help that I'm a coat of many colours in terms of races...I know those old people respect me, that there's mutual respect and they'll support me because I'm the up-front leader. But I'm not the boss.'

But you've been involved in Aboriginal decision-making, I say.

'I've been involved in all decision-making, but not to the extent that it's me who's making the decision. I'm basically a front. I get my instructions to do things and I have to work within that charter. The moment I work outside that charter I get rapped on the knuckles. That's what Broome culture is all about—we all have our roles.

'For people like me and Peter Yu and Jimmy Chi, this is one time where multiculturalism is a big disadvantage. This is what I keep coming back to, in terms of what table you're at, because at the end of the day Peter Yu will never have the same credentials or acceptance—he's accepted, don't get me wrong—but not the same *sort* of acceptance.'

He'll never be an elder?

'No. Well, he'll be an elder in one sense, strategically, but not culturally or in how the real system works. Likewise, I will never be. But we will go down as great people, in getting things through. That's our role, so we're not doing anything special. If we died tomorrow we'd be regarded as a couple of people who opened the gates in different areas of opportunities. But we'll never ever have that thing where we can say "oo-ay". (A sort of Kriol "hey you!")

'How do you find that middle ground when you've got those complex dynamics going on? That's the challenge, I guess.'

Height of the season

The narrow Broome roads are chocker with retirees and their monster caravans, a stream of them edging their way around the Guy Street roundabout on their way to the Town Beach caravan park. The population of the town has more than trebled. It's almost impossible to get a park in Chinatown's main street. The calendar is packed with activities: concerts, gallery openings, book launches, balls.

On the way to the markets, we ran into Anne Deveson, just arrived from Sydney and getting back into Broome ways. She's here to write the last draft of her novel. It's her third Broome sojourn, so she already knows you have to be early at the markets for the vegies and the fresh-baked bread. She was feeling guilty about not working. No, no, we chorused, you shouldn't start work straight away. Acclimatise, relax into Broometime.

On the way home we called in on Perpetua. She was at her most Perpetua—the habitual hesitancies and elaborate courtesies shot through with bouts of incisiveness and outbursts of naturalness. She had got Anne D, Susan and me tickets to the Linney's function at the races, so the four of us went out together for Broome Cup Day.

Linney's had a marquee, an elegant white structure with open sides, beside the 'rails' (actually wires). The horses' hooves threw up clouds of red dust as they went past. The Linney's tent was some distance from the hoi polloi of the betting ring and main building. There was a band and good food and waiters going around with champagne and wine. The guests were almost entirely white; most of the notables around town—Magda Male, Lyn Page, Greg Powell. Some very smart outfits and elaborate hats.

The whole day must have cost Bill Reed a pretty penny. But you would never know it was his show. He moved among his guests in his modest, low-key way. (Although we've heard that Bill is not always as mild as he appears—that there's a hardness beneath the amiable exterior.)

The races are another true-Broome experience. What looks like outback larrikinism suddenly transforms into slick sophistication; small-town innocence rubs up against streetsmart wiliness.

I didn't enjoy Cup Day much—nowhere to hide. Racing is so high energy and frantic and so *public*. I do like the gleam of the horses, the jockey's colours, the clamour of the betting ring and the faintly disreputable air of the bookies with their bags. But I'd had enough after half an hour. The beer cans, the debris and the crowd—7211 people, the loudspeaker announced—a record! I hated the tarted-up be-hatted women teetering coyly on a platform waiting to be judged for their outfits, the 'Couple of the Day' prize, the special marquees where 'the gentry' can get away from the riff raff and inject a bit of tone.

You and Anne Deveson enjoyed it; Perpetua and I wilted.

I've recently seen Broome described in metropolitan papers—once as a 'resort town', another time as an 'outback town'. It is neither, although there are elements of both.

Once a week we take a look at the 'resort town'. Our hour on Cable Beach on a Sunday afternoon has become a little ritual. For the first few weeks I insisted on hiring a two-dollar-an-hour umbrella, but now that it's cooler we just lie on the sand, which is usually damp from the last high tide and has the colour and consistency of fine brown sugar. I suspect that we keep going back to that same stretch of beach each Sunday because it never varies. We can relax and not have to be on the lookout for things that are new or 'say something' about Broome. Cable Beach, with its tourists from the resort on their striped green and red towels, its lifesavers, board-riders and bodysurfers, is just a typical resort of the nineties, complete with umbrellas, chairs, beach tents, kayaks and bottled water. After an hour we go up to the kiosk and have a Coffee Chill while watching the ocean.

Another reason we like Cable on a Sunday is that with a bit of luck we don't meet a single person we know. As someone said to us, Broome people don't go to the beach (at least not in the tourist season). Bruce goes—sometimes two or three times a day. But while he's there he's hardly out of the water.

Sometimes as we come home the ABC radio will be giving the tides and forecast for the whole of the Western Australian coast, a long, long list of places I've never heard of, with their swells and winds and barometers rising and falling. It takes nearly fifteen minutes to get through them all, the announcer's voice droning on and on.

Before coming here I never appreciated just how very long the Western Australian coast is, and how very far away this State is from anywhere else. The news, particularly the television news, is totally dominated by what is happening here. The rest of the country hardly seems to exist, let alone the rest of the world. 'The Government' always means the State Government; the 'Minister for Transport' means the Western Australian Minister for Transport.

Cable is a thoroughly modern beach. Tourists lie on the sand with their mobiles, casually ringing home to Melbourne or Paris. We hear quite a few French voices. I can see why the French wash up at the Club: a long white beach, the desert almost at their doorstep, yet all the comforts of civilisation. The romance of *Australie* without the hardship.

Broome is becoming quite a sophisticated mini-metropolis, at least in winter. The art world is thriving—a new show opens nearly every week at one of the four main galleries. Robert Juniper lives here for part of the year; John Olsen has a house up here.

The day Princess Di came to Broome

A story from Perpetua. In 1995, for the twentieth anniversary of International Women's Year, Perpetua organised an exhibition of women's art. She asked Jo Mellick, a talented local actress and singer, if she would open it and do a Germaine Greer impersonation.

Jo is tall and lanky with short straight hair. She said she couldn't do G.G. but she could do Princess Di. So the invitations, with gold lettering, went out announcing that Princess Di was to open the exhibition at the Durack Gallery. People immediately took it for the real thing. The whole town was talking about it. (Does this say something about the perceived power of the Durack connections?)

The local media was very excited; journalists began ringing from all over the country. Ray Martin rang then realised it was a joke. But the local people took it for real. The ABC TV stringer, David Battey, said: 'This is going to be so big, Perpetua. I was in Alice Springs when Charles and Di came and it was *huge.*'

The manager of the Cable Club rang and asked if it was true and where would Princess Di be staying?

'On the Royal Yacht,' Perpetua said. 'They'll be anchoring off Cable Beach, but they'll be wanting to dine at the Club.'

The manager then rang the British Consulate in Perth and ascertained that the Royal Family was not expected in Western Australia. But he joined in the spirit and arranged for a box of small Union Jacks to be sent up for distribution to the crowd.

David Battey started to talk about keeping the outside media out, keeping the scoop for the local journos. He thought it would be a good idea to close down the airport so they couldn't fly in. At this point Perpetua thought things were getting a little out of hand, but she still didn't say anything.

Donny D'Antoine, who works in the Coast Watch spotter plane, started to get a bit suspicious because he hadn't sighted the Royal Yacht. His son and daughter were lined up to present a bouquet to Princess Di.

In the last couple of days before the big event it was impossible to get an appointment at the hairdressers.

On the day, the police set up barricades along Robinson Street. The crowds began to arrive early. Flags were distributed for people to wave. It was the biggest thing Broome had seen since the Queen came in 1963.

Then 'Princess Di' arrived, in Broome's one and only stretch limo. She fluttered her eyelashes and looked demure. And she gave an excellent speech. Jo Mellick had had her hair lightened for the occasion. But it was still evident that this was not quite the real thing.

A few people, when they realised the deception, turned away in disgust. 'I had my hair done specially,' one woman said. But most people thought it a great joke. One who did not was Maria Mann, then the journo on the *Advertiser*. Perpetua says she wrote a scathing report for the paper.

But maybe it gave her an idea. Three years later, when Jimmy Pike and Pat Lowe were launching *Jimmy and Pat meet the Queen*, who should dress up as the Queen, complete with corgis? Maria Mann.

Ten

Looking ahead—Vanessa and Goolarri—Get 'em working—
Phillipa's kids—Baamba's career—Chez Lyn—
Cissy's stories

On the other side of busy Guy Street, across the road from the house, is a heavily laden tree full of tiny green fruit like miniature apples. In the past couple of days groups of countrymen, adults and children, have stopped to pick the fallen fruit, putting them in their bags, oblivious to the heavy traffic roaring past a metre away. One old man told me the fruit are called Taylor fruit; he picks them as a treat for his grandchildren.

Another old man, Aboriginal/Japanese, or maybe Malay, takes a morning constitutional down the street every day. When I pass him on the footpath he turns and smiles. He always wears the same yellow and white baseball cap, and sunglasses. He looks as if he was once a bit of a dandy; now he's rather frayed and down at heel. The first morning I saw him he was wearing faded pink trousers and a wine-coloured jacket. The next, clean pressed jeans and a bright blue shirt.

Thursday, July 30

A very strange night last night. Out at the Club a director of Sothebys from London was giving a lecture on valuing great art. What on earth was he doing here? Maybe a mate of McAlpine's? He was a typical upper-crust Pom, but not overly pretentious. Tall, slim, pink-skinned, youthful-looking, although he's probably in his early forties.

An eclectic little bunch gathered in the Sam Male Room: John Olsen and his wife and daughter, Perpetua, Anne Deveson, an ageing hippy type, a couple of tourists in shorts who wandered in. About fifteen of us in all. The Sothebys' man gave the lecture, complete with slides, as if he was talking to a couple of hundred wealthy connoisseurs.

Then we called in at Gordy's flat to see if Damien's birthday party was on. Damien wants to have it on the big verandah overlooking Sheba Lane restaurant and the chatter of diners. Gordy answered the door looking dishevelled in shorts and singlet. He'd been out drinking till 4 a.m. and had been woken at seven by the guy he was supposed to be defending in Derby, two hours drive away. He slept it off in the back seat while the defendant drove. By the time they got there he'd sobered up enough to win the case!

There was no sign of Damien when Gordy got back. Gordy said he was in no condition for a party anyway. We had a beer with him, then left him to recover.

Looking ahead

Coconut Wells is just a scattering of houses and small mango plantations on the coast about twenty kilometres north of Broome. The other day we drove out there for a picnic on the dunes and didn't see a soul all day, just a few tyre marks in the sand.

But there are big plans for the area. There's a million acres out there, the former Waterbank Station, and it's been bought by the State Government to provide space for Broome to grow.

'You get one chance to carve up Waterbank,' Angus Murray told me, 'so you really have to look ahead and have a bit of vision.'

The idea is that once Broome's population reaches about twenty-five thousand (still a long way off!), development will leapfrog to Coconut Wells and Willie Creek. There are also plans for a big coastal park, living areas for Aboriginal people and maybe the new airport, although there's still a fight about that.

Discoveries of oil and gas off the coast have the potential to double Broome's population in the next decade or so. The town might end up with an administration centre, a port, service vessels, choppers flying people in and out, and spin-off industries—but the refinery would probably be down south, at Dampier, so as not to spoil Broome for tourism.

Lyn Page is on the side of those pushing for more development. But despite this, and despite her connections with McAlpine and the Sydney social scene (or maybe even because of them), she has never been entirely accepted by the Broome 'establishment'.

'The Murrays, the Reids, the Telfords, the Kennedys, the Haynes. And the Males of course—I never get invited to their homes. Maybe once, to Kim and Magda's.'

But Lyn works closely with Angus Murray and in that sense she's part of the establishment faction.

She says, 'We've got the numbers on Council: that's Angus, me—going around the table—Kim Male, Brad Sounness, Tom Vinnicombe. Five.'

'The numbers to do what?' I ask.

'Anything we want to do.'

'But you say there's no party politics.'

'It's not a "party". That's the division. Chris Mitchell actually caused that. He flouted the establishment. You can't do it!' she says emphatically. 'Know the rules and play by them.' She taps it out. 'That's what you've got to do.'

'So you've decided to go with the establishment?'

'I'm part of the establishment on Council at the moment, yes.'

'Why? For you, why?'

'Because I think they are progressive. Even though they don't back me on heritage issues. I'm the only one who's interested in preservation. The rest of them couldn't give a stuff.'

'So why are you backing their agenda?'

'Because I am pro-development. Controlled development. I'm also a capitalist—a socialistic capitalist. You've got to move forward. Move slowly. Keep your infrastructure growing at the same pace as your development, so it can cope with it. I've seen Broome when it could *not* cope with it.'

'What do the other councillors want, the ones who aren't in your group?'

'Chris Mitchell—he's hard to fathom. He swings. He's a fence-sitter. Marty [Sibosado] I like. And I think he's pretty open minded. He's on CDEP, topped up. The other part of the establishment that I'm aligned with... I know he's not trusted by them. I suspect he might be too bloody smart for them.'

I remember something that Marty said to me about the Shire and Rubibi: 'If there was no native title, there would be no relationship. Without native title the Shire would have had to be dragged kicking and screaming to the negotiating table.'

But Lyn has moved on to the next councillor: 'As for Nolan [Hunter], I like Nolan but he has really shat in his own nest. As of NAIDOC Week (the speech he made at the dinner, criticising the Shire) it has become rather apparent that Nolan has a huge chip on his shoulder. He's an angry young man.'

Susan: 'Don't you think that even though Council didn't get formally invited to the NAIDOC dinner, it should have been the sort of thing that councillors automatically went to?'

Lyn: 'You don't automatically go to things. There's a protocol...'

Me: 'You don't need an invitation to go to the races, to go to the pearling do...

Lyn: 'Even Pat Dodson said that the Reconciliation Council was remiss. NAIDOC here was *very* remiss. You don't *expect* people to come if they're not invited...There's no reason for Nolan to stand up and say what he did, that Council's effort at reconciliation was tokenism. You don't say that.'

Me: 'Maybe he spoke out at the NAIDOC dinner out of frustration. Maybe he doesn't say much at council meetings because he knows he's in the minority block and what's the point.'

'Marty speaks up,' Lyn says. 'Marty speaks up and challenges Angus. And I can tell you, Angus does not like being challenged by anyone.'

She says that at times she has more time for people like Marty Sibosado than the ones who are on her side.

'So why do you go along with them?' I ask.

'I suppose because I was included in it. Know the game and play it.'

Vanessa and Goolarri

It is the brief conversations, the throwaway lines, that often give the clearest insights. Like yesterday, when Vanessa was saying that the new Goolarri Radio is a big disappointment, 'always playing dreadful music, not giving people any information, hardly any news'.

According to Vanessa, Goolarri hasn't got the funding it was expecting to train news and other staff. 'I said to Fongie, "You come up against a brick wall, you gotta jump over it. You come up against ATSIC, you gotta jump over it. You're supposed to know about money; you're the Chinaman."'

It sounds like the old story: you can get ATSIC funding to set things up, but no money to keep them going. Goolarri needs to look beyond ATSIC for funding—to advertising, for example. But that leap into the commercial world is one that Aboriginal people and organisations seem to find difficult.

Vanessa also talked about the cattle stations bought by the Aboriginal Development Commission. 'Useless,' she said. 'Useless country.' She has a cousin out on one of the stations. 'Hard work, and for what? No-one wants to run cattle stations. You've got to maintain fences and wells, and there's not the labour, not like when they had our old people working them for nothing.' Most of the stations are now just places for families to live.

Vanessa crystallised something I've begun to feel about a number of the enterprises up here. People are trying to establish Aboriginal organisations that to a certain extent mirror those in the white community, and often the surface looks good. Buying cattle properties, establishing a radio station, a television station. The problem is, it's so often hollow. The radio station is a shell without the skills to make it a self-sustaining thing. Maybe you put up the shell and eventually it gains substance. But does it work that way?

It is those things that grow organically that seem to be the most successful. Like Broome music: Jimmy Chi, the Pigram Brothers, the now-defunct band Kuckles that got them started. And Mark Bin Bakar's hugely successful radio character, Mary Geddardyu. Mary Geddardyu is the best thing Goolarri has going for it because Mark has a true talent for what he does. It's genuine and spontaneous. He is an innovator. He started up the first Aboriginal music school in Perth.

Mark and Kevin knew each other right through school, lost touch, then both ended up back in Broome after having kind of breakdowns. 'I came back and sat under a mango tree, then he came back and sat under a mango tree.'

He said Kevin was always confident, always a leader.

But I'm not sure about Goolarri Media Enterprises. It's real success seems to be in organising festivals, events, short-term PR exercises. The only time Goolarri feels busy is when there's an event on. This is Kevin's talent: bringing people together, organising them, being the front man.

He told me, 'At the end of the day, if we don't start setting up an economic base, no-one's going to take any notice of us. When it became obvious that the Western Australian Government wasn't going to grant land rights, we started buying land—Mount Barnett Station, Leopold Downs, Gibb River Station. And other things—the Fitzroy Crossing pub joint venture, the supermarket, the caravan park. The entire loan for the Fitzroy supermarket will be paid out by 2000. Mount Barnett paid their loan out five years in advance.'

I am bemused that the old Fitzroy pub, that destroyer of so many lives, that blight on the landscape, surrounded by its sea of red Emu Export cans, is partly Aboriginal owned. Making money out of their own annihilation? The rationale might be that if they're going to drink anyway, why give the money to a whitefella. But still...

Get 'em working

A few Aboriginal girls work at the supermarkets, and there are people around town running small businesses who clearly have some Aboriginal blood. But these are the exceptions. Most of the Aboriginal people around town are not 'employed'; they may have jobs but they are CDEP work-for-the-dole jobs.

Angus Murray was telling me that he went to the Police Citizens Youth Club one day and saw about twenty young Aboriginal men playing basketball, surrounded by an equal number of their friends and girl-friends. 'And I looked around and thought, "I've never seen anywhere where these people are working. You never see them across a counter or what-ever". And I thought to myself, "What are their aspirations? What are they thinking in twenty years time that they will be doing, that they will have achieved?" And I didn't know the answer. So I sat down with Pat Dodson and Peter Yu one day and asked them.'

I can picture that: Angus with his smooth, round face and long socks; concerned, well-meaning but at a loss.

'Well, they didn't have a clue either,' he said. 'They said that that is the biggest problem that confronts Aboriginal people in Broome at the moment. These people are wandering aimlessly. Peter Yu's comment was that he thought it was going to be a forty-year problem, to fix it, a couple of generations. That would be terribly sad.

'I don't think it's the employers,' Angus said. 'My feeling is that the tourism operators understand that the multi-racial flavour of Broome is crucial to the continued prosperity of tourism. They would love to have those young girls working in their hotels. I think it's more a matter of confidence and training. There's been trial schemes at the Cable Beach Club, for example. They've had ten or fifteen kids through and at the end of it none of them have wanted a job. That's pretty disappointing and I think it comes back to confidence. Give those kids the confidence while they are in school that they can participate in the tourism industry.'

The thing about Angus is that he always expresses the right sentiments, but there is a sense that he is removed. Aborigines will always be the Other.

One solution he proposed was that kids be given scholarships. 'So they can go and get a good education, go to university, then come back as role models.'

It sounds familiar. It's what the Church was doing in the fifties, sixties and seventies.

Councillor Marty Sibosado is one of those who did his training down south, got himself a trade, then came back. Most of them got themselves a trade but hardly any are using it. They are too bright to be boilermakers and mechanics for long. Instead, they've been roped in to run indigenous organisations. Marty runs Nirrumbuk, which administers the CDEP programs for more than thirty groups on the peninsula.

Nirrumbuk is a spartan blokey place with a few old vinyl lounges, mugs of coffee going cold on tabletops. They've just started up a mechanics workshop and a building company. At the moment CDEP is their only funding. But Marty hopes the businesses will start making money soon.

Nirrumbuk acts as the link between ATSIC, which provides the funds, and the community groups who employ people. Marty doesn't have a lot of time for ATSIC—even though he used to work for it. 'They're not proactive enough. All they do is process paperwork. They're not out there in the community. They're just a bureaucracy . . . Two years ago we marched on their offices because they stopped our wages. They victimise those who stand up for themselves.'

I remember seeing Marty at the KLC conference, this nuggety little bloke at the back of the room, standing and haranguing ATSIC, saying, 'The results just aren't hitting the ground.'

Like Peter Yu and Kevin Fong, he wants to see ATSIC's role devolved to a regional authority. 'They're totally inflexible,' he told me. 'They say "housing" and everyone has to spend on housing, even if their housing needs have already been met.'

Phillipa's kids

When it comes to employment for Aboriginal youth, Phillipa Cook's kids are doing well. All four of them have jobs around town, although I'm not sure how many of them are CDEP jobs. Samantha is a designer at Magabala Books, having finished a traineeship there—one of the Aboriginal traineeships which David Kemp has since abolished. Kylie is a graphic designer and a secretary at Heatworks, the theatre group which is a creative offshoot of the Aboriginal medical service. The third, Bianca, is a choreographer and dance teacher with the Modern Dreamtime Dancers. The boy, the youngest, is an assistant manager with Chicken Treat. Phillipa says that watching her struggle to survive as a single mother may have given her children some mettle, more motivation to find work.

Phillipa is one of a band of indigenous women around Broome who seem to spend their lives running from one meeting to another. She's co-ordinator of the regional domestic violence committee and is also on the board of Magabala Books, as well as holding down two other part-time jobs, as a reparative mediator and as a tutor at Curtin University. She says she needs all her jobs to keep things going, although the kids (by her ex- husband, Senator Peter Cook) are more or less grown. Even with everyone working, Phillipa says it's hard to make ends meet. The cost of living is extraordinarily high, and much higher since the advent of McAlpine and increased tourism. Vegetables are expensive, especially now the local Japanese market gardens no longer exist. Meat has shot up since the meatworks closed down in the eighties. Water and electricity are dearer than elsewhere. In the worst months, when air-conditioning is essential, her electricity bill climbs to eight hundred dollars.

I'm always struck by the deep circles under Phillipa's eyes and her way of being simultaneously eager and weary. She has a look that's more Indian than Aboriginal. The family origins are totally mixed: Afro-American, white, Sri Lankan, Mexican, Aboriginal. Despite the mix, she says the family feel themselves 'at base Aboriginal'. That's what they hold on to.

I don't know what to make of Phillipa. One moment she's sophisticated, very much in control, the next a poor put-upon black woman. But she's a dogged and inveterate lobbyist. She's currently campaigning to get a female lawyer for the Kimberley because, she says, the ALS (i.e. Gordy!) routinely defends the perpetrator, while the indigenous (usually female) victim is missing out on help.

In many ways Phillipa and her kids are the sort of role models Angus Murray is looking for. All with jobs that may hold a future. Even the youngest boy could work his way up in the Chicken Treat hierarchy. They are gifted, motivated kids. There are more like them out there, but there are not enough challenging jobs in small Broome to go around.

*

Last night we saw Jimmy Chi's *Corrugation Road*. We adored it—so snappy and sassy and tuneful and *tolerant*. The whole message was tolerance, of all sorts, but done with the lightest of touches. It was affecting, serious even from time to time, but not a solemn or saccharine moment.

Most of the action takes place in a mental hospital. Jimmy Chi himself has spent time in such places with bouts of schizophrenia.

A cast of every hue. Apart from Jimmy Chi and his fellow composers, and Baamba, of course, only a few actors were from Broome, but what a Broome flavour nonetheless—the sea and sun and up yours to pretension and prejudice.

The musical was staged in the garden of the Mangrove Hotel; under the stars, with the mangroves and mudflats at the back of us. It was lovely seeing it with a home-town audience. Not only did they get every reference and in-joke, but there were those extra little moans and laughs—'Ooh, there's Baamba acting crazy', 'Ooh, there's So-and-so dressed up as a gay', 'Fancy saying that'...Even the title, *Corrugation Road,* is an in-reference to the deeply corrugated pindan road leading north from Broome to Lombadina.

Afterwards, Baamba beaming his almost toothless grin, clasping every second person's hands. He's got that *je ne sais quoi.* People's eyes stay on him and his voice has great warmth and expressiveness. He's only in Broome for a week, then back on the road on a highly successful national tour.

Baamba's career

I caught up with Baamba before he left town again. We sat in his and Pam's small neat house, drinking bottled water from the fridge.

Pam wants someone to write up Baamba's story, particularly the way his life interweaves with Jimmy Chi's. 'They're like two old women, always squabbling and making up,' she told me. 'Sometimes it gets a bit much.'

And occasionally it gets violent. The other day there was a real fight; she had to separate them. Jimmy gets jealous, accuses Baamba of stealing his songs. Baamba says, 'But I thought you *wanted* me to promote them!' And later it's patched up and forgotten again. Pam thinks that Jimmy is jealous of Baamba's social skills, his ability to go out into the wider world.

I asked Baamba about Jimmy. 'Pam says you're always having little quarrels and making up.'

Baamba didn't miss a beat. 'Yes, that happens. We're pretty close. Me and Jimmy, we've been family since we were kids. His mum was brought up the same way as my mum, close to the Church. We're related through our parents, so we're not only bubblies [Broome Kriol for buddies], we're also cousins. We're from the same traditional country. And the other thing, too, we sort of complement each other; I've been there for him and he's been there for me. When I split up with Wendy I used to stay with Jimmy and Glenny at their place when I was in dire straits.'

Baamba and Jimmy were schoolmates together at Rossmoyne, a Catholic hostel in Perth. Then while Jimmy went to university, Baamba took up an apprenticeship as a diesel mechanic. He'd thought about the priesthood, as had Jimmy, but decided against it. 'But my other cousin, Patrick Dodson, went through it; he was the first one.

'Then Jimmy had this car accident, and that's when he started to get paranoid. They diagnosed schizophrenia. The accident brought it on. He realised he couldn't finish his goal—he wanted to become a civil engineer—and he became frustrated. He was under all this pressure; he was the first Aboriginal person from here to go to university. He had all that weight on his back to be successful...He was nineteen or twenty.'

Baamba's career as a diesel mechanic never really got going. He started travelling around, and ended up in Alice Springs where he met and married Wendy. In the seventies he enrolled at Adelaide University to study sociology, psychology and community development. He'd only been there eighteen months when Canberra headhunted him to become the inaugural Chair of the National Aboriginal Education Committee, advising the Federal Government.

'I was twenty-seven. I knew nothing about chairing meetings...All my friends had a gambling night and raised about $800 and they gave it to me, plus Chairman Mao's Little Red Book!

'I think they got me because they didn't want any academics on the committee to compete with them. I think they gave me twelve months, but they didn't expect that I was going to play another game. Because that's all it is—playing games within the politics.

'First time I met Eddie Mabo, he called me 'a black fat cat from Canberra'. So I got him on my committee the next year and then I said, "Now you're a black fat cat!".'

While Baamba was in Canberra, 'Jimmy and them went to Adelaide to do their music lessons and to learn how to read music and produce music— Jimmy, Steve Pigram, the Kuckles band. And while they were in Adelaide I was able to get funding for them through the Aboriginal Studies Grant because I was in charge.' He giggles, then more seriously: 'But the cycle turns, because years later when I was broke they gave me a job in the show.'

After his years with the Canberra bureaucracy Baamba returned to live in Broome. But not long after that he and Wendy broke up and Baamba fled down to Perth.

'I started busking. Jimmy found me. Me and my mate were doing a gig in Moora. I don't know how the hell Jimmy found me. He said, "Come straight up." He paid for my air fare—I was going to catch a bus. So I came up here and we started rehearsing *Bran Nue Dae,* and that's when my life changed. My only regret is that my mum has not seen this part of my life, but I know she's watching now.

'My aunties come up to me and they cry. They don't see me on stage, they see her... They reckon she used to be an actor as a kid. With what I do, they remember her.'

*

A dry intense heat today. But this morning at Town Beach a little breeze was blowing off the water and the trees were giving shade. The water was so soft that you barely felt your limbs parting it. There were four distinct bands of colour—milky turquoise next to the shore, then a deeper strong green-blue, then a real, pure blue, then the gentle pale blue of the sky. On the right as I swam, the small man-made promontory of red earth, rocks and rubble; on the left, the submerged mangroves, and in front of me the park with its swings and little memorials to people drowned at sea. As always, plenty going on—kids, caravanners, hippies and tourists—yet such peace, such quiet, lazy enjoyment.

Chez Lyn

Lyn is her usual, casually elegant self, in checked shorts and a navy T-shirt with 'Chanel' across the front. She says the time might be coming for her to leave Broome. She recently sacked her largest client and she's in two minds about tendering to produce the Shire Directory this year. The directory is a cross between a local telephone book, trade directory and a council information kit. Extremely useful. Lyn's desktop publishing outfit, Magnolia Associates, has been producing it for the past few years. She does a stylish job and has won awards for it.

One reason Lyn is thinking of not tendering for the directory is that her last tarot session with Chi brought up the words, 'Don't pay attention to the dollar.'

But later she talks about investing in a piece of land in Chinatown and putting a building on it with a flat for herself upstairs, done Tuscan style.

She already knows how it would look—quite a different decor from the present house.

If she does leave Broome, she says, it won't be for Sydney or Perth, but somewhere overseas: Italy, France, who knows?

She's telling us all this sitting on her kitchen bench, legs drawn up, bare feet, an ageing but glamorous imp.

On Saturday evening we called in on Gordy and Damien. They were stretched out in the darkened room in front of the TV, side by side on thin swags topped by boomerang-shaped pink pillows. As always, the room was virtually empty, except for two chairs ranged behind the swags on the floor—the stalls and the dress circle, as Anne called them.

Gordy had been out on the piss seriously the night before. He wasn't drinking now. He made himself a coffee, groaned a lot and acted rueful. He says he's going to stay off the grog for a while. Starting Thursday, he's got a series of heavy trials: rape, grievous bodily harm, fraud. 'Trouble is, most of them are guilty as hell,' he says, and laughs. I know by now that that laugh of Gordon's is a mixed message.

We mentioned *Corrugation Road*. Neither of them had got around to seeing it. When we left, Annie said, 'They are so frustrating! Why didn't they go? Damien would have adored it!'

Gordon and Damien almost never go out together. Gordy says he won't do it because he feels ridiculous, is embarrassed on Damien's behalf. All Damien's friends are his age and Gordy has nothing in common with them.

The other day Damien had his long black locks crimped and Gordy paid for it—$142—then had to cough up some more so Damien could go out and show off his hair to his friends.

'This is what it's like,' Gordy said. But he wasn't really complaining.

'He's my bank,' Damien said cheerfully, referring to Gordy. It's a joke that's not a joke between them.

Gordy knows precisely where Damien will be at any hour of the day or night. He sleeps till noon, goes to the Tote in the afternoon, and maybe up to the dealer who lives in Guy Street for some gunja. He meets up with Gordy after work, around five, usually to get some money so he can go partying. Gordy calls it 'being taken for my evening walk to the auto-bank'. Damien might go back to the Tote till about 8 p.m. Then home for a sleep. He goes out again at about 11 p.m., to the Pearlers Bar at the Roebuck, then on to one of the two clubs till three or four in the morning. Then he goes home to wherever Gordon is sleeping.

Monday, August 3

A discussion on the radio this morning about the Broome cricket season. The cricket is to start soon, playing both Saturdays and Sundays. They used to start around the normal cricket season, then stop for eight weeks at Christmas and start up again later. 'But a lot of the blokes don't ever come back.' This way they manage to get a whole season of games over by Christmas, after which it's 'too bloody hot'.

Wednesday

I've never worn so much white as I wear here. Even the thought of black makes me hot. But because it's always hot and sticky and dusty, whites don't last long. So I'm always doing the washing, much to Susan's amusement. I don't go near the washing machine at home.

The pearling masters always wore white drill suits (some of them with gold sovereigns for buttons), which they had laundered in Singapore back in the days when a good water supply had not yet been found here. Broome water turned clothes red. So the pearling masters sent their suits on the regular boats plying between Broome and Singapore and Perth. A few weeks later they'd get them back clean.

Kim Male still wears all-white, although now it's an open-necked shirt, shorts and long socks. I've not seen so many men in long socks since about 1965!

*

Angela, the Legal Aid lawyer from Melbourne, has been promising us a home-cooked Thai meal for ages. She's been taking Thai cooking lessons as part of her acclimatisation to Broome. Angela's house is in Sayonara Drive, Sunset Park—worth living there for the name alone! It's Broome's newest suburb and suitably surreal. Opposite the large but totally characterless government house that goes with her job at Legal Aid are two others, very similar. Beyond them, nothing, a flatness of bare bush, as if the great northern wilderness starts just beyond the kerb and guttering.

Angela acquitted herself of the cooking ordeal admirably while telling us tales of the Broome underworld. The Coffin Cheaters, who run the drugs and prostitution in town, have been wanting to buy the Nippon Inn, but the guy who owns both the Nippon and the other less lucrative nightclub,

Tokyo Joe's, wants them to buy both. So far, no deal. Dope has been a bit hard to get this year and the bikies have been flooding the town with amphetamines instead. Lots of cocaine and Ecstasy about, too.

During NAIDOC Week some people were suspicious that both nightclubs were closed because of all the extra countrymen in town. But it was also the week that the Gypsy Jokers arrived in Broome, and the nightclub owner and the cops were worried that the two gangs might have a bust-up at either place. So the closures were nothing to do with NAIDOC influx at all, as it turns out.

Cissy's stories

Some people over at Cable Beach have been ringing Mary, wanting help to get rid of a bad presence hanging around their house. The figure of a sixteen-year-old boy kept appearing. They reckoned they were being haunted.

'Gardiya people?' I asked.

'Yeah.'

After several weeks of being pestered, Mary got two old countrymen to go over there. In a couple of hours they had exorcised the place. 'Those old people, they're amazing the things they can do,' Mary said, shaking her head.

She lent me two books of stories by her mother. *The First Fire* (part of the Dampierland Oral History Project) is about a man named Loom who was the first to use fire. The second, *How the One-eyed Snake got its Power* ('a Jukun Yawuru story, told by Cissy Djiagween'); is about a seasnake who lives off Minyirr, or Gantheaume Point, and the one-eyed Rainbow snake.

Mary's face fills with absolute delight when she relates the stories. She has a very expressive face. She gets a faraway look in her eyes and her voice becomes quiet and clipped.

We're on a couple of chairs outside her office. Mary's having a fag.

'The old people are so wise,' she says. 'They've got so much wisdom.'

I ask her if they are sometimes reluctant to hand that knowledge on.

'Knowledge is dangerous,' she says. 'It's dangerous to know things before you're ready to know them. That's why stuff is secret. There's a progression.'

I mention by name a Yawuru elder who disappeared into the desert some time back, and Mary shooshes me. His name should not be spoken. It is now accepted that he is dead. He took over as senior Yawuru man from Mary's grandfather, Paddy Djiagween. Now there is a break in the chain because the elder had not named a successor.

We talk about why some people drink. 'They can see things that white people can't,' Mary says. There is a whole other world that Aboriginal people have access to. It's why they don't care if the drink kills them. According to Mary, they know where they are going and that nothing will change that; it doesn't matter what they do.

I try to argue with her. Surely the drinking must be a sign of them not being happy in their spirit? She won't agree. As far as spiritual evolution goes, 'they're already there'.

'I'm not saying people shouldn't think about their health,' she says. 'It's good to be healthy because you live longer.' But she thinks whitefellas are overly concerned with their physical bodies, to the detriment of the spiritual.

The spirit world is a busy place. Her mother Cissy often sees things, apparitions. They don't scare her. 'Nothing scares her,' Mary says, and laughs loudly.

Eleven

Quiet as lambs—Broome burial—Beach idyll

A lot of people run away to Broome. It is the perfect place to run to. So far away, so remote, so of itself and nowhere else. A lot of them come here because they don't fit anywhere else. This place is very tolerant of strangeness. Some come because they are depressed, and the depression is not entirely left behind.

But you can change your life here. That is Broome's promise. I think of Angela, leaving a tortuous love affair in Melbourne to come and work for Legal Aid here. I think of Lyn Page, of the life she lived in Sydney as the socialite who spent five-hundred dollars a week on clothes, and the life she lives in Broome.

It takes guts to expose yourself to the differentness of the place and not just survive but make it work. I asked Lyn how she coped when she first made the decision to stay. Was she ever bored or alienated?

'Nope. I wouldn't allow myself to be. I had an attitude. I knew I wanted to stay here. I knew it was right that I was here. But at first people were not welcoming. But I just thought, "Damn it! I choose to be here."'

After working for McAlpine for a year or so, Lyn went back east for a few months, then decided to move to Broome permanently. When she got back she went down to the post office to get a post box and was told there was a three-month wait. 'Uh-huh,' she thought, and arranged for her mail to be held till a box became available. That was when the post office was opposite the prison, and tourists dispatching their postcards would gawk at the prisoners sitting on the lawn outside the gaol.

After a week the post mistress rang her and said they had a post box for her after all, one at the front, at a nice height.

'You sure it's for me?' Lyn said.

'Yes,' said the woman. 'A nice one at the front. We must look after the locals.'

'And I thought, YES! And from that moment everything changed. That was the turning point. People realised I was here to stay.'

At the time, she was living in a little cottage on a dirt road out in what was then the backblocks, now a busy part of the light-industrial area around Clementson Street.

'A bit different from what you were used to,' I say.

'The apartment in Elizabeth Bay with the most gorgeous views over the Cruising Yacht Club?' She chuckles. 'Yeah, a bit of a change. But it was good. I loved it.'

Quiet as lambs

One of the first things that visitors remark on when they arrive in Broome—after the colour of the sea, the colour of the earth—is the prison. Slap bang in the middle of town. In Hammersley Street, which used to be the main street until Chinatown took over as the chief shopping area.

A few days after we arrived here I was coming out of the library and ran into a group of green-uniformed men on their way in. At first I thought they were council workers, but they were prisoners. Trustworthy convicts are allowed out on their own. The less trustworthy go 'on the truck' with a staff supervisor. They do clean-up jobs around the parks and the foreshore, help out if a community group needs a hand with anything, do odd-jobs for pensioners. There has been some suggestion that the practice should stop but no-one is taking much notice of that. The prisoners are a Broome institution.

No-one worries that they will try to escape. Where would they go? There's only one road out of town.

The prison office is a long, simple building facing the street, with a lawn in front of it and a low brick fence. When I arrive there's a group of prisoners sitting on the fence, and a few people on the lawn. This is the visiting area. There's a good view of the lawn from the watch-room, 'But most of the time we don't even bother to watch 'em,' says one of the warders, Garry Fitzpatrick.

Fitzpatrick is a big, ginger-haired, ruddy faced man who has worked at the Broome prison for five years. He says they average maybe one escape a year. 'Usually it's because of a woman. A woman from one of the remote communities will come into town to see her man, then she'll get on the piss and come to the prison in the middle of the night, yelling and screaming for him. He'll start to wonder what she's getting up to, who she's screwing, and will break out so he can go and bash 'em up.'

Garry Fitzpatrick is a rough-gruff sort of bloke but tolerant and non-judgemental about his charges. Part of the easygoing ethos of the prison. Visiting days are meant to be weekends and public holidays, but no-one takes much notice of that. 'Aboriginal people don't have much sense of time,' he says. 'A truck from Balgo might roll up and they'll want to see their boys. Of course we let 'em. It'll often be a weekday because that's when the people come in from communities to do their shopping.'

Sixty to seventy per cent of the prisoners are Aboriginal. Most are there because of the effects of grog. 'If it wasn't for the grog, we'd be out of a job,' says Charlie, another of the warders. Unlike Fitzpatrick, Charlie is in his prison uniform. He's a swarthy skinned guy, possibly of Lebanese extraction. He says Aborigines shouldn't be allowed grog, that they just can't handle it.

Most of the Aboriginal inmates are there because of crimes of violence when drunk, usually against family members, usually their female partners.

'Their foreplay is violence,' Fitzpatrick says, somewhat cynically.

But by the time they get to prison, they're sober. 'They're as quiet as lambs when we get them,' Charlie says. He starts going on about the grog again. Fitzpatrick looks at the floor. He doesn't blame the prisoners for their predicament, he just accepts the human variety he sees around him.

There has only been one death in custody in Broome to date—a guy who couldn't get parole because no-one outside would take him back.

'The families don't want them. But then as soon as they do that to themselves, the families come and blame us.'

This, they say, is the great unspoken about Aboriginal deaths in custody. That and the fact that, relative to their numbers in prison, white deaths in custody are a much bigger problem. But that never gets talked about. Fitzpatrick says that he's been to three inquests for deaths in custody: one white and two Aboriginal. The white guy's inquest was over in eight minutes. The two black inquests each lasted five days.

All the non-Aboriginal prisoners—with the exception of a handful of whites—are Indonesian fishermen gaoled for illegally fishing in Australian waters. There are so many Indonesians at the moment that there's no room for women prisoners, so they are being sent down to Roebourne. Like every prison in the State, Broome is massively overcrowded.

During the day the prisoners stick to their own groups. The Indonesian fishermen stay with their crew and expect their skipper to look after them. They eat earlier than the others, because they have their own food prepared for them. The prison employs a chef and he has two teams of helpers for the two sorts of food.

To be caught illegally fishing is a bit of a scam, some people say. Prisoners can actually save more money during their prison term in Australia, if they work, than they would earn in Indonesia. Fitzpatrick doesn't know about that. But he says he knows of one skipper who has been jailed nine times.

Last week, Angela defended some Indonesian fishermen charged with smuggling illegal immigrants into Western Australia. They were getting less than a hundred dollars each to do it. The prosecutor said that 'the current economic climate in Indonesia is forcing them to do anything for money'.

In the men's defence, Angela said, 'They took a perilous journey with little regard for their own safety to secure an amount under one hundred dollars. They are traditional fishermen and normally fish in northern waters. They navigated by sight and had no idea how long the journey would take them.'

The magistrate, Col Roberts, was not convinced. 'This was not a simple case of catching fish to feed your family,' he said. 'It was a deliberate breach of Australia's law to make a profit.' He gave them eight months gaol each, to be served in the Broome prison.

*

Saturday evening at Gordon's. Remains of takeaway Chinese scattered over the kitchen bench. Looking for a clean glass on the sink, for the beer we've brought. Give up and drink from the bottle.

Damien was on one of the bedrolls in front of the TV. The news was on, and he appeared to watch avidly. But it's hard to tell with Damien. I suspect he looks at the TV but has his ears open to what we are saying behind him.

These evenings at Gordon's have a particular atmosphere. The lack of furniture, the general mess, the TV going, all eyes fixed on it. On top of the tele, videos of evidence from Gordon's clients, a copy of *Rolling Stone* on the kitchen bench next to copies of our books, and the *Australian* spread out on the floor. The French doors to the verandah open, and across the way the long red neon slash that lights up the roof of the Roebuck's bottle shop, an attempt at a Chinese-style roofline. And voices and laughter drifting up from the Sheba Lane restaurant next door.

Monday, August 10

I went to see Dr Harp Singh today. He's an Australian-born Sikh, an aristocratic looking man with his beard and turban. He hasn't been in Broome long. He wonders why so many retiree caravaners come up here—he wishes they wouldn't. He has seen three heart attacks in the past month, all of them old caravaners. He says there is a lot of stress and depression in Broome. People come here thinking it's a tropical paradise and it's not at all. It is actually a hard place to live.

Dr Singh lives near Fong's Store, an area he describes as 'properly Broome'. Lyn calls it 'salt and pepper territory', meaning black and white. She lives there, too.

Dr Singh said the flutter in one of my eyes was a result of 'too much looking'. A good description of my life here! Maybe we need to get away for a few days. The stresses of this enterprise are showing with both of us—we're edgy with one another, our moods are all over the place.

Things aren't helped by the political situation. Watching the progression of the Pauline Hanson caravanserai—who's attached themselves to her this week, who's undecided, which politicians are balancing their fear of her against their fear of a reactionary electorate—is both depressing and electrifying.

It's frightening to watch the emergence in this country of right-wing populism, to see 'liberal' politicians duck and weave rather than condemn Hanson outright. They know that her diatribes against 'Asianisation' and 'multiculturalism' strike a chord. There are tens of thousands of Australians who believe, as she does, that Aborigines receive 'privileges' denied to white Australians, that Asian gangs are taking over our cities.

Hanson is playing on people's fears. Whenever people feel insecure they lash out at those who are lower down the peg, those whose grasp on the mainstream is even more tenuous than their own. No wonder, in such a climate, that Howard has been able to decimate native title rights, to 'raise the pole' so that fewer and fewer Aborigines have any chance of proving their ties to country. It was the white authorities who tried so hard to break those ties; now it's indigenous people who have to try to prove they still exist.

∫ Pauline Hanson was on ABC regional radio a couple of days ago, just after her triumphal march through Kim Beazley's electorate of Brand. It was a talkback session. I could feel the sympathy for her pouring down the airwaves as the superior, cultured tones of the interviewer contrasted to her trembling mispronunciations. For all that, she's getting smoother. And she's dogged. I can see why people identify with her. When asked exactly what she meant by 'the Australian way of life', she said, 'Beaches, the barbie, the English language, "g'day mate".' Then, 'Australia is a multicultural society, but multiculturalism will destroy us.'

One caller, a reasonable-sounding, caring woman from Kununurra, said she'd spent forty years ministering to Aboriginal kids, many of whom have done very well. She claimed to have ten Aboriginal grandchildren. Then she praised Hanson in the warmest of terms.

I don't understand what's going on.

*

A nine-year-old boy has hanged himself. No-one seems to know why. The town is stunned. At St Mary's they are trying to work out how to commemorate this awful event in a way that's 'culturally sensitive' and won't encourage copycat suicides.

In Northern Ireland three young boys have been burnt to death in their beds because their mother is a Catholic living in a Protestant area. The children were being brought up Protestants. Now they are to be given Catholic funerals.

After such a weekend, what does the ABC radio news run as its lead story on Monday morning? The outcry in Perth over the installation of parking meters at Cottesloe Beach! Annie was so disgusted she rang the newsroom in Perth and blasted the chief-of-staff.

Broome burial

At the funeral for Trevor Roe, the bishop told a story about him. Trevor, a bright, ebullient, emotional kid, came up to him after mass one Sunday and said, bold as anything, 'Do you remember me, Bishop?'

'No,' said the bishop, 'why should I?' That brusqueness of his again. But Trevor wasn't put off.

'Because I'm the first child you baptised as Bishop of Broome.'

'And then it came back to me suddenly,' the bishop told the mourners. 'Trevor. Trevor Roe.'

At the service the bishop was solemn, sincere, very much the upright man of religion, offering hope in a hopeless situation. Does he truly believe, I keep asking myself?

I don't know if I can write about the funeral. What to say in the face of so much sadness and futility? Except that the church was packed with sombre and sincerely grieving people. Even those who barely knew the child seemed to be grieving for him.

Most of the speakers and most of the congregation were Aboriginal, although there was a sprinkling of whites. Standing just outside the church, a white woman dabbed her eyes frequently. A stocky blond man in a shirt and tie was comforting a light-skinned Aboriginal child—his daughter? Inside, an Aboriginal woman sat at the side of the pulpit, her face covered by one long elegant hand in a constant attitude of sorrow, her mouth working occasionally. Little kids sat solemnly on the floor. Others awkwardly read out their tributes to Trevor from the dais. Songs, prayers, flowers, the Aboriginal Lord's Prayer, the spare beauty of which grows on you.

A special booklet was handed to everyone, a kind of program with Trevor's colour photo on it. Inside, scattered among the prayers, hymns and order of service, were more colour photos: Trevor as a gorgeous baby, Trevor with his family.

I saw Phillipa Cook, singing all the hymns, joining in all the responses. Her Catholic education must have been thorough. She cried briefly. I often felt like crying myself, such was the heavy mood. You only had to glance at the open friendly face of this child to feel overwhelmed by his tragedy.

No-one really knows why this lively rush-at-life child hanged himself. His parents were separated, and he'd recently had to leave his home in Derby to live with relatives here and go to a new school. But nothing else has come to light; no neglect or hardship or abuse. Just a sensitive kid having a hard time.

We were dubious about going to the cemetery, but there were so many people going we decided we wouldn't be noticed. If anything there were even more people at the graveside, perhaps five hundred.

It's an anarchic kind of cemetery. No neat rows. Just gum trees and dirt tracks, names and nationalities higgledy-piggledy. The sort of cemetery one wouldn't mind being buried in.

People of all sorts stood around, some with their offerings of flowers—single roses, plastic wreaths, mixed bunches. The principal of St Mary's, Cath Hegny, who we met once at the Soroptimists, stood diffidently at the back with her official wreath. A white man in shorts, thongs and ragged singlet stood by; old ladies sat on folding chairs brought for them by relatives. A few smokers stood at the back, lighting up for relief from the tension.

Over it all the repeated 'Hail Mary full of grace, blessed is the fruit of thy womb Jesus' read over a portable mike by a small group of Aboriginal women. The men took turns to shovel the red earth into the grave. A brief high-pitched wailing of women, a sudden eerie return to the Aboriginal, before the Hail Marys and rosary took over again. The bishop at the graveside throughout.

We left while some were still taking up flowers, others trailing away, back to their cars.

Later in the evening we called in on Gordon, to see if his promised but much delayed party for Damien's birthday was finally happening. His face saddened. 'It didn't seem appropriate,' he said, (Gordon, who flouts all conventions) 'with that kid's funeral on.'

*

I was taken aback by Vanessa's angry reaction to Trevor Roe's funeral. She was incensed that so many showed up for the funeral when the very same people might be neglecting their own kids. The biggest turn-outs these days, she said, are not for weddings or for a kid's birthday party but for funerals. People flit from one funeral to another. They think nothing of travelling vast distances—down to Hedland 600 kilometres away, or even further. 'Socialites of death, that's what they are,' Vanessa says scornfully.

No wonder she's angry about death. Suicide seems to be decimating a whole generation of Aboriginal youth here, including her own younger brother.

I suggested we might meet again this weekend. Saturdays are normally good, she said, but she has to go to a funeral at Derby. Then she grinned at the irony of what she'd just said. But this young man was different, she said—a good friend who'd supported her family through both her mother's and father's deaths.

Vanessa has a rapport with young people. Her home always has a passing population of them, black and white. She worries about young Aboriginal men killing themselves on an almost daily basis. How to give them a hold on their future, a sense of self-worth? Her brother's suicide hangs heavily on her heart.

She talks of the terrible pressures on teenage couples with young babies. The strain is greatest on the boys—'they're normally the ones that commit suicide.'

I mention the very young couple and their baby that I saw outside the Seaview Supermarket yesterday. The boy looked no more than fourteen.

'Yeah, they're the ones I want to try and support. The social pressures make it worse. Children are dumped with the parents, who may not have any parenting skills because they themselves were taken away, y'know, and the grannies are looking after kids. It just goes on and on and on...

'The image of Aboriginal men—it's like, where are they? This whole society is profiled by white males. In terms of indigenous men, they don't even have their own law to be able to govern by. They don't have an image, and I think that's why a lot of them vie for black politics, because at least you can sit up there and be seen on TV or be quoted as saying this or that. Then it becomes like "Oh, that's Puggy Hunter's territory", or, "Oh yes, that's Marty Sibosado's territory". It becomes territorial.

'A lot of it comes down to anger with the bureaucracy. The men who are in their little community and just rassling to get by from day to day, they're the ones that get angry, and then come the wife bashings and the abuse. It's their own internalised oppression that they have to deal with, and they don't have the skills to interpret it.'

*

Vanessa didn't get to the funeral at Derby after all. Her brakes failed. But another funeral next weekend might take her out of town. Is this where the bitterness about funerals comes from? Her life seems ruled by them as much as anyone else's in the Aboriginal community.

The bishop's weekend was funeral-bound, too. A young man's suicide by hanging at Beagle Bay. Bishop Chris flew up in his plane. He knew the young man and his family well. At the service many of the young man's friends were weeping, but as one of the old women said afterwards, 'Within an hour they'll be off to mull up or start drinking, and prepare for the next death.'

Two days later there was another attempted suicide at Beagle Bay, this time unsuccessful.

Beach idyll

We're taking three days off at Eco Beach. It's a new 'ecologically sound' resort over an hour's drive from Broome. Here at Eco the air is cooler, there's a constant little breeze off the shining ocean, and the beach is even longer and far more deserted than Cable. The food is good, the beds comfortable and we haven't had a cross word for three days.

We've met Lyn's ex-husband, Carl. He owns the resort along with a silent partner. Carl is personable and easygoing; also smart and driven. In

Susan at Eco Beach

Broome he used to manage the Backpackers. According to Perpetua, when Lyn took him up he was a young nobody. There must have been a bit of a scandal when they married, because of the hefty age difference. Once again you have to admire Lyn's guts. He and Lyn remain good friends.

It was nice having Anne Deveson here for the first two days. We all warmed to each other further, got to know each other better. The combination of vagueness and smart, self-deprecation and a certain steeliness, of warmth and reserve, is an attractive one. We discovered two things in common—a mutual lover from way back in our pasts (not at the same time!), and first novels coming out. Similar reactions to both. To the lover, short-lived obsession, to the novel, apprehension mixed naturally with hope...

*

Since getting back from Eco Beach it has come home to us that we can't live here just as observers. We can't live here and not be touched by the place. Friday night was a case in point. We were supposed to have dinner with Angela and Gordon, but Gordon never showed up. We tracked him down afterwards at the Lugger Bar. He was in a bad mood, had already had too much to drink. At some point and for no clear reason he started being mean to me. In my usual observer mode I wouldn't take such a thing too seriously. But it upset me, a lot—out of all proportion really.

There was a band playing at the Lugger Bar. A tableful of countrymen were obviously dying to get up and dance but were reluctant to in this room full of whites. So I went over and asked a couple of them up, first a woman then a man, and within a few minutes most of them were up and dancing. One of the things I've found since being in Broome is that I am actually a lot more comfortable with Aboriginal people than I thought I might be. I had all the usual fears and nervousness. I'm relieved to find that it's challenging but not scarily so.

Since our break away, the book has gone into the background a bit, and we're more relaxed and fond with one another—having fewer little snipes. You said to me that Gordon was probably shitty because he was thinking, 'You're not really my friends, you're just writers', just interested in him for material. But maybe it's more that you and I have got something that he certainly doesn't have with Damien and he's jealous of that.

ʃ Yes, you've got it in one, the essence of it anyway. He was all over the place that night, showing the different parts of himself in frighteningly quick succession—kind and caring Gordy, don't-give-a-stuff Gordy, insecure and despairing Gordon, mean and aggressive Gordon. I think perhaps he was jealous of you on many scores that night, which was why he 'turned'. He doesn't really like anyone but himself making overtures to and being easy with Aboriginal people. He didn't really like seeing you dancing when he doesn't and when he saw me reluctant to. He became protective of me over your 'youth' and over-identified you with Damien, even though I reminded him you were forty-one years old!

But yes, he said it himself: we have a relationship where we can talk to each other as equals and friends. He doesn't have that and would give anything to have it. The despair that emanates from that man sometimes breaks my heart. Yet it is far from too late for him.

You're bolder than I with the Aboriginal people you meet. I'm still straining every nerve to find the right response and it renders me passive.

At Eco Beach I read back over what you wrote in the double journal early in the year. You were prescient about the risks of this venture. And at that stage we didn't understand the two major ones—the occasional sense of falseness we've had in being here, and the extent of our reliance on each other and the extra stress that puts on us. It's stretching us, but in ways we won't understand for some time yet.

Twelve

The real estate agent's shack—Tropical summer—
Lyn on Elsta—Mary—Bob's bad leg—Ménage à trois—
Shinju countdown

The real estate agent's shack

Tony Hutchinson has been in the real estate game since he was sixteen and chauffeured Lord McAlpine around town, watching him buy up dozens of properties. He realised then how much money could be made out of Broome.

Lyn took us to Tony's house last night for a gathering in honour of visitors from Perth and Melbourne. She was very keen to meet the Perth people, but was tight-lipped and mysterious as to why.

Tony must be the only real estate agent in Australia to live in such a marvellous tumble-down house. It's the same basic style as the Rat Palazzo, with shuttered verandahs and sagging floorboards, only it's not quite as decrepit, and it's furnished with some consciousness of its charms.

Outside, in the overgrown, shadowy garden, a Broome whitefella evening was in progress. Mountains of fish and crabs freshly caught that (weekday) afternoon by Tony, huge bowls of salad, everyone hoeing in with their fingers. Suntans glowing in the dark. Amiable chat and discussions of last night's hangover.

Tropical summer

Tourist Broome is all around us and will be for a month or so yet while the milder weather lasts, but we generally ignore it, so fascinated are we by the other 'old' Broome. Yet tourism is the biggest thing in Broome, the source of many livelihoods. The problem for the shopkeepers and tour operators is how to make a year-round living out of it. The season really only lasts from May to September, after which Broome begins to shrink to a third of its winter size. Shops close, people go fishing or down south. And many locals heave a sigh of relief because this is how Broome is meant to be.

The latest attempt to change Broome into an all-year resort is the 'Tropical Summer' campaign. It's not the first, but so far all others have failed. A meeting has been called at the Shire offices. The idea is to go on the offensive. If tourists can be persuaded to go to Bali in summer, where it's even hotter, why not Broome?

The marketing man, a confident young fellow employed by Cable Beach Club, assures the audience that while the first season will be hard, the dollar rewards will be there in the long run. His key idea is a Kimberley Passport, which guarantees tourists cheap fares, discounted accommodation and shopping, and stores that stay open.

There are mixed reactions in the room. Some are keen, others dismayed; they want to keep the Wet sacred for quiet times and recovery. Lyn speaks as President of the Chamber of Commerce. It's the first time I've seen her professional persona. She's casually dressed in black jeans and an elegant white shirt, and she's self-possessed and fluent and subtly but powerfully sexy. She says the chamber is behind the idea one hundred per cent, and her own experience as the former proprietor of Mango Jack's takeaway is that long hours and persistence pay off.

The ice-cream shop man advocates planting shade trees in Chinatown. 'Right now the tourists bake on those streets,' he says. 'All they want is to scuttle back to their air-conditioned hotel and swimming pool.'

Lyn proposes the town reinstate siesta hours, as of old. A two to three hour siesta in the middle of the day was once a Broome institution. But Chinatown shopkeepers won't get behind that idea; they can't agree amongst themselves.

'Do you think this Tropical Summer idea will work?' we ask Perpetua.
'Oh, I hope not!'
'Too bloody hot,' says someone else.
The meeting breaks up. Lyn gets behind the bar and helps dispense

drinks. We ask her about the siesta idea. 'No-one will take it seriously,' she says, 'but I keep bringing it up year after year, just for the hell of it.'

As we're leaving, she stops us and says, 'I didn't get the tender for the Shire Directory.' She sounds bemused. She was sure she'd get the contract once she'd decided to tender.

We remind her that she was ambivalent about tendering anyway. 'It might lead you on to new things,' we say.

'Yes, it might,' she says absently.

Friday, August 21

I spent an hour at court this morning. Angela was there for a brief mention. She said that after our last drinking session with Gordy, she swore she would never drink so much again. I told her that Anne and Gordy had agreed not to take their recent little falling-out too seriously. 'I don't think one should take anything Gordy says too seriously,' she said ruefully before disappearing into court.

Gordy was around and about, leading two Aboriginal women into the court office, putting in a guilty plea for a youth charged with assaulting a policeman, etcetera. In between he brought me up to speed on the latest in his personal life. His lady friend from Perth who buys him women's clothes has arrived in town, but she already has the shits because she suspects him of playing along with an Aboriginal girl called Sharon. The woman from Perth offered him a free week's holiday to a mystery destination, but Gordy refused.

'I can't be bought,' he says, laughing in his self-derisive way.

Gordy likes Sharon. But there are complicating factors. She is young (although she's Damien's senior by four years), and worse, she's Damien's niece.

'I can't get involved with young ones again,' Gordy told her.

'Well at least I'm older than Damien!' she said.

Gordy thinks for a minute, then muses, 'I think I might turn heterosexual for a while.' He does seem rather taken with this Sharon. She's cleaned up his flat beautifully, and he likes the feel of her lying next to him. ('It's years since I lay next to a woman; they're such little things. Men are great lumps.')

At first I think he's serious. But then it becomes clear that Sharon's main function is to make Damien jealous. Damien hasn't been home since Saturday, and Gordy's getting worried.

'You're only using that girl as a ploy,' I say, cottoning on.

'Yes, probably,' he said, 'poor little thing...'

'Going "hetero" for a while mightn't be such a bad thing, but not with Damien's niece! Think of the jealousy, the rows!'

'Yes,' he says, and falls into a reverie, his eyes glinting at the sport of it.

If you warn Gordon of danger it becomes an immediate temptation. Perhaps his real interest in life is finding new ways of skating close to the edge without finally and fatally falling over it.

Outside the courthouse I noticed a stringy looking man with a messy white beard picking up debris from under the trees. From Annie's description, it had to be local identity and former diver, Dave Dureau. I went up to say hello. He was apologetic that we still hadn't got together. He's only just back from the long walk he does each year in a different part of the Kimberley. This time it was the Mitchell Plateau. Normally the walk takes a month and the walkers carry their supplies in with them, but this year Dave allowed himself to be dropped there by helicopter and to have extra supplies dropped, too, so the walk took only two weeks and there was less to carry.

Dave must be in his sixties, thin and a bit bent, but he's tougher and stronger than he looks. He now earns his living doing gardening and rubbish collection around town. He's married to Elsta Foy, one of the three Aboriginal people on Council. He's a keen botanist, conservationist and intellectual. His father was a Melbourne businessman who was instrumental in setting up the cultured pearl industry. Dureau senior is one of the figures memorialised in bronze in the main street.

I'm intrigued by Dave's story—wealthy businessman's son turned odd-job man. He seems to cross class and race frontiers very easily. In the five minutes we were together he greeted a young black man and talked to a mixed-race woman who told him she was thinking of buying a fast food shop in Derby and getting her daughter to run it, 'but that daughter of mine, she's likely to give free hamburgers to all the rellies and friends, so I don't know...'

They agreed that Derby, where Dave spent a week after his walking trip, was a lovely little place—'like Broome was a few years ago.'

'Broome's finished,' Dave said. His friend nodded gloomily.

Lyn on Elsta

'What's Elsta Foy like?' I asked Lyn. 'How's she on council?'

'Look, I don't even know where to start,' Lyn said.

So she starts where she always starts. 'I like the lady. I have wonderful chats with her. I want to go camping with her. I wish to Christ she wasn't on council. She doesn't read her agenda...'

Lyn's dog Georgie interrupts, snuffling for nibblies.

'That's mine, George! Elsta comes from a community. She thought she wouldn't stand last time and I said, "Yes, you must. The council needs you. Got to get in there." She said, "I come from the little fella, the community." I said. "Yep. Necessary voice." But she specialises in it, and to hell with everything else. She harped and harped about the cemetery, said we had to do something about it. Right. Who ended up on the cemetery committee, has to go to meetings every two weeks?'

'You did?'

'Mmm. She doesn't pull her weight, she's not up to date. Council's not a paid position. But if you read your papers, go and talk to people, ask the right questions and put something to council, it's likely to get up. She doesn't know enough about the processes. Same goes for Nolan. If he had a problem he should have raised it in council. But he hasn't done it. He still hasn't done it!'

Mary

The other day Mary asked me if I would give her a hand in getting things going with the culture centre. The whole thing has been stagnating for a long time, maybe in part because it hasn't been high on Rubibi's agenda.

Mary has now decided to take things more into her own hands. This morning, just as I was sitting down to sort out my desk and get to work, an old mustard-coloured Holden pulled up at the gate and Mary and a white woman got out. I was in my sarong and went out barefoot to meet them.

'Sorry to just call in like this,' said Mary, 'but Lyn Devereaux rang. She wants us to go there for a meeting at ten. Can you come?'

I went inside and threw on some clothes.

Lyn Devereaux is the Shire's community development officer—'A nice woman,' Mary said on the way there. It was Lyn who had suggested that Mary should apply to the Department of Land Administration for some land in Clementson Street. Mary's idea is that if she could get hold of this piece of land, she could clean it up and set up an office for the culture centre on it, as well as a camping ground for people coming into town for cultural events.

Mary took me to have a look at it yesterday. It's between the former meatworks site (now the new foreshore housing estate) and the sewerage treatment works. There are a couple of tracks where people drive their cars down to the shore to go fishing. Local people have always fished here. Part of the dunes were washed away when the sewerage settling ponds flooded during a huge fall of rain. The whole area is a mess and needs cleaning up.

These are the dunes where Kevin Fong's family and many others lived up until the 1970s. There was once an unofficial market in the shacks here. People would buy and sell them among themselves, like in a shanty town. The shacks are all gone now but there are old camp sites, places where corroborees have been held. Bush medicine is still collected here.

Mary taught me about some of the trees: the Jarradung, which is a spindly tree with long narrow leaves; the Bundarrung, which is a medicine tree, graceful with a weeping habit and rough bark. Strips of the bark are cut off and stewed in water for a long time until the sap comes out and makes a form of natural iodine, which is then poured over wounds. Then there's the Jigily, which is a common tree around here, bushy, with small, round leaves. And Meda, which has smooth, pale bark, a nice shape and loses all its leaves at this time of year. When they grow back they are green and slightly waxy.

Mary wants to apply for a Land Care grant once they get the land, if they get it. She also has her eye on a large block opposite, which would be good as a site for the culture centre itself.

Lyn Devereaux, the community development officer, works in an airy set of offices halfway between the old town and Cable Beach. She's a pleasant, largish woman, smartly dressed all in taupe. She knows Mary and treats her with respect.

After discussing the Clementson Street land, talk turns to the racecourse. Lyn Devereaux says the State Government intends to offer it for tourist development and is going to invite expressions of interest. The Turf Club is not keen—they don't want to move.

Mary says she would like the culture centre to be built out that way, but not on the racecourse because it's too close to sacred Gantheaume. 'A bit back from the racecourse would be okay.'

I worry about Mary trying to find a site for the culture centre on her own, independently of Rubibi. Rubibi is meant to be the overarching body for land claims. But Mary's not worried.

'Rubibi won't mind,' she says. 'They'll support me.' Then she laughs. 'Or most of them!'

I wonder where all this is heading. Sometimes she seems to know exactly what is required: the acronyms, the granting bodies, and so on. At other times it is like the ball hasn't even got rolling because quite basic things have not been done, preliminary meetings have not been held. Mary clearly wants me there at these meetings with the white bureaucrats. When we talked about it, I thought my involvement would just be to write a few letters. But today it seems she wants me for back-up. By default I have become almost a 'white adviser'.

*

The regional manager for the Department of Land Administration (DOLA) rang me at seven-thirty this morning, so I was able to tee up a meeting between him and Mary and a senior DOLA man from Perth.

They were both nice, greying, slightly portly men. Sympathetic. Mary started by telling them a bit about the culture centre. She handled it well. Then she talked about the Clementson Street land. About setting up a walking trail, an interpretation point to tell visitors about the area, camping facilities and an office where she could be based. They said the land could be vested in Rubibi, then leased back to the culture centre. 'It will still have to go through the native title process,' they said. Mary agreed.

Then I shoved her a bit towards the racecourse. They reassured her that they're only calling for preliminary interest and that Rubibi would be consulted intensively during the process.

One of them went to get a large aerial photo from the car. He showed us how the racecourse could be moved back from Gantheaume Point, up towards Cable Beach. That would free up a lot of land on the coast.

It also frees up exactly the bit of land that Mary said yesterday she'd like for the cultural centre. It would be next to the new racecourse.

Mary got out the plans for the culture centre. The two government men were quite excited by its extraordinary turtle-shaped design.

'Having it close to the beach would be perfect,' Mary said, 'because Cable is the Turtle Dreaming.'

Cissy, Mary's mum, came to the door. Cissy is small, shy, a little stooped. Mary beckoned her in and introduced her. Cissy was enticed up to the photo. She pointed out two high rocky points which were old camping grounds. Then smiled shyly again and backed out.

I'd like to know, when Mary looks down at one of those aerial photos, what does she see? What does Cissy see?

After the others had gone, Mary told me a story about her mother predicting a big Wet months in advance. And another story about going fishing with the old people. She likes to be always there with the old people, listening and learning. She's still learning.

These stories are dropped into Mary's conversation in ways which I at first took to be ad hoc and accidental. But I'm beginning to see that even if there is no apparent connection between the story and other things we have been discussing, they are there for a purpose. Sometimes the purpose is simply a kind of thank you, a gift to me. When I got up to leave we gave each other a hug.

Bob's bad leg

Bob's in hospital. He went in for an unspecified operation, then took himself back a few days later because his leg was becoming gangrenous.

'I caught a whiff of it a couple of times,' he said, pointing to his bandaged leg, 'and it made me a bit suspicious, then I saw a fly on it. I know that smell. Smelt it on cattle lots of times. You know what cleans it out? You put the maggots on it. Cleans it out in no time.'

He was sitting up on his hospital bed in his usual ancient shorts and stained T-shirt. Says he doesn't own a pair of pyjamas. I took him a box of chocolates labelled 'Mon Chéri'. He was delighted because he'll be able to tease his pretty French therapist with them.

He told me that when Shama started Bloom's café, he considered buying into the business—'the turnover was terrific'—but decided against it because Shama was spending too much on wages and on supplies, especially meat.

'Besides, there were too many of those ta-ta people employed,' Bob does a limp wrist movement, which also imitates the head movements of the local ta-ta lizard, 'and I didn't like that.'

'Oh, you old bigot,' I say.

He nods amiable assent to the description.

'When I went around to your place I found at least five young blokes sitting in your lounge room.'

He is unsurprised. 'Taken over, have they?' He's more worried about his dog, a huge gentle beast, but I told him he seemed happy enough.

'I'm still trying to meet up with your daughter Coralie,' I say.

'She's a good girl, Coralie.'

Coralie married into the Kennedys, a respected old Broome family. Bob is proud of the Kennedy connection, and that they in turn are connected with the Haines family, another branch of Broome aristocracy. Old man Kennedy didn't approve of Bob and didn't want him at the wedding. Coralie insisted. But once Bob had led his daughter down the aisle, old Kennedy said, 'All right, Bob, you'd better go now.'

Bob didn't leave, of course.

The Kennedys didn't have the same objections to Bob's wife, 'Bub'.

'Bub was of a different temperament, you see. I was a bit of a wild man in those days. But I didn't like things Kennedy did, either. He had a brother who was a bit funny in the head. But he was a nice bloke, I liked him. They kept him in a tin shed in the back. In the end they sent him away, down to a home in Perth. I didn't like that. No, I didn't like that.'

Ménage à trois?

Sharon, the girl who's keen on Gordy, was at the flat when we dropped by last night. She's a dark, thin, feisty young woman. She talks fast, confidentially, with the same swift glancing from topic to topic, not waiting for you to follow, that I've noticed before with many Aboriginal women. Although Sharon doesn't want to be called an Aboriginal woman. She prefers 'black woman'; there's more pride in that. Or in lighter mode, 'Call me a little black bitch from the bush'. Grinning a wide, brilliant grin.

Even more than Vanessa, Sharon is full of strong and immediate contrasts. One moment very much the full-blood Aboriginal girl, full of family and custom and things we whites can't latch onto, then within seconds, sophisticated, white-educated, talking of her work as a teacher (she did her teacher training in Perth), her stint in Sport and Recreation, her plans for future jobs and business ventures, her funding applications, her opinion of native title (ruining relations between Aborigines). 'You used to be able to stop anywhere, go anywhere. If you wanted to swim, to fish, you could just go places. Now people say, "Hey, this is my land".'

She is critical of some Asian-Aborigines like Peter Yu, who she says are not working for the grass roots. The real black people, like her and Damien and their families, get nothing. 'Everything that's happening here in Broome is for the yellowfellas. But they should be working for *us*!'

As she talks, she nervously sips Passion Pop. 'I'm trying drinking a bit,' she says defensively (she's supposed to be a non-drinker). She's feeling discouraged. She's thirty-one years old and feels she's run out of opportunities. She recently tried to get a cultural enterprise going on the land her family lives on, but got no support from them. Her father set his mind against it, and the brothers and sisters are all 'too busy drinking and drugging' to be interested.

Sharon is waiting for Monday when she'll learn about a possible job. 'If this opportunity doesn't happen, I'm getting out of Broome,' she says. 'There's too much infighting, too many people on the grog.'

She has had a couple of relationships, one disastrous, and a promised husband who died. She doesn't want kids; she sees how they've trapped her sisters and many other Aboriginal women.

Things seemed friendly, if a little febrile, between Sharon and Damien, with much chiacking about a local copper who's after her. Damien is doing everything in his power to promote the match—to get her out of his hair!

'Gordon and I have been together six years now,' he says happily, a dreamy little smile on his face. 'We had our anniversary the other day. I hope it goes on forever.' Yet there's no sign of romantic behaviour *towards* Gordy, only when he talks *about* him.

Sharon says the family adores 'Uncle Gordy' and approves the match with Damien. Yes, Damien avers, they haven't liked any of his other boyfriends, only Gordy. Sharon and he reel off some family nicknames. Gordy's nickname is 'Junior', thus Damien's is 'Senior'. Damien's dad calls Gordy 'General Custer' and Damien 'Crazy Horse'.

Damien talks about his promised wife, who was hugely older than him. 'Even older than you,' he says, smiling at me innocently. 'She's dead now. She was in her seventies. I looked after her till she died. I still think about her, you know?' Then he becomes flippant again. 'After she died I looked around and everyone had two left feet, so I thought I might as well become gay!'

We eat some spag bol that Gordy has made. I root around in the kitchen for a plastic fork. The spaghetti is quite good. Damien plays with his food, eating it slowly. Gordy doesn't eat, says he's already had some.

I don't believe him. He almost never eats. He says you can't do both— eat and drink—without putting on too much weight, and he'd rather drink.

Shinju countdown

Over at the Goolarri offices a Shinju meeting is in progress. The opening ceremony is only nine days away. Kevin and half a dozen of his team are going through the program, ironing out problems, filling one another in. In the last few weeks these meetings have become frequent.

Kevin is in fine form, firing questions at people in a staccato fashion, keeping the pace up. He seems able to hold a huge range of figures in his head: how much individual sponsors have promised, the cost of various items, right down to how much prize money was given in the children's pet parade last year—was it $50 or $100?

The Shinju programs are nearly ready. Kevin wants to see them before they go out. He asks what has happened to the tickets for the Teen Ball: 'Why aren't they printed yet? What's Michael doing? Send him an email from me.'

His last advice before the meeting breaks up: 'Sit down at your computers and think it through—Do, Think, Do. If you do that now, you'll cruise through and enjoy it. If you don't, I'll be saying to you "Told you so", and there's nothing worse to hear on the night.'

*

Allowing myself to become involved with the life here has been a bit like flicking a switch. Suddenly, it's happening. Now that, too, will have its dangers. For example, Mary. She rang this afternoon, sounding excited, and asked me to come down to her office because she had some news. She's been elected to the executive of the Kimberley Land Council, nominated by Pat Dodson. I told her she was being groomed for big things.

She wants my help with a presentation she has to do to the ATSIC regional council. She's hoping to get their support for the culture centre, perhaps even some funding.

It became clear a while ago that not only was Mary prepared to talk to me, she also wanted something from me—help in negotiating those parts of the white world that she still finds difficult. I said to her, 'I help you; you help me.' It's not that simple of course. She doesn't know how I'll use the help she gives me, although she knows what I'm doing and I don't think she'd mind the story of 'How Mary got a culture centre for Broome' being recorded. But we are close to being friends now and that does complicate things. As with Gordon—are we friends or are we writers?—similarly with Lyn. I used to think I had to keep the two roles separate but that is not possible here. Susan is better than I at negotiating these fluid boundaries. It has always seemed simpler to me to keep things separate. Simpler, but no longer realistic.

Thirteen

Festival of the Pearl—Art matters—The bird observatory—
Post-Shinju—A gathering of beauties—Grilling Perpetua

It is just turning dark at Gordy's. From the verandah you can see a neon-lit mini panorama of downtown Broome. To the right are the mangroves on the edge of the bay where a couple of old luggers are being restored, then the pagoda-like roof of the Roey's bottle shop, then the two-storey latticed Backpackers (towels on the verandah, a stream of young itinerants going in and out), then the Westpac bank. Across the road is the park where at all times of the day and night countrymen sit in companionable circles under the trees, and to the far left, the floodlit oval.

Damien has gone out—it's his turn. They seem to have settled to an amicable routine since moving to the flat. Gordy is in an affable mood. He's in pink singlet and shorts, barefoot, his legs beautifully shaved and smooth.

He goes over to the Roey to get some cigarettes. As he wanders back across the road, Annie calls out, 'Here comes the blond bombshell!' Gordy flicks back his long blond hair skittishly.

Sharon has put in an appearance again. 'She's still after my bottom,' Gordon says. She plans to put some sort of hex on Damien, courtesy of an old aunty of hers, to make Damien drink so much that even Gordy will go off him. 'So I'll be watching for any changes in his drinking patterns with some interest.' Gordon laughs, but he's half serious, too.

All is on a serendipitous roll at the flat. The ALS powers-that-be have announced they are going to send him some furniture—the cast-offs from the former solicitor at Kununurra. Gordy has bought a bed, already authorised, which he shows us with some pride. Quite a nifty black metal job. (He makes much of the fact that head office told him to buy 'a queen-size bed'.) So he's settling in, although there's still no official confirmation that he's got the permanent job in Broome.

The other night Gordy went out to a posh dinner with the State president of the Law Society. Damien wanted to go, too, but Gordy said it wasn't his kind of do. Damien sulked. 'At least bring me a plate of food home.'

So at 3 a.m., Gordon rolled home 'gloriously drunk' and chucked a greasy hamburger Damien's way. Damien threw it back and flounced off to the spare room, banging the door behind him.

As we're leaving, Gordon asks us to do him a little favour: could we take two videos back to the shop? One is a gay porno video that Damien borrowed. Gordy doesn't want to be seen taking it back.

What a strange and touching mixture Gordy is. On the one hand, living on the edge, daring the world to find him unacceptable; on the other, quite discreet. Leading both a 'depraved, degenerate' life, and also one of curious domestication—cooking spag bol for Damien, doing his washing, taking turns to go out, watching telly alone on the nights he's at home...

Festival of the Pearl

For the opening of Shinju Matsuri, Carnarvon Street is cordoned off. In the park, groups of countrymen are sitting on the ground, some drinking, some not. One noisy group is hard up against the toilet block, taking no notice of the proceedings. The cop car arrives to quieten them down.

Centre stage at the opening ceremony is Pearl's brother-in-law, Ahmat Fidel, this year's patron. Ahmat came to Broome thirty-six years ago to work on the pearl boats and never left. He is a neat, benign, handsome little man, immaculate in a light pink shirt and trousers, a gold and black embroidered cap and a gorgeous cummerbund in the same material. He's thrilled to have been asked to be patron. He reads a heartfelt, civilised speech in excellent but accented English. (I think his partner Sally vetted it for him.) In the old days, he says, Malay became the lingua franca of the divers, being the easiest to learn of all the languages, and is still used by the old-timers. And he cites the Malay contribution to the local cuisine—the fish curries and satays.

There are only a handful of full-blood Malays left in the town, but lots of descendants. A group of young girls sit on the dais, dressed in versions of the national dress, looking bored or shy. To their right, the Shinju Princesses, blue and gold sashes over their chests. Behind them, immaculate in their new Shinju T-shirts, is the organising committee, overwhelmingly young and mixed-race. Vanessa is amongst them, casually elegant in her well-cut shorts, her gorgeous blister pearl necklace at her throat. Her brother Neville, who has the same handsome, defined Poelina features, gives a closing address. He mentions the recent deaths of two old divers, and his own father, Simon, who died last year.

The Shire President, Angus Murray, does his *de rigueur* praise of multiculturalism, then a State Minister delivers much the same message. It all begins to sound hollow when you know more about the complications and problems here. Bill Reed speaks, trying hard to sound non-paternalistic and man-of-the-people. He praises the Broome-ites for having reclaimed their festival from the commercialism of the whites.

Some old-timers are called up to give speeches. A handsome old man talks about being the last Aboriginal diver on the boats. Another, a jolly extrovert with almost no teeth left, promises endless tales, but not in front of a mike. His English still isn't too good, he says, and sits down. Peter Ghouse, the MC, sums it up: 'Our English isn't very good but we speak it very well!'

A dignified matriarch sings a lilting song half in Malay, half in English. Then Sammy the Dragon, long and resplendent in red, green and gold, with a dozen sweating tourist volunteers under him, snakes his way up the main street, leading us into the Roey for free drinks.

There's more mingling of the races in the pub than usual. Maybe people feel they have to live up to the multiculturalism of the occasion. A group of white tourists listens avidly to the stories of the old Aboriginal diver. Vanessa is being maternal with another group of old-timers.

Who are they, I ask? 'Old lugger buggers!' she says, embracing them with her smile.

Pearl and Hama were there. Out in public, at such an event, it is clear that the Hamaguchis are something in this town. Later I saw them at the Kids' Pet Parade, sitting in state in the middle of the park on folding chairs, looking out for one of their grandchildren.

No doubt in a couple of years, when the Shinju theme is the Japanese, Hama will be the patron.

On Friday afternoon I went over to the Boulevard to help put up the decorations for the opening ball. A lot of people had doubts about holding a ball in a shopping centre, me included. But it looked terrific by the time the design team had finished with it. At the entrance was a large blue rice-paper boat with a sail, lit up from within. The boat turned up again in the grand parade next day, carried by, among others, Angus Murray and at least one State Minister.

The best bit of the parade were the kids from St Mary's Primary School, walking in costume according to ethnic group, each with a flag and banner. Mary's daughter was with the Yawuru, Pearl's granddaughter with the Scots, Kevin's daughter with the Chinese. There were at least half a dozen Aboriginal tribes represented.

There was a rather familiar looking man, a bearded wild-haired Englishman, watching the parade as it passed the prison. He turned out to be the English writer Howard Jacobson, in town doing some research for a British TV documentary. All the prisoners in their green uniforms were sitting on or in front of the prison's brick fence, waving at the floats; the people on the floats waved back. Once the parade was over, the prisoners turned and began strolling back into the gaol. A few girlfriends took the opportunity to run over and kiss their fellas. Perfect Broome.

Art matters

On the radio this morning, Howard Jacobson's wife, Rosalin Sadler, was talking about the Shinju art prize. Ros, who writes for a leading art magazine in England, was roped in to judge the prize along with Perpetua and Nolan Hunter. Ros is Australian, although she's lived in England for twenty-odd years. She said Broome was the most confronting and stimulating visual environment she'd been in for a long time, so much so that 'I need to go south soon, for a rest'!

She was immensely enthusiastic about last night's Performance Body Art show.

'How does it compare to London?' asked Angela, the local ABC presenter, quite innocently.

'Better!' exclaimed Ros. 'Much better!'

She went on to praise the wealth of creative talent in this little town. And it was certainly the overwhelming impression from last night's performance. It was an exhilarating mix of fashion, body art, cabaret, social comment and pure fun. Inspiration came from take-offs of tourist culture, from Aboriginal myths, and the evening's 'Sea Change' theme. And all done with sheer invention, a bit of glitter, smoke and lighting.

Vanessa was the occasional MC in a deliberately loud oversized shirt, all grin, jollying the crowd along, announcing the winners in a cheerfully disorganised rush at the end.

Thursday, September 10

I spoke to Gordy this morning on the phone. He sounded a little tired, but surviving.

'We've been busy with Shinju,' I said.

'Yes, I've had fallout from Shinju, too. I was defending a client who bashed his wife. "He was just carried away by the gaiety of Shinju, your honour," I told the magistrate. Even the client smiled.' Gordy gave his self-mocking, self-delighted laugh.

He hasn't seen Sharon for nearly a week. 'She's disappeared. Damien must have exerted his authority. She wanted the receptionist's job in the ALS office. Yeah, that's what she was after.'

She didn't get it. Instead, some other young male relative of Damien's has got the job.

We agreed that Sharon was best out of the way, that maybe Gordon was not quite that much of a risk-taker after all.

I told him how entranced we'd been by the Performance Body Art. 'Why doesn't Damien get involved in something like that? He'd be in his element.'

Gordy sighed. 'Yes, but how to motivate him? God knows I've tried.'

He thinks there's a big lack of confidence underneath Damien's chutzpah, especially when he's not on the grog.

The bird observatory

At first I thought we'd landed in the midst of a hellish scene from an early Bergman movie—a group of sweating red-faced people lugging telescopes up burning sandhills in the hottest part of the day, slipping and sliding on the fiery sand, peering at flocks of nondescript birds hundreds of metres away. We'd gone out to Crab Creek because the Broome bird observatory is world famous, but after just ten minutes I was searching for a scrap of shade, wondering how the next two and a half hours were to be endured.

But then it got me in. It was the names of the birds that did it: Red-capped Plover, Greater Sand Plover, Ruddy Turnstone, Sooty Oyster Catcher, White-faced Heron, Crested Terns and Lesser Crested Terns, the White-bellied Sea Eagle, Great White Egret, Terrik Sandpiper, Whimbrels, Grey-tailed Tattler and, best of all, the Bar-tailed Godwit.

Once I was enchanted by their names, I looked at them with a literally new eye. And got used to the telescope. Then it was exciting, being able to catch them in repose more intimately than with the naked eye, and to see three or four different species crowding each other on a rock or lone piece of sand.

The wader birds come here for their non-breeding season, to rest and to put on an enormous amount of body weight which will fuel them on their epic journey to China's north coast. In March they will fly three to four days without stopping to eat, drink or sleep, averaging seventy kilometres an hour. Birds that have been tagged here in Broome have been known to turn up in China four days later.

I told Howard Jacobson that learning the names of the birds made me see them differently. He's the same. The world made real through words. Things have to be named, then the names catch the imagination, then the thing itself comes into focus.

*

Everyone says the Wet is going to start early this year. Among the signs: the unusually heavy dews, and the crocodiles starting to nest early at Windjana Gorge.

This morning we began the day earlier. Up drinking tea on the verandah by six-thirty, but by the time we took the dogs for a walk, around seven-thirty, it was already hot—an oppressive glare in the sun, a stickiness to the air.

At Town Beach we saw several people who'd walked so far out into the bay at low tide that they looked like stick figures. We thought they were crabbing, but then we made out the outlines of two wrecked Dutch Catalinas destroyed by the Japanese in Word War II. You can only see them at extremely low tide.

The Catalinas were among sixteen flying boats destroyed in a single fifteen-minute air attack in 1942. Many were carrying Dutch women and children evacuated from Indonesia. Anthony, the manager of Matso's, told us about the little Dutch girl whose body was found

in the mangroves after the air raid. Her ghost is sometimes seen in Matso's garden. She has fair, shoulder-length hair and enormous blue eyes.

Imagine Broome at that time. The Japanese, who were part of the fabric of the place, were suddenly the enemy. When Japan entered the war, Broome's Japanese population was interned, although Sam Male, Kim's father, apologised to them as he was doing it. But after the air raid the town was devastated: dozens of bodies to be buried, the road south cut because of the Wet, only a short stretch of water separating Broome from the advancing enemy. Australia's front line, yet such mixed allegiances within the town. The whites desperate to flee, the Asiatics treated with suspicion, the Aborigines forgotten.

*

The Sea of Hands has been going around the country and has finally reached Broome. We went over with Bruce to see it. A team of volunteers spent the morning laying it out on Cable Beach, and what a sight! Each hand signed by someone committing himself or herself to reconciliation. Thousands and thousands of them—multi-hued, laid out along the beach in long curving lines, a rainbow serpent of colour against the sand, with a black circle at one end and a white circle at the other end.

At a stall at the top of the steps, people were still 'buying' hands, pledging themselves. There we ran into Sarah Yu, Peter Yu's wife. She's a blonde woman with curly hair and an alert, matter-of-fact air about her, an anthropologist by trade. She does some work with the KLC on land rights matters. It's intriguing, the number of anthropologists around Broome, most of them married to indigenous people.

We're becoming increasingly convivial with the Jacobsons. We had drinks on our verandah with them before the Batik Ball and discussed our reactions to Broome. Similar highs and lows, much the same kind of love–hate.

Ros has a rambunctious, omnivorous intelligence, at times piercing sharp, at times full of bullshit. Howard seems quieter—although possibly he just knows when to concede her the limelight—but he is engaging, keen-minded, sceptical. She has quite a bit of a rampaging ruthless Germaine Greer about her but is a softy at heart, I suspect.

The ball was at the Chinese-inspired Civic Centre. There was a lot of dress-up in ethnically inspired costume, some of it very gorgeous indeed. And so many good-looking people! Among them Ros, who has a handsome lioness look about her. Howard, too, was looking winsome in his long Malay-style skirt, his wild hair tied back in a ponytail.

We sat at long tables and were served Peter Ghouse's food. The waiters were all smart in bow ties but the food was served on paper plates. Ahmat, again immaculate in national dress, gave another little speech followed by a demonstration of Malay martial arts, which looks rather like speeded up Tai Chi.

Annie got roped in for judging—as she did a few nights ago for the Performance Poetry—this time for the best-dressed costume, male and female. Is it to do with her natural air of authority, compounded by her height?

Kevin Fong gave a telling speech. 'I'm appalled that there are no white entrants for Shinju Princess whenever there's a coloured Shinju committee,' he said, 'and no coloured entrants when it's a white committee. It has to stop.'

The band played golden oldies from the sixties and seventies. Everyone got up for 'Peggy Sue', even us. We left as most of the hall was up in a big circle, doing the hokey-pokey. Angela was in the thick of it, pink-faced and jolly, as if the night was just beginning. Gordy and Damien were nowhere to be seen. They shun all such 'official' events.

Post-Shinju

Certain scenes from Shinju that seemed to contain the essence of Broome: the gorgeous teenager Zaripha Poelina (one of Vanessa's nieces) at the Performance Body Art in her Queen of Hearts dress, made from one hundred packs of playing cards; Kevin doing a TV interview and behind him thirty-one flag poles flying all the national flags of

Broome's people; grey-haired, august Bill Reed saying at the opening ceremony, 'Let Pauline Hanson come and see what we have here, and what we have here can happen elsewhere.'

There are such odd juxtapositions of sophistication and its opposite in Broome—that unworldly charm that takes no heed of what the rest of the world is doing, that in-Broome-we-do-it-this-way insouciance. Just as I'd be thinking how 'quaint' and old-fashioned Shinju was, suddenly there'd be an image that was original and powerful. We saw it time and again. At the Batik Ball, when I was asked to judge the 'Best Dressed', I at first thought I'd strayed onto a sixties film set. But then I looked again. No 1960s Australian ball would have presented such a sight: Malay, Aboriginal, Chinese, white—the full kaleidoscope—in their gorgeous fabrics, heads held high. The handsome young women and beautiful men, elegant matrons in high heels, elderly men proudly modelling their national dress. Pearlshell cleaners and ATSIC commissioners, schoolteachers and divers' sons.

Peter Ghouse was everywhere. I'm amazed at that man's energy: Master of Ceremonies at the opening, marshalling the grand parade, zipping here and there on a white scooter, handing out showbags for the kids at the Pet Parade. Not to mention cooking the food for the Batik Ball! And the next morning, he was there again cleaning up, together with the prisoners from the gaol.

Kevin is pleased with Shinju. 'Looks like we'll have fifteen thousand in the kitty for next year,' he tells me when I go to see him at Goolarri for a Shinju post-mortem.

I ask him if he enjoyed it.

'I don't enjoy an event as an event, but how it compares to what we had planned.'

He spent most of the festival rectifying problems, making sure things ran smoothly. But he did enjoy getting dressed up in full Malay costume, living a while inside his Malay self.

Monday

I've been throwing myself into things more, recording less. More the participant, less the observer. While you stay in your room typing, I've been getting out—helping with Shinju, giving Mary a hand at the culture centre. Sometimes I feel I'm beginning to understand certain people and aspects of the place better as a result. But that's not much comfort when I look at my sparse notebook.

I still have moments of feeling dislocated and depressed, wondering what we're doing here, but they disappear the moment I leave the house. Because outside there's always something happening. Outside, you can't be depressed in Broome—the colours won't allow it.

A gathering of beauties

A strong cooling breeze in the late afternoon, so we walk the dogs up to Lyn's. Jacko knows by now not even to try to enter Georgie-Girl's territory. She sits quietly by the open door. Scruffy walks in like a prince and has large Georgie bounding after him, skittish and flirty. Then he mistakes one of the handsome wooden structural posts in the middle of Lyn's house for a tree and cocks his leg!

Lyn is unfazed: 'He's not the first.'

Lyn is in a grey leotard, barefoot, no make-up, and looking terrific. She's still working, as she has been all weekend. A male colleague and she are bending over the computer. Papers and brochures lie all over the dining room table. Lyn is friendly but ignores us; she's busy. So we talk to her old friend Jeanie, who recently turned up in town, fleeing an awful marriage down south. Jeanie is an ageing ethereal beauty. She arrived at Lyn's with a dozen suitcases of designer clothes and severe depression. But she's beginning to relax, and today a feyly humorous person emerges.

She tells us a story from Lyn's Sydney life: Lyn wearing nothing but bikini pants, vacuuming the family swimming pool, when her sons arrived home with their adolescent friends. The boys were slack-jawed.

Lyn overhears and laughs loudly. 'Barry said maybe I should wear my top in future.'

It's not long before the gorgeous Chi turns up with a bottle of wine (it's at least the third time we've run into her here on a Sunday). I feel as if we're in a home for superannuated models, all three women are so careful of their looks and figures.

Every time we've seen Chi at Lyn's she's struck me as engagingly weird. Lyn seems to think a lot of her, and of her psychic powers. Chi spouts all the crappy lingo, but there's probably a hard-headed realist underneath it all. She sees her clients in a little house full of cheap new-agey incense, pictures, scarves, throws and artificial flowers. She reckons the lumps on my arms and legs are due to liver problems. If I gave up alcohol, went on a really good diet…

Apart from Chi, there's a dozen or more practitioners in Broome offering combinations of massage, reiki, psychic healing and tarot cards, not to mention yoga and Tai Chi. After I pulled a muscle in my back last week I ended up at Vedant's.

'The Healing Touch,' crooned a deep resonant voice when I phoned for my appointment. Vedant lives in a neat block of two-storey units, done agreeably in Broome style; lots of lattice and verandahs. His place is very clean, minimalist and soothing. He's a small wiry man, deeply olive skin, large dark eyes, a very alive face. He could be part Spanish, part Moroccan, Aboriginal or Afghan, or none of the above. His voice is gorgeous, stagily so, and he calls you 'love' and makes groaning and 'aah' and 'ooh' noises as he massages you. 'Don't be put off by the noises I make, love, it's just my way of working.'

The massage is vigorous, energetic, almost sexual, if Vedant were not so clearly professional. I'm supposed to breathe through my mouth which somehow makes me feel more vulnerable, especially as I'm lying on my side with only my pants on. But while he is vigorous, Vedant is entirely unaggressive, and his hands are small and soft.

Although Vedant has lived in many different places, overseas as well, it turns out he's Kimberley born and bred. His mum lives in Derby.

I have to ask him about his fruity voice. He tells me he trained as an opera singer, worked as one too, and as an actor, and as a horticulturalist. I forget the fourth career path. He only took up massage professionally in his forties.

'The human body doesn't have to age, love. That's just nonsense.'

Grilling Perpetua

Dinner at the Jacobsons'. Perpetua there, too. An interesting night.

Ros is fascinated by Perpetua's mother, Elizabeth Durack; by her role as artist-witness of Aboriginal life on the Kimberley stations, where she lived when young. Ros sees her as a marginalised artist on three fronts—as a woman, as a woman of the privileged classes, and as a maker of a now unfashionable style of art. All this, suspects Ros, masks her true importance.

Ros replayed the video about Elizabeth Durack recently shown on SBS. I think it was a chance for her to question Perpetua, with us there for back-up. We all tried to get Perpetua to tell us why her mother persisted with Eddie Burrup to the point of entering 'him' for the biggest Aboriginal Art prize—the point at which the four of us agreed that Eddie Burrup became fatally compromised. Perpetua was not as upset or as flustered as I thought she'd be—she seemed almost relieved to have it brought up. She held up remarkably well under fire and told us nothing really new. No, they had never really thought through what would happen if Eddie won—they knew that to be almost impossible. Yes, she admitted, not only had she originally put the idea to her mother, but they'd collaborated every step of the way.

'Why did Elizabeth do it?' we kept pestering her.

'Why don't you ask her?' Perpetua said. 'She'll be here on Friday.'

We discussed the Burrup business some more after Perpetua went home. I can make out a credible scenario whereby the idea, once hit upon, became irresistible, for a range of reasons: chagrin at Elizabeth's failure to be taken seriously by the art world, anger over the focus on an artist's personality or race rather than the work itself, a touch of mischievousness, a commercial opportunity, a burst of new creativity combined with a genuine empathy and closeness to the Aboriginal world. And once Eddie Burrup was conceived, he took on a momentum of his own. The art prize entry was just a logical last step.

But all this is just deduction or outright speculation. We stopped short of *really* pushing Perpetua. Will we be harder with the old lady when we meet her on Friday? We'll see.

*

The Society of Authors are in town to drum up membership and they put on a lunchtime seminar. The Rav was in for a service so we hitched a ride with Pat and Jimmy, in the back of Pat's old Suzuki.

'Don't expect Jimmy to give up his seat for you,' said Pat, as she threw a blanket in the back for us.

We felt ourselves almost initiated Broome-ites, in the back of the rusty ute, hooning down Guy Street towards Lotteries House. Maybe twenty locals turned up, a good number for Broome. A sprinkling of indigenous people, including Phillipa Cook and her daughter Sam from Magabala, and three or four aspiring writers.

Jimmy spent his time either drawing on Pat's pad or with his eyes closed. I tried to listen to the talk through his ears—copyright, agents, electronic rights, authors' websites, government policy, PLR, ELR...

Pat asked him if he wanted to join us for dinner that night. He shook his head and said, 'Too much gardiya talk'.

Fourteen

Midlagon—Friends of Gantheaume Point—The bishop's pasta sauce—Communication—At Blooms

We were due for dinner at Perpetua's to meet her mother but I slipped away to see if Gordy was okay. We'd had a rather alarming phone conversation. The night before, Damien had stabbed him in the lip with a fork at Murray's restaurant—some kind of lover's tiff. This put Gordon in such a lousy mood that he got into a fight at the Nippon and was beaten up by a guy who proved to be one of the bouncers. Gordy called the cops, determined to nail the bouncer. Then he woke up in the morning and decided to drop the charges.

Gordy was doing his hysterical 'aren't I an amazingly bad boy' laugh throughout this recital. 'I wanted to hang myself this morning,' he said, 'but I couldn't find the rope.' Laugh.

He was in pain, too, he said, from bleeding heels. 'You get it when you walk around a lot barefoot. Aborigines get it, too.'

So I went around to see how he was. I took some Vaseline Intensive Care for his heels and a couple of beers.

And there he and Damien are, doing their own version of domestic bliss, a drink in hand, two chairs arranged around the telly in the otherwise empty room, obviously companionable and fond. Gordy has one foot bandaged but is otherwise looking fine; no outward sign of the fork stabbing, nor of the beating, just the bandaged foot and a rueful grin. I remind myself to take his stories with a pinch of salt in future.

Damien is sitting there looking like a black Madonna, seductive, innocent and slightly sinister all at once. He's in a communicative mood—jokey, serious, flirty and confiding. When Gordy pads off to buy cigarettes, Damien says that once, when he tried to leave, Gordy let himself go—grew red-eyed, let his beard and belly grow.

'I can't leave him. He won't accept it,' Damien says. (But note Gordy's version—of *his* trying to leave and *Damien* saying 'I can't accept it'.)

A couple of minutes later Damien is recounting with shining eyes how he and Gordy met. 'It was love at first sight. We made love that night. And now here I am, six years later. I could have had other men—there were at least twelve men who wanted me—but I ended up with a lawyer.' He smiles his angelic smile. 'My family says he loves me. I say he knows me inside out, inside out.'

What about the fork incident? Damien does his half-playful half-sinister look. 'He accused me of something I hadn't done and I don't like that, so I stabbed him. That's all. I like arguing with him.'

Gordy looks rueful. 'Yes, he likes arguing with me.'

After the fight at the Nippon, Gordy told the cops someone had stabbed him with a fork earlier in the night.

'Why don't you charge him, too?' the cops asked.

'I can't,' he told them. 'It was Damien.'

'You're going to be the talk of the town, man,' says Damien, teasing. He repeats this a few times, then, 'I felt so sorry for him when he was beaten up.'

'Did you take him home?' I ask.

'No, he's a grown up boy. He can look after himself.'

Just before I go, Damien admires my white cotton trousers. I should give them to him when I've finished with them, he says. It doesn't matter that they'd be too short for him. He likes cotton.

Gordy lights my way down the stairs; the light has blown. He often displays these rather nice old world courtesies.

I was there just fifteen minutes.

At Perpetua's we ate under the stars in the natural courtyard between the gallery and her little air-conditioned room. Perpetua always describes her living arrangements as 'camping', and it's true they are extremely simple. A kitchen, a closed-in verandah where she sleeps, an outside loo and a small separate air-conditioned building of just one room—her office, where she keeps her papers. She also sleeps there occasionally when it's very hot, on a camp bed.

The evening was arranged partly so that Ros and Howard could meet Elizabeth Durack. Ros is thinking of writing a big piece about her for the British publication *Modern Painters*.

Elizabeth was much as I expected: elegant, lively, in her eighties but full of zest. A combination of idiosyncrasy and conservatism. She'd been reading my book *Sex and Anarchy* and launched into a tale of her Communist youth both here and in Sydney, where she met Perpetua's father, Frank Clancy. In the Kimberley in the 1930s the young Duracks were voracious readers of works from the London radical publishers, Gollancz. I suspect the young Elizabeth was taken not so much by the ideas that she was reading as by the delicious adventurousness of reading such ideas. She and Perpetua are still basically conservatives.

Susan mentioned having read Ernestine Hill's *The Great Australian Loneliness*.

'Oh yes, she was a very close friend. She often stayed with us in Perth,' Elizabeth said.

'It's a good book,' Susan said, 'but there's so much unconscious racism in it.'

'Really? I don't remember that...'

While we were sitting there in the balmy night, the faint fragrances from Perpetua's garden mixing with the fumes from the mosquito coils at our feet, we looked up to see wave after wave of wader birds flying over, high up, flying towards their night roost near Cable Beach. They just kept on coming, Godwits and Bar-tailed Godwits and Red Pikes, thousands and thousands of them, crossing the peninsula from the bay to the coast.

As for Eddie Burrup, he never did get discussed at length. Susan says that while both Perpetua and her mother are quite worldly—intelligent, well read—they are not really politicised. They wouldn't have conceived of the moral and political hand grenade they were launching with the creation of Burrup. It's clear that Elizabeth has no regrets. It might be a scandal, but she is unrepentant. Eddie Burrup lives on, still painting busily. And maybe, in time, this alter ego of hers will be her most enduring achievement as an artist.

*

These past few days we've both been sinking into a lethargy that is not altogether unpleasant, but it is a bit disorienting. As though we're adrift. I'm finding it hard to focus on anything very much.

This was meant to be the year we stretched ourselves, and maybe we're shirking. But who knows from what direction challenges come? Maybe even this slow, almost empty time, this quiet ennui, is part of the Broome experience. Maybe we have to slow down to understand the place.

Midlagon

My sister Jenny and her husband Ian have come over for a holiday. Almost as soon as they arrived we took them up to Midlagon for a couple of days. I've been wanting to get back there ever since flying over it with the bishop and being captivated by that perfect curve of sand and sea, and the small huts on the hill above.

The little resort has been renamed 'Middle Lagoon' for the tourists. The word 'Midlagon' comes from an Aboriginal legend about a snake.

It was as perfect as expected: swimming in water of an unimaginable colour and softness; clambering around mangroves and mudbanks with Ian in search of mud crabs; watching the dawn through the shadecloth walls of our hut; eating around the camp fire with Kiri Te Kanawa blasting from the Rav's tape deck.

But our return to Broome was traumatic. We discovered that we'd been burgled—gone was the TV, portable CD/radio and my laptop. It was an old computer but I was attached to it because it was so simple. It started in a jiffy, not like the new ones which seem to take forever to boot up.

To get over the trauma we went out to the art auction that Perpetua was co-organising. I thought it would be a relatively low-key affair, but the big room at Matso's filled up rapidly. There was a buzz in the air—people busily marking their catalogues, clapping if there was a good price achieved. We bid on a few things that seemed to be going ridiculously cheap. Ros seemed to be attracted to many of the same pieces, in particular the bright, messy paintings by some of the older Aboriginal women from Fitzroy Crossing.

There was a group of people from Mowanjum who had been brought down 'to see how an auction works'. They stood out on the Matso's verandah watching through the barred windows. Occasionally the auctioneer introduced one of them—'the artist is here', pointing to a door—but it didn't seem to raise the price any. Faces peering through the bars.

'I wish they wouldn't do that,' Ros said. 'I wish they'd just come into the room and sit down.' But none of them did.

*

Yesterday I arranged to meet Clare Chang for a coffee at Bloom's. While I was waiting for her I talked to Perpetua's friend, Alison Lawrence. There is something sweetly anachronistic about Alison, as if she's just stepped complete from a 1930s *Girls' Own* yearbook, with her waddle and her gorgeous auburn hair. She puts me in mind of high teas and hockey sticks. I can't imagine her being anything but a school librarian. But she's bright, very on the ball.

I told her how we'd been robbed. She said she was robbed three weeks ago. 'A man came into the house while I was in the shower. I glimpsed him going into my bedroom. Then I saw him come out with what I thought was my brand new laptop. I was so angry I chased after him, stark naked!'

The man got away, of course. It turned out that he had taken not her laptop but her satchel, and in it were the keys to the school.

'But some kids found it near the cemetery. Yeah, I was lucky. I got everything back except thirty-five dollars cash.'

Alison thinks our burglary was probably an outside job. Most of the thieving in Broome is just kids taking small amounts of cash. Often they're after food, too. Large items like televisions don't normally get stolen—there's nowhere to flog them without getting caught. Our things are probably on their way to Perth.

Clare arrived as Alison was leaving. Clare must be about forty-eight, a blonde, weary, intelligent woman, thin. Up until last year she was in Kevin's position at Goolarri. In the early days at Goolarri the committee was dominated by women, but when it started attracting big grants the men took over.

'This is a woman's town,' Clare said. 'The energy here is very female. It's women who are active, who carry the load. Pat Lowe once said, "The egos of Broome men are built on sand".'

Clare's been in Broome sixteen years. She was married to a Chinese Indonesian man from Lombok who now runs a Mr Whippy van in Fitzroy Crossing. Clare knows Broome and how it works. 'The intricacy of the cultural relationships in Broome is such that even people with good intentions stuff up, offend the protocols.'

She is now the events co-ordinator at the Shire, a strange position given that the Shire itself does not run any 'events'. It was created after the local people took back control of Shinju. 'Basically the Shire was waiting for Shinju to fall over. They thought they'd have to pick up the pieces.'

But Shinju hadn't fallen over, which left her with no real role. The community groups don't want her—they want to run their own shows.

'People are very suspicious of the Shire and of people who work for the Shire, and they are quite justified in that. The Shire doesn't have a good record.'

Everyone expects Clare and Kevin Fong to loathe each other, but they don't. In fact her relationship with her bosses at the Shire is far worse than that with her usurper at Goolarri. 'Angus Murray is a nice person, and he's committed to Broome, but he's one of those business people who can't see beyond their own square.'

As for the CEO, Greg Powell, 'I think Greg hates Broome. If I say, "I'd like to do up the Civic Centre", he'll say, "Burn it down". If I say, "I want to do such-and-such", he'll say "Why bother?". He refuses to delegate anything. Every piece of paper addressed to the Shire goes across his desk. Capable people are reduced to playing at the edges.'

Friends of Gantheaume Point

For months I've been hearing talk about what might happen to the expanse of land out near Gantheaume Point. Ripe for development, say some. Sacred country, say the Yawuru. I've heard the Department of Land Administration officials talk about moving the racecourse, of finding some land for the culture centre.

Now the Government's agenda is clear. There's been a big advertisement in the national papers (and international ones too, I hear) showing an aerial photo of Gantheaume, the coastline, the racecourse behind, and the bushland between it and the town. They're calling for expressions of interest in developing the land.

Mary's mother, Cissy, is the custodian of this area. She is the only one of her family left. The last two of Mary's uncles died after Corrie Fong's house was built. Mary thinks it killed them. One reason she opposes the racecourse development is that she fears it could kill her mother. Whenever Mary speaks of Gantheaume, she calls it Minyirr, then adds 'Gantheaume Point' if she is speaking to a white person.

Mary is meeting with a newly formed group, Friends of Gantheaume Point, to talk about ways they can work together to stop the development. The leader of the Friends, Kerry Marvell, is a petite woman with short black shaggy hair. She's an artist and one of the Shinju prize winners. Mary tells her how Corrie Fong once demanded forty hectares or $600 000 in exchange for the land at Gantheaume Point where she subsequently built her house.

'We told her, "We don't have no land yet, we don't have no land in our own country. We've got no land rights in this State."'

Mary says she's happy for the culture centre and the Friends to support each other and she shows Kerry one developer's plan: tourist housing right up to the beach, the road pushed back, a golf course, even a backpackers near Reddell Beach.

And the lolly? A tiny culture centre.

'No way,' says Mary. 'All that...and they give us this!'

Kerry says that the Premier, Richard Court, and Angus Murray secretly flew over Gantheaume recently and that Court said he'd make sure the development happened.

Mary appears distracted, moving things around on her desk, not concentrating on the job to hand, making a phone call. When she does start talking again it's in that way that I find difficult. We two white women sit trying to understand and not really understanding, till Mary suddenly says, 'Sometimes I wish I were a man!' and we crack up.

The other night, late, a group of us ended up at Perpetua's, eating ice-cream and drinking wine. Pat Lowe was there. She'd been on the bus back from Hedland all day and hadn't eaten. She nibbled on some pâté, and livened up when talk came to the bishop. She was quite bitchy about him. Did we know that Bishop Chris was a member of Norforce and had guns in the house? She contrasted him with Father Mac, who somehow in the politics of it all was forced out of Broome. Mac never had a fence around his place. You could drop in any time for a cup of tea, whereas Chris has had the effrontery to build a fence around his house. Pat said she actually felt sorry for Chris early on, because everyone was comparing him, to his detriment, with Father Mac. She decided to go and see him, only to be told that she had to have an appointment!

Howard recited his bawdy ballad 'The Bishop of Hall's Creek' while Perpetua looked on nervously. He was particularly fetching last night in his black and yellow sarong, his hair in a top knot.

Perpetua was upset at the negative press the 'poor old bishop' was getting, although even she remarked, gently, that he does like to spend time with other bishops down in Melbourne, Sydney and even overseas. He's also seen as liking to spend time with the 'upper end' of town. Another source of talk—his love of food and wine and his dramatic fluctuations in weight.

People seem to love or hate the bishop. Some see him as too much of a businessman, others as too much of a politician—altogether more a man of the world than of the Church. Which is why I like him.

The bishop's pasta sauce

I always check with the bishop's office at the back of his house before going in through the garden. This is part of the formality that people object to. But this morning as I walked into the office I was scared by the loud croakings of a frog—a plastic frog that the bishop had hidden under a chair to make visitors jump. It was a running joke all morning.

In the garden two young Aboriginal guys were working on creating new beds. Bishop Chris has ambitious plans for the garden and I see developments each time I come.

The bishop was in the kitchen stirring a pasta sauce. Each Thursday he cooks for lunch after the weekly staff meeting. Cooking is his device for keeping the meetings short—he serves up lunch at twelve-thirty on the dot.

He gave me a copy of a press release, signed by churchmen of several persuasions, calling for a new commitment to reconciliation and 'an end to attacks on ATSIC'. He said he fought for two days to get rid of the adjective 'unjust' with 'attacks'. 'It's got to be acknowledged that ATSIC has real problems with nepotism, and some dodgy practices. And not all attacks on it are "unjust". Aborigines themselves criticise ATSIC roundly and often. If you have an uncle in ATSIC, your community will get more funds; if not, you might get a few beans. That's partly a cultural phenomenon. But they are survivalists, they know they have to clean up their act. And they'll do so, given time.'

On the Federal election coming up in October, he concurred with me that there is probably a 'gentleman's agreement' between the major parties to keep the question of race out of the limelight. He predicts that more people will vote Labor this time but that nonetheless, on the seat count, the Libs will get in 'by a short nose'.

He loves talking about politics—I can see the polly in him straining at the leash.

I asked him about his informal, occasionally irreverent style that I find so disarming. He's been able to escape the 'clericalist mode', he says, because he's spent so much of his priesthood alone in the bush. 'In the cities, I would have been under much more pressure to conform.

'Another bishop saw me officiating at Mass not long ago and he said, "You better watch it, you've been in the bush too long—you were carrying the body of Christ in one hand as if it were the Olympic torch!".' So he's been more conscious lately of the correct form of reverential behaviour.

Suddenly I see the serious churchman again, conscious of his authority, and just as suddenly it disappears again, and Chris of the lively mind and slightly larrikin manners is back.

He lends me a book on Aboriginal religions. I invite him to dinner. I tell him he'll meet another (his second!) Jew in Howard Jacobson. He says he'd love to come to dinner if his fishing trip is cancelled due to bad weather. He sometimes goes for an overnight fishing trip with a couple of Aboriginal mates and sleeps in a swag under the stars.

Communication

Living in this part of the world you encounter communication difficulties all the time. Every day I'm straining to hear and understand. I remember the time with Jimmy and Pat when Pat said, 'Just stop Jimmy if you don't understand something he's saying.' But we didn't, because it would have meant interrupting him at every sentence. Only by listening carefully back to the tape could we make him out, with difficulty. Even with Vanessa, whose English is rich, colourful and quick, it's only when I listen again on tape that I get the full import, the full range of reference. We're better with Damien, now we've got used to his style and his extraordinary hybrid accent.

Does it work the other way? Do countrymen understand only half of what we say but are too polite to say so? Do we constantly make references to things they are not familiar with?

It's not something that should surprise me. I've lived with half-language, with parents whose English, even after fifty years in Australia, has never matched their ease with their mother tongue. So we talked a kind of Kriol— half-Hungarian, half-English—with our own abbreviations and self-created expressions. Yet stupidly, I've never understood the problem within Australia, with indigenous people. I've assumed that if countrymen went to school here from the start, and heard English constantly around them, everything would be fine. I've been mystified how some lose all traces of 'accent' and some remain hard to understand. I've not really understood the divide between what is spoken at home and what's learnt at school. I've not taken into account remote locations and inadequate schooling. Or that an Aboriginal person may speak four or five languages, with varying degrees of skill— their mother's, their father's, Kriol and High English, just for starters.

Historically, white Australia has always been mono-lingual. When I was growing up, speaking a language other than English was somehow shameful. We migrant kids tried hard to forget our first language so we'd fit in better. At high school even learning French or German was a bit suspect, while it was positively nerdish to try to emulate a proper French accent. Who needed other languages in fortress White Australia?

Things have changed somewhat. In schools, kids are now learning the Asian languages of our own region. And in Broome, of course, the whole notion of a mono-lingual Australia is stood on its head.

The back blurb of *Jimmy and Pat meet the Queen* rather sums it up:

> 'Jimmy's first language is Walmajarri, but he also speaks
> several other desert languages and Kriol. He learnt
> English much later, so he doesn't speak High English.
> Pat speaks High English and rusty French, but
> her Walmajarri is not as good as Jimmy's English.
> Kilu [their dog] is a large dog of mixed descent. He is white
> with irregular black spots and one black ear...He barks
> in Walmajarri and English.'

*

Wednesday, September 29

Broome is suddenly much quieter. There's collective relief in the air. Some shops are closing at odd unannounced times, then opening again, for a while. The town is beginning to relax. Small green mangoes, ripening quickly— too quickly the locals say—are everywhere on the trees. The green-necked parrots are still stripping the blossoms and leaves from the flowering gums, leaving pretty litter on the pavements—prettier, anyway, than the beer cans and soft drink containers I compulsively pick up.

Ah, how we continue to adapt...We've put the folding bed out on the side terrace, covered in a piece of batik and a pillow. How shocked we were initially at Donny's garden strewn with beds. Now we see it as suitable for siesta and a better way of surviving stifling nights than air-conditioning. I've bought my first mu-mu—a seer-sucker cotton number, lots of room for air, can't tell whether you're wearing a bra or not. Now I understand why so many Aboriginal women wear something similarly shapeless. Also why the windows and doors of houses are often taken off, and why the houses themselves are neglected. They are no use, apart from their roof. The doors and walls obstruct the precious breeze, the windows help keep it hot. Apart from their kitchen and bathroom facilities, what earthly use are they, at least in their present box form?

The Federal election campaign continues. Oddly, I don't even care too much if Labor doesn't win. Maybe they will eventually do a better job, as Annie says, with a couple more years in the wilderness.

At Blooms

In the evening, at Shama's invitation, a large group of us gather for dinner at Blooms. Among others at the long table: Bob, Tony Hutchinson and his blonde bombshell girlfriend, and a pleasant youngish woman from New Zealand who settled here eleven years ago and is Shama's best friend.

Bob is beaming, delighted to be included with all the young people. He is dressed quite smartly in a mustard-coloured shirt and long pants, the first time I've seen him in anything but shorts and thongs. Shama has sat him at the head of the table next to her mother, who's up from Perth visiting.

When I ask about his wife, Bob is serious for a moment. 'I did the wrong thing by her, and after that, that was the end of it.' But he won't be drawn on what the 'wrong thing' was.

The Hanson topic comes up, of course. To my relief, but not altogether to my surprise by now, Bob hates her.

'That bloody woman. What would this country be without its immigrants?'

About 9 p.m. a rather fierce looking hippy with dreadlocks and a flourishing moustache wanders into the café and begins deftly arranging some flowers he pulls out of a plastic shopping bag. It seems he comes by when he feels like it and does the flowers in exchange for cappuccinos.

All night Bob teases Shama, who teases and flirts with him. She says to us as we're leaving, 'I haven't felt so close to him for years'—as if she's rediscovered him all over again.

Build up

Fifteen

Lyn's surprise move—Beach picnic—Who are you?
Where you come from? What country you belong?—
Little black books—The Directory Wars—The Anne Street
Reserve—Houseproud

At the polling booth at Cable Beach Primary School we were handing out how-to-votes for Labor. Lyn Page was a few metres down the street, handing out cards for the Liberals. We ribbed each other but there was no ill-will. Lyn was in shorts, T-shirt, baseball cap, and silver pumps. A large jolly young woman was handing out gumpf for the Greens, trilling 'One for the planet! We need your vote in the Senate—Dee Margets,' or, 'Social justice—vote Greens.' Alison Lawrence was there, too, in her role as Labor Party activist, fussing about, thanking us profusely for helping out.

It was a more mixed bunch of voters than we anticipated. A superficial drive through the Cable Beach area spells youngish, upwardly mobile Liberal-voting suburbia. Lots of green lawns and modern houses with reticulated watering systems and air-conditioning, two innovations that make life bearable for newcomers from the south. But it's not so homogenous on closer acquaintance: quite a few Aborigines, some poor, some not, quite a few white working class, a sprinkling of tourists as well as some alternative types.

Because of the two-hour time difference between east and west we could have known the early trends by five o'clock, but I wanted to preserve the excitement of it all unrolling on TV, and to ward off the inevitable disappointment a bit longer. But the news spread, of course, and by the time we got to the election night dinner we'd been invited to I was as flat as a tack.

On Monday afternoon Alison called by with the figures for Cable Beach booth (Labor slightly ahead), plus the news that Labor might well win in our electorate, Kalgoorlie. Alison has been telling the Party bosses down in Perth for years that Kalgoorlie was a winnable seat if only they put some time, effort and money into it. But they never have.

Perversely, we're both interested again in the elections now they're over. In this the biggest electorate in the world, the renegade Campbell is out after eighteen years, and the porky Labor millionaire with his own plane (a prerequisite in Kalgoorlie) might scrape in.

Wednesday, October 7

Yesterday, Lyn said: 'I don't force my political opinions on people. I've voted Labor in the past. When there is absolutely no-one else. I won't vote Independent. I've voted Labor a number of times.' She thought about it. 'Three. When there's been no-one decent in the Liberal ranks. Anyway, Liberal and Labor are not that far apart these days.'

I didn't argue with her, but the two parties are still very far apart on some things: industrial relations, social justice issues, and the current flashpoints—the GST and reconciliation. But I never had much hope that Labor would make it this time. And although I wanted them to win, I also felt that it might be better if they didn't. For all the talk about rethinking policy there hasn't been sufficient change within the Party. They are still dancing on the same old drum.

Here in Kalgoorlie the Libs have won after all.

*

Life has speeded up again. The humidity is bearing down on us, the mangoes are ripening, bats circle in the trees at night, making their eerie calls. The big lizard that lives part-time in the roof is making a great deal more noise. Perhaps building a nest? Do lizards build nests?

The other day I was talking to one of the Fongs (a Fong by marriage) and she said that because of the intensity of this place, things can go from being very very good to very very bad quite quickly. And that's when people get out of town for a while. Despite the laid-back 'Broometime', there *is* an intensity here. In part it's the climate. In the wet season some people really do 'go troppo', particularly in a bad Wet, when the humidity builds and builds without rain.

But it's not just the climate. It's an intensity that comes from being a small town in an isolated place; people forced into close and continual contact with one another. There's a lovely side to that—familiarity, lots of energy combined with ease. But if something went wrong it could turn nightmarish.

Lyn's surprise move

Lyn has struck out with her own Shire Directory! She's taken the town by surprise. A glossy brochure on classy paper arrived in the mail:

BE IN YOUR AWARD WINNING DIRECTORY
This year Magnolia Associates will be publishing the
BROOME COMMUNITY AND BUSINESS DIRECTORY
independent of the Broome Shire Council

Followed by reasons why people should sign up with her, plus an advertising order form and a business and personal listing form.

What chutzpah! And this from a woman who was saying she was sick of doing the directory and wasn't at all sure if she wanted to tender this year. But now she's refusing to take defeat lying down. She reckons that she still has the database for the directory and also, according to her legal advice, the copyright.

The bloke who won the Shire tender, one Ian Moore, is not taking it lying down either. Last night Perpetua and other business people in town got a heated fax declaring war on Lyn. Perpetua saved it at our request and brought it around, beautifully preserved in a plastic sleeve.

It was headlined:

DO NOT BE FOOLED!!!
The Broome Community and Business Directory
IS NOT YOUR SHIRE DIRECTORY.
Disregard all information received last week...

And we're off soon for a few weeks at home, so we won't be here to monitor the skirmishes!

Beach picnic

An evening picnic on the beach organised by Lyn Devereaux. It was supposed to be a farewell for Ros and Howard, although they've now postponed leaving for another week because of the gas crisis in Melbourne. Mary Tarran and Nolan Hunter were there. Mary's first comment, repeated a couple of times with a bemused and gentle smile: 'I'm not used to sitting on a beach with chairs!' She was sending us whitefellas up—our overly elaborate arrangements for watching the sunset, our portable chairs and eskies.

Nolan Hunter was a surprise. He doesn't seem to be highly regarded as a councillor—not saying much, not pulling his weight etc. Then there was his outburst at the NAIDOC dinner which was impressive at the time but ended up backfiring. But at this first social meeting he was delightful—bright, fluent, good sense of humour. He joked with Howard about crocodiles, exchanged news with Lyn Devereaux and Mary.

Nolan is leaving Broome soon to study law in Perth. He talked a little of his schooling with the Catholic brothers; how they didn't believe an Aboriginal kid like him could write the poetry he did.

Later I heard Mary say to Nolan, 'Hey, brother, this culture centre—you know, it's going to happen. Yep, it's really going to happen.'

'Good on you,' he said, and gave her a nudge.

With Mary, Nolan's exchange of news and gossip was in that rapid Kriol shorthand that Broome-ites use amongst themselves. Almost impossible to follow. They're not necessarily terribly friendly to each other as it's happening—it's all done quickly, almost furtively while whites are around. Then Nolan returns with ease to the white discourse. He's one of the few locals who can 'talk white' without effort. I've noticed that even Kevin gets into a kind of uneasy garble when he's in a roomful of whites and under pressure.

On to the next do. There's always something on! This time it's Bev Kinney's fiftieth birthday party. I was intrigued to lay eyes on the woman Perpetua has described as the Queen of Broome. Beverley is wealthy, sophisticated and from an old Broome mixed-race family, the Fongs (the other Fongs, not Kevin's). She owns Kinney's store and a pearl farm up the peninsula. Her sister Dianne owns FongSam's Bakery; her other sister, Corrie (the owner of the infamous house on Gantheaume Point), has a couple of shoe stores, here and in Perth.

Bev is lovely to look at. She has an innate elegance, a graceful figure and a pleasant, strangely magnetic face without a skerrick of make-up. She is an astute businesswoman. Early in her career she's said to have done a stint carting off Broome's night soil. You'd never guess it now! As she twirls in her simple red dress, she has, as Perpetua says, something of the classic elegance of Jackie O.

And homage was being paid her. The glossy presents were piled high on a special table near the entrance, a mini jukebox was playing and Bev was constantly on her feet, dancing graciously as the guests milled around the swimming pool.

Lyn Page was there—the only person from council, I think. Pearl was there, too. And Sally and Ahmat. (Sally refuses to marry him in case it spoils their relationship.) And we met Joyce Fong, Bev's mother, who is another of Broome's endless supply of lively, indomitable women in their sixties.

There were lots of business people and professionals, white and mixed-race. Not the top-echelon whites, but no full-blood blacks, either. It was, as we remarked afterwards, strolling the block-and-a-half home, the alternative elite of Broome, the ones who've made it but don't take themselves too seriously. There was just a touch of film-set about it all, what with the floodlit green pool, the stylish open cabana for guests to loll in, the open-air kitchen where the hors d'oeuvres were being warmed and served up by personable young waiters, the gorgeous dense well-tended garden, the caressing night air. It was très atmospheric, and we were content just to have had a look at it.

Who are you? Where you come from? What country you belong?

A Bev's mother, Joyce Fong, has a brother called Jack Lee. He is one of the renegades from the Rubibi process. He's claiming some land across the bay in opposition to Rubibi. It looks like the competing claims may end up in the Federal Court.

Pat Torres is another dissenter. Pat is a forceful presence—intelligent, combative eyes, a forthright manner and a fluent, sophisticated intellect. She is perhaps forty, smartly dressed, long strands of dark hair across her face. Pat was enthusiastic about Rubibi when it started; she was one of the signatories to the initial constitution. But now she's disenchanted.

'It's all about expediency,' she said. 'It's about getting a structure that the white lawyers can do something with within the white legislation.'

You hear a lot of bagging of 'the white lawyers' around town, but talking to Pat I got my first real grasp of the structural and conceptual problems faced by Aboriginal organisations employing them. The lawyers try to make Aboriginal organisations operate inside the parameters of white law, structuring them in a way antithetical to traditional methods of decision making.

For example, Pat says Rubibi should be inclusive of all the family groups rather than just made up of people from the three organisations—the Yawuru, Djugan and Goolarabooloo corporations—that preceded Rubibi. But the lawyers won't take the time to get everyone involved and let them talk it through till consensus is reached. Part of the problem is the different European and Aboriginal attitudes to time.

Pat and her mother, Theresa Barker, run the women's co-op Jarndu Yawuru. They feel they've been excluded from the decision-making process because they ask too many questions and are not compliant. In the complex manoeuvring and power struggles around Rubibi and native title, they've been sidelined.

Pat Torres's vision is matrilineal. The local Broome people are indigenous, she says, regardless of who their fathers were, 'because the mothers grew us up'. Fathers came and went. Even when the men didn't go away but stayed on as loving fathers and husbands, the cultural glue was still the indigenous mothers.

Often the men stayed on as illegal immigrants. They sometimes bought land. Often the title was not secure—because they were in the country illegally, maybe never paid the rates—and after they died the land was lost. Many widows did not inherit, perhaps because they were Aboriginal, perhaps because there had never been a wedding. It's hard to divine the truth here on the frontier where the law was applied arbitrarily and to further whitefella interests.

There's great bitterness about the lost property, still, in Broome. People point and say, 'That was my grandfather's house.'

One way or another, the fathers disappeared and the women and children carried on, and with them, the names: Torres, Sibosado, Chi, Fong, Lee...And besides them, their cousins, the descendants of whitefellas: Hunter, Roe, McKenzie, D'Antoine...

Amongst 'indigenous' people in Broome there are those who have always seen themselves as Aboriginal and those who passed for a time as 'Asiatic'; there are those whose families have always been here and those whose forebears were brought here.

And now there is Rubibi, which is ultimately about having control of the land, having the right to be consulted on what might be done to it. It's about permission being asked and compensation paid.

Theresa and Pat are thinking of using Jarndu Yawuru as an alternative land-owning corporation, separate from Rubibi. Their own patch of turf.

And why not? Why shouldn't family groups own title to land? The only problem is, if there are too many breakaways Rubibi will fall in a heap. And if that happens the power of the local people to negotiate with the Shire and the State will dissolve.

Little black books

Theresa Barker remembers that there was still a curfew until she was about sixteen. That would put the end of the curfew about 1960. This is as close as I can get to pinning it down. It's hard to know what the regulations were because often white authority was imposed arbitrarily. Individual police could order blacks around at will, stop them while they were walking down the street to check their papers, ask them where they were going. One sees that occasionally even now.

There were two little black books. The smaller one was an Exemption pass. This allowed Aboriginal people to be in town for work. The bigger black book was for Citizenship. Having your citizenship allowed you to drink.

There's a story about Mary's grandfather, Paddy Djiagween, when the Queen visited Broome in 1963. He asked Her Majesty if he was the equal of any of her subjects. The Queen said 'Yes'. Paddy rushed straight down to the Governor of Broome hotel and demanded a beer, which the barman, nonplussed, served him.

Mary told me how proud her father was of his Citizenship pass, how he always kept it in his jacket pocket.

*

An item on the radio: talk of winding back ATSIC, taking away its funding power and giving it back to individual government departments. This is the exact opposite of what Peter Yu wants. He believes that the only way to make funding work effectively is not to centralise it federally but to give it to regional authorities.

Kevin is having his own problems with ATSIC. I managed to get hold of him on his mobile earlier this afternoon and asked if he had any news yet about Goolarri's funding.

He said, 'Someone is making a presentation to the chairman as we speak.'

If the outcome isn't good, Goolarri might be ready to make a public protest.

'I'll get back to you,' he said.

*

According to one of the 'white lawyers', Dave Lavery, the Kimberley Land Council has spent a lot of time tying the State Government down so that Rubibi will have the right to be consulted on developments, including the racecourse site, even after the removal of the 'right to negotiate' following the Wik amendments'.

Dave said that the right to be consulted may in the end amount to the same thing as the right to negotiate. 'The framework agreement between the State and Rubibi gives us leverage and may help keep the Rubibi claims out of court. Going to court is to no-one's advantage.'

He told me a story about plans to redevelop the Cable Beach kiosk, to turn it from a little shop selling chips and ice-creams into a full-blown restaurant. One of the tenderers was the Cable Beach resort. They asked advice of the CEO, Greg Powell. But it was the deputy CEO who sorted the tenders, and he excluded it on a technicality. Powell was furious with his deputy and the Cable Club was furious with Powell.

'He's been hiding in his office all week,' Dave said.

The Club is not giving up. They've brought in a big firm of lawyers from Perth, who'll be at the council meeting on Tuesday.

The Directory Wars

The Shire Directory Wars have erupted.

Last night Lyn said, 'I've been injuncted.' She sounded tense. I told her she shouldn't be surprised—she who lives dangerously.

Her rival, Ian Moore, was on air this morning to give his side of it. The man clearly hadn't made up his mind as to his tactics. On the one hand he tried to minimise the affair, called it a 'hiccup,' and never mentioned Lyn by name. On the other he said it was unfair and underhand, and made threats of legal action.

In the evening we went around to Lyn's to see how she was going. She was looking weary and grim and didn't even have any wine, far less champagne in the house. So she and her friend Jeanie came down to our place for a drink and an impromptu meal.

Lyn won't go on radio to rebut Ian Moore's attack. She reckons dignified silence is best.

She recapped for us how it all happened. Ian Moore offered the Shire $40 000, compared to Lyn's $28 000, for the tender, which gives the tenderer the right to produce the directory and collect the advertising revenue it generates. The Shire went for the bigger money. Lyn says the Shire didn't bother to find out anything about Ian Moore, whose company,

Sportswreck, runs a car wrecking outfit on the New South Wales central coast. They didn't ask how her database might be transferred if he won, nor who had copyright on it.

She rang Moore and offered to sell him her database and help him set up. He refused. People began to whisper that the directory would never come out because he was so late getting started. She was worried, but she swears she was prepared to give the whole thing away when she suddenly woke up at 2 a.m. one morning and heard a voice saying, 'Bring out your own directory. It will be called the *Community and Business Directory*.' There followed clear concise thoughts as to its layout, direction and so on.

Lyn has checked it out with the lawyers and she's going ahead, although she's worried about what this will do to her support around town. But at least Kim Male seems to be treating her with new respect. 'For the first time ever in a council meeting he called me by my name! I nearly fell over backwards. I don't think he'll go so far as to support me, but he's at least amused by it.'

Jeanie says, 'He never thought you'd have the balls.'

If so, Kim Male can't be overly observant. Balls is about the first thing you notice about Lyn.

*

October 20, Council meeting, Shire chambers, noon

A big crowd: some Aboriginal people, including Mary; Friends of Gantheaume Point; Dave Dureau in his ratty pigtail and long maroon work socks.

There's no sign of Lyn Page at the councillors' table. Angus Murray is in the president's chair at the top table; Greg Powell in the CEO's spot beside him. Powell's colour is never good but today it's terrible. He's pale and pasty, and somehow more jowly. He's looking fierce and angry and not at all well.

Angus opens the meeting and announces that discussion of the Cable Beach kiosk tenders will be in camera because of legal action against the Shire.

Still no sign of Lyn but she must be around because I saw her little maroon four-wheel-drive outside.

Question time. Suddenly Lyn appears through a door at the back of the room, stands next to the public seating and makes a statement: 'I have received legal advice that I may speak during question time as a public citizen, then take my place at the council table.'

A flicker of impatience crosses Angus's smooth, round face.

Lyn has a list of eight questions. She passes a copy up to Angus, who says, 'These are very long and we won't be able to answer them now.'

He puts the piece of paper down.

Lyn, very vehement, says, 'May I read my questions?'

Again he says they won't be able to deal with them now.

Again she says: 'May I read my questions?'

He sighs. 'Go on then.'

The questions are to do with the method by which the council assessed the tenders for the Shire directory: Did the council ask what Ian Moore's previous career had been? Did they ask if he had produced such a directory before? Did they know that the copyright was with Magnolia Associates? Does Mr Moore intend to use local staff? etc etc.

When she's finished, Angus says the questions will be answered in due course. Lyn then takes her seat, grinning widely, as if she's had a minor victory.

Several people, including Dave Dureau, ask questions about the coastal park. Protection of the local vegetation is one of Dave's passions—that and keeping an eagle eye on the Shire. His wife, councillor Elsta Foy, is present today. Elsta has been unwell this year and has missed quite a few meetings.

Before coming to Broome I thought it was standard practice for in-coming correspondence to be listed in council agenda. Not here. Dave Dureau has a go at Greg Powell about people sending letters to the Shire and getting no reply.

Greg is angry: 'You had better have proof of what you're saying, because I object to my professional reputation being impugned and I'll take it further.'

Dave says again that people don't get information, that decisions are made which they never hear about.

The development at Gantheaume Point is raised. Angus says, 'It's been assumed for some time by council that there will be some development on the racecourse site.' There are murmurs. Someone in the public seating mutters, 'It's never been discussed by council.'

Then it's on with the agenda. A long time is spent on an item about converting part of the Cable Club resort to strata-title apartments. Angus declares a conflict of interest and leaves the room—no doubt his real estate agency will be selling them. Kim Male takes the chair.

Two Americans (the resort is now owned by Intercontinental) are at the meeting representing The Club. They object to one of the conditions of approval recommended by the town planner—that The Club provides a public walkway to the beach. The younger man—a slight, fair-haired, all-American-boy—speaks. They want the requirement for the footpath removed, he says. He accuses the town planner of asking for something that is not an appropriate condition of approval.

One of the councillors, searching for a compromise, suggests that a bit of land could be taken from the school camp next door and a bit from The Club. But The Club won't budge.

'Why are we being asked to make a decision now?' asks Elsta. 'Why hasn't it gone through the committee?'

'Because of time constraints,' Greg says. 'The president and I discussed it and decided it should come straight to council.'

'Is that right?' Elsta asks, meaning: Is that okay, given that the president had an interest in it?

Kim says: 'It's not wrong.'

Sounds like Angus and Greg wanting to rush it through.

Elsta is performing well. The rest of them don't ask the obvious questions. Or ask them but then just go to water if they are opposed.

And that is what happens—The Club gets its own way.

The Anne Street Reserve

After a hot afternoon, just as it begins to cool, we take the dogs for a walk to the old Aboriginal reserve. A rough piece of bushland with low trees and shrubs; clumps of tall, dry grass with tracks running through it, the red pindan showing through. It has the look of urban bushland, well used but not particularly cared for. There is litter here and there—plastic bottles and rusty tins and crushed aluminium. Tracks criss-cross this bit of open space, maybe four hectares in all. The only indication that it was once the reserve is the remains of a road that enters from Anne Street and ends abruptly in a clearing. Nearby is an old electricity pole, the meter box still hanging from it.

Around the edge of the bushland, facing the street, are the houses that replaced those on the old reserve. Small cottages with a few large trees and bushes and not much of a front yard.

We move slowly through the bush, keeping an eye on the dogs. We talk of the Aboriginal people we have met, of those with get-up-and-go, of those who lack confidence. We talk of white domination on the Shire, and the reasons for black reticence. Who has the skills to mount a challenge? Who the chutzpah? Here, on the patch of dirt where white administrators corralled them, we can better understand why even the 'successful' blacks still seem stymied from seeking power.

The shadows stretch from one side of the reserve to the other; the air lightens, a tiny puff of coolness. You pause to gather wildflowers, snap a fragrant grey-green branch. In the west, where the tourists will be watching the sunset from Cable Beach, the clouds are mauve and gold.

We come out onto the road not far from Mary's, put the leads on the dogs' collars, and head up Forrest Street towards home. Forrest Street, named after a white explorer, a white politician, a white dynasty.

Houseproud

Mary was about five when her parents married in the Catholic church in Broome. They went to live on Kennedy Hill in a rough bough shed two metres by three, while waiting for a house. In cold weather the dew would drip through, so they laid sheets of iron across the top of the bed, an old hospital bed, and slept under that. While they were living in the bough shed, family would come and go all the time. The Bardi side of the family would come down from One Arm Point.

A couple of years later they moved into a house on the Anne Street reserve, just Mary and her parents and brother. They were the first to move onto the 'new' reserve and Mary was very proud. It was only a couple of rooms, but after the bough shed it was a palace. There were twelve houses on the reserve, three for each of four tribal groups. Mary's extended family of Yawuru came soon after, then Karajarri, Bardi and Nyulnyul families.

Mary's parents always worked—her father at the council depot, her mother in the convent laundry. She started school at the old St Mary's in Barker Street. She liked going to school, and she liked the fact that her mother worked close.

The Welfare were always checking up on kids not going to school. 'I didn't miss one day at school,' says Mary, 'except a couple of times when I was sick. One time I remember I couldn't run in the school sports 'cos I had a boil on my bum! I was a good runner.'

Was her mother ever afraid that she might be taken away?

'As a kid you don't think about those things. But living on the reserve, I saw things...the Welfare, they'd always be showing up. You'd be afraid.'

There was one nun who was around a lot. 'She kept an eye on us. She was part of the system.'

Sixteen

*An extraordinary trial—All eyes on Gantheaume—Dinner
at Sheba Lane with the Yus—Aunty Bella's rosary*

Goolarri Media is running out of money. They are getting the same funding now as when they were just doing a couple of hours on the ABC each morning. And they're meant to be running a full-time operation.

The Goolarri offices are quiet. I find Kevin in the upstairs office. He's wearing a T-shirt and shorts and he's growing a beard. But there's nothing relaxed about him. He's sounding very tense, and he becomes more emphatic the more tense he is.

'The people that haven't been funded are all on notice,' he tells me. 'Our technician is going. There'll only be seven of us left, out of twenty-nine. We've carried some people on the income we've brought in but we can't do that any longer so we've had to put people off.

'ATSIC are still being their unresponsive bureaucratic self. We need a commitment from them for $1.8 million over three years. But they won't come up with recurrent or operational costs. It's the old thing—build me a house but don't put any furniture or power or water in.'

His voice is clipped and aggressive.

I unwisely comment that people are saying they're not getting the same level of information about indigenous affairs as when Goolarri had a timeslot every morning on the ABC.

'If people want to know what is going on in indigenous affairs,' he snaps, 'they really should come and ask us. I don't think we need to air what we feel about things...The real issue is that quite a few non-indigenous people are interfering in indigenous issues that don't concern them. A lot of the people who are coming to live here who have the empathy— the ferals or the mung beans—are actually starting to think that they're black, and they're forgetting the demarcation, the jurisdiction of what role they actually play.'

Having got that off his chest, he seems to calm down, so I ask him, 'So how close to the line is Goolarri?'

'Very close. We might have to go back to five hours [on-air] a day. The whole thing is extremely frustrating. Mark and I have no vested interest but we're probably going to get so frustrated that they won't keep us. We're a package. If I go, he'll go, and if he goes, I'll go. Sometimes I get a bit cynical and think that's what they want. For some reason we threaten a lot of people.'

Friday

We had an appointment at Greg Powell's office but he rang and seemed more interested in lunch, so we met him at the Mangrove. There's no such thing as a private lunch in Broome: Lyn was in a meeting on the other side of the room with people from the Kimberley Performing Arts Council.

Regarding the directory imbroglio, Greg thinks that in the end it will be a financial decision. Either Lyn or Ian Moore will pull out, depending on who gets more advertisers.

He said it was good to see Mary and other Aboriginal people at the Shire meeting the other day. He hasn't seen them come to a meeting and speak on their own behalf before. 'Usually it's the white lawyers.'

He dislikes the white lawyers—has been known to storm out of meetings with them. He gets frustrated by how slow Rubibi is at making up their minds. He's not used to working with councillors, either. Before coming to Broome he was the administrator of the Cocos and Christmas Islands— maybe that explains his governing style. Councillors irritate him. He thinks they go to water whenever they get any opposition.

'You were there the other day when the Cable Club pedestrian access came up,' he said. 'I left the way open for them to give approval, but attach the condition that an access path be found. Instead, they let The Club get away with providing a footpath around the outside, so that now people will have to walk all the way around to get to the beach.'

Greg is not sure what the future holds for him. His wife isn't very happy here. 'She'd rather be in Perth.' His oldest child is going to school in Perth soon. But he can't bear the thought of going south. He hates the cold.

*

Lyn is very unhappy with an article about the Shire Directory on the front page of today's *Advertiser*. She claims the article defames her. 'It's saying that people felt misled because I sent them the same application form as last time [when she did the official Shire directory]. But I stated clearly, on the top of the letter, that the *Business and Community Directory* was independent of the Shire,' she says in that high, precisely enunciated way she has when she's on the defensive. Then more darkly, 'I'm going to get the *Advertiser* now. I'm just devastated. I value my good character and my standing in the community above everything else.'

I suggest she could bow out now, citing too much community confusion and division.

'I won't do that.' Black eyes blazing.

'I know you won't.'

But I wish she would. I see no good coming out of it.

In the evening we call in on Gordon and Damien. The flat looks much better—the ALS has sent the cast-off furniture from Kununurra. Cane, with blue-grey cushions, fortuitously colour-coordinated with the walls and vinyl floor. Gordy has the place looking quite smart. But there's still a bedroll on the floor in front of the TV.

An extraordinary trial

I've been sitting in on a trial that has raised all sorts of questions for me—about how the courts work, cross-cultural interactions, family relationships. I came across the case accidentally. I'd just dropped into court to find Gordy, and was struck by the dignified old man with intelligent eyes in the dock—the disjunction between his demeanour and the sordid act he was accused of. Tom Wiggan, a Bardi man from One Arm Point, was on trial for indecently touching his de facto wife's granddaughter, with whom he had a grandfather–granddaughter relationship.

Once the trial got underway, I was even more struck by Tom Wiggan's de facto, a handsome woman with longish grey curling hair. She was giving evidence for the prosecution. She had great presence and spoke excellent, elegant English. At first I didn't realise that she was Esther Bevan, whom I'd heard giving an impressive address at Notre Dame not long after we arrived. Esther works as a fundraiser for the university, does teacher inductions, and each year conducts an alcohol rehabilitation course at the centre just outside Broome. Tom Wiggan lives partly with her in town and partly at his home at One Arm Point.

At the time, Esther's grandchildren were living with them in Broome. Their mother was in Perth. One day Esther's granddaughter told her that 'something was happening that she didn't like, something I should know about. Something sexual.' Esther reported Tom to the police.

Gordon cross-examined Esther:

'How long have you and Tom been together?'

'Fifteen years.'

'Would you describe Tom as a caring man?'

'Yes.'

'A loving man?'

'Yes.'

Esther looked sadly across at Tom, without hatred. He looked straight ahead of him without expression.

'Would you describe him as a man who was caring and loving to his grandchildren?'

'Yes.'

Outside the courthouse a thin old Aboriginal lady began to chat to me about the weather, then about the case. It seems very sad, I said. Yes, she agreed. 'It's been going on for three years. But then it came out in the open.'

Tom Wiggan is her brother-in-law. He's staying with her on Kennedy Hill at the moment. (When the judge asks Gordy for a more precise address than Kennedy Hill, he says, 'Everyone in Broome knows Kennedy Hill, your honour. It's pretty precise in Broome. Just at the back of my place.')

After the break the granddaughter took the stand, solemn and scared, but composed too. She's an intelligent ten-year-old, big and well developed for her age. She was very shy and embarrassed when it came to details of the three instances she alleges, when she was eight and nine years old—basically, that the old man touched her on the breast and the vaginal area, underneath her clothes, for a time she guessed variously to be between one minute and five minutes.

When Gordy cross-examined her, he was matter of fact but gentle. She agreed that her grandfather 'growled' at her for coming home late a few times, even though she said she came home in daylight.

'Do you love your grandfather?'

'Yes.'

'Were there good times?'

'Yes.'

'Was it a fast touch near your nanya and minni?' (Both white lawyers used the Aboriginal terms for vagina and breast with her, even though the child's English is excellent, and indistinguishable from any other ten-year-old's.)

'Did he say, be careful, I'm worried bad things can happen to you?'

'Yes, he did.'

When the prosecutor re-examined her, he asked her how long were the fast touches. She couldn't remember for sure—maybe five minutes. At the end, and in a rush, and this was the only time I wondered if the sentence had been rehearsed, she said that her grandfather told her after the touching, 'Now if you get a boyfriend you'll be good enough for him.'

All this time, a big screen (the Far North's substitute for videoed evidence) has protected her from seeing the old man, who continues to stare ahead of him as if elsewhere.

It is clear how painful and serious the whole thing is for the child. The jury listens to her intently. I notice that Eirlys Richards, our blue-eyed linguist friend, is one of the jurors.

Angela comes into court. Gordy whispers in her ear. She comes back to where I'm sitting.

'Do you have any Panadol for Gordy?'

Just for once, I don't. 'Hard night, was it?' I whisper back.

'Damien kicked him. He thinks he might have a broken rib.'

In the break Gordon is looking pale, says he's in pain. I go off to Mango Jack's to get him 'something very sweet to drink' and some fags.

Next on the stand is the cop who interviewed Tom at One Arm Point. The tape of the interview is played. The judge warns the jury that it's hard to understand. It seems that a transcript was mooted, but never acted upon. Extraordinary, because Tom is almost impossible to understand unless you have had long exposure to Aboriginal English. But you get the feel of it, and it's unexpected and disconcerting. Tom is unconcerned, voluble, almost casual. Yes, he did touch the child, and it was to warn her of the dangers out there once she started to grow up. What he did was part of his culture; his right and duty.

This relaxed, talkative Tom is nothing like the stunned old man sitting impassive behind his white lawyer.

The next day, Tom takes the stand. Several times he is asked to speak louder and slower. He gives similar evidence to that on the video. He touched the child only to warn her. He was angry with her for staying out late; he was worried that the same thing would happen to her as happened to another child who disappeared. He did not touch her under her clothes.

There is no evasion about him. His puzzlement about what is happening is patent.

The prosecution does him no real damage. What looked like an open and shut case when the child gave evidence now looks much more complicated.

There is just one character witness for the defence—Malcolm Douglas, a tall, bearded white man with a lispy voice. He is a film maker and ex-crocodile shooter who now runs the croc park in Broome. He's known Tom for thirty years, sometimes spending weeks alone with him as a guide in remote country—'times when you can't get to know anyone any better'. He speaks of him as an honourable, traditional man, devoted to family, concerned always for the welfare and morals of the young. He says that apart from a brief time when Tom and Esther were on the grog together, early in their relationship, Tom has always been an exemplary person. He speaks emotionally of the detrimental effect of a conviction on Tom and Esther's teenage son. He breaks down.

The Prosecutor rises to object, but Gordon waves him away impatiently. His witness has already had the desired effect.

Annie has come by to listen in until the adjournment. As we emerge into the steamy air on the verandah, a thin young woman hurls herself at us. 'Suzie! Annie!'

It's Sharon, Damien's niece, who'd left town but has come back for the trial of her 'Dad', who on further talking turns out to be her uncle Tom. She's here to vouch for him. She's angry with several family members who have failed to show up to do the same. Tom has raised dozens of kids, she says—herself and her sisters and many others not his blood relatives— and not one of them has ever been afraid of him, but have gone to him for love, cuddles and advice. She is very dark about Esther, who she claims didn't do much for her own grandchildren; it was really Tom who raised them.

To my surprise Esther is also out on the verandah, chatting away with Tom! At first I'm not sure if it's her; her hair is tied back in a knot today, and her clothes are shabbier. Today she looks more like Tom's wife than the high-powered woman attached to the Catholic university. With the relations on the verandah she speaks Aboriginal English. She and Tom look perfectly content in each other's company, as if she'd never brought charges against him that could send him to gaol.

I'm flummoxed. In white society the hostility would be total. Here, even though his relatives give her a bit of berth, there is no outright ostracism or aggro towards her. It's the fact that this charge is possible within the white system that angers them more.

As the day wears on the tension gets to people. There is railing against white justice, at the inability of whites to understand Aboriginal law. Yet it's Esther who brought the charge in the first place. Was it the white, Catholic part of her that felt obliged to do so? Maybe she thought it best to let the white man decide the right and wrongs of it; she would have at least done what was expected of her. What complicated moral shoals someone like her must negotiate.

It's time for Gordy to address the jury. He doesn't deny that Tom touched the young girl, but the whole question is, was it innocent or indecent touching? He is dismissive of the disputed times of the touching. Aborigines are far more imprecise about time than we are, he says. What is important is that the child has agreed that it was a 'fast touching'.

He makes much of the fact that Tom did not have to give evidence, but took the stand despite his poor English and the strangeness of a court-room. 'His first language is not English and he cannot instruct me as fully as he would like,' Gordy says. He reminds the jury that Tom's concern for his 'granddaughter' was genuine, even though they were not blood relations, Aboriginal concepts of family being much broader than our own. Here is a family that still clearly loves each other, despite what has happened.

His address verges on the sentimental, but it escapes being so because he speaks with brusque passion and a patent love of Aboriginal people. And to the heart of things, without legalisms. Angela tells me later that there were a couple of 'weepers' in the jury as Gordon spoke.

In contrast, the prosecutor loses the jury altogether. He bores them.

The judge does a scrupulous summing up. The jury goes out.

Sharon suddenly reappears, having been absent all morning, breathlessly bearing a passionate letter of support for her uncle. It's eloquent and well spelled but the phrasing is at times eccentric. She is running around, asking her relatives to sign it, getting it crumpled and damp. She then thrusts it at Gordy. He says he'll use it if there is a guilty verdict. Otherwise, her effort is too late.

Half an hour turns into an hour, turns into two hours. The relatives speak in hushed tones with Malcolm Douglas, the croc man, with whom they appear at ease. Douglas is worried by the composition of the jury: 'There's not enough indigenous people and too many older white women who are going to be set in their ideas.'

The tension on the verandah gets to people. Tom's younger brother goes from person to person, emitting sharp angry verbal volleys. Why don't people understand, what sort of justice is this, what can the jury be thinking of?

Sharon's sisters come up to talk. Her sister Katie invites us up to One Arm Point to see what traditional life is like up there. She points to young Albert, Tom and Esther's son. 'I sang for him all day and all night, traditional way. I sang for him.'

Nearly three hours after the jury filed out, they're coming back in. They look pale and exhausted. The forewoman is ashen.

The first 'not guilty' verdict is barely audible. Not guilty on all three counts.

The relatives are so tense that they can't believe their ears. As the members of the jury file out, they thank them, clasping their hands. Sharon hugs me and introduces me to Tom's younger brother, who has tears in his eyes. He holds my hand and tells me how important this 'not guilty' verdict is.

Tom comes out surrounded by family, head bowed, crying with relief. Till now his features have given nothing away. Gordy tells me later that he refused to eat for a week before the trial.

Esther looks composed. I suspect she is relieved, too.

Thank yous to Gordon, a round of cigarettes, then everyone melts away. It's been a hell of a day.

As I leave I notice the forewoman of the jury sitting in her car, her head resting on the steering wheel, motionless.

*

The more I've thought about and discussed this trial, the more complicated it gets.

For instance, a little scene I glimpsed at the beginning of the proceedings: two old men outside the courthouse were being schooled by the prosecutor to give evidence. All they had to say, the prosecutor told them, was that it was not Aboriginal custom for grandfathers to teach their grandchildren about sexual matters; they would not have to attack Tom himself. The two old men took this in, silently.

They never appeared in court. I assumed it was because they were not willing to give that kind of evidence. But it turns out that Gordy persuaded the judge to exclude their evidence, on the grounds that what was and wasn't custom was not relevant for the jury; the crucial thing was what was in Tom's mind.

'We could have been sunk if those two had testified,' said Gordy.

Later, when I talked to Eirlys Richards over coffee about the trial, it got more complicated again. Contrary to what Malcolm Douglas had feared, it was not the older white women on the jury who wanted a guilty verdict. Eirlys and most of the others thought there was sufficient doubt to acquit. It was the sole Aboriginal (or part-Aboriginal) woman on the jury who held out. She was from down south. She effectively shut Eirlys up, denying that this kind of teaching was Aboriginal custom—as she knew it, anyway. But she also admitted that she might be the wrong person for this jury, as she'd been sexually molested as a child. Nonetheless she wanted a guilty verdict, as did the white hairdresser from the Seaview shopping centre.

The jury did wonder why there was no evidence on what was and wasn't customary. And as to why so few Aborigines were empanelled—it seems many were called up but nearly all of them said, 'I'd rather not, he's my relative,' or, 'I know him.'

A After the case we went home with Gordy for a beer but we didn't stay long. He was worn out. He didn't even feel like a drink.

'Every now and again there's a case that takes it out of you more than the others.'

All eyes on Gantheaume

There's to be a public meeting to discuss the Gantheaume Point development, which we'll miss because we're going home for some R and R for a few weeks. The Western Australian Land Minister has been quoted as saying that the Gantheaume site would be ideal for all sorts of tourist development: a golf course, a five-star resort, a caravan park, a backpackers' hostel. The area for redevelopment is big enough for the lot—one hundred and twenty hectares, covering the racecourse and beyond.

This is a rich spoil for the Government. Where else in the world is there such a piece of land available on such a coastline, close to an established tourist town?

Rubibi has released a statement, moderate in tone, saying, 'The area around Gantheaume Point is rich in cultural heritage sites and places of significance.' It points out that a land use study done jointly by the Shire and Rubibi has shown that high-density development on the racecourse site would be inappropriate. The racecourse should either stay as it is or become a nature reserve.

So far, not a peep from the Shire about it.

I see now why Mary was so ambivalent when we talked to the State

Government men. Their offer of a site for the culture centre behind the Cable Beach dunes was contingent on the land closer to Gantheaume Point being developed for tourism. But there's no way that Mary will go along with development that close to Minyirr. 'We've identified twelve sites there, and there's more,' she says. 'Why should we tell them about them?'

There's always this tension in Mary between telling and not telling. If she is to act on the public stage, working to secure rights for the Yawuru, then the gardiya way requires that she present proof—by telling stories, identifying important Aboriginal sites. But as a Yawuru woman she knows such things should not be talked about.

I ask her why her mother speaks out, is active, while her father remains silent. 'He's a traditional man,' she says. 'But Mum, she knows, she knows you gotta do it. To save the country.'

A few months ago, seeing that tract of land so close to the town and the beach, seeing it with eyes that could still not 'see', I thought to myself, 'bound to be developed'. Now I wonder what would be the effect of such a development, eight or ten times the size of the Cable Beach resort? It would transform the town, wipe out its character by sheer volume. Broome can absorb a gradual growth in tourism, maybe one or two small new hotels or blocks of holiday units a year. Even that is changing its character. But one hundred and twenty hectares of development! They are talking of keeping it low-scale, no buildings on the dunes or overlooking the beach; of having 'an Aboriginal theme'. What good will that be to the local people who now wander through the bush collecting bush tucker?

Early Sunday morning

The build-up to the Wet has begun. Most mornings now the sky is a misty mauve with heat and cloud. It clears later in the morning to bright sunshine, then in the afternoon large cottonwool clouds appear over Roebuck Bay. So far, no rain.

We're eating the first mangoes. 'The first are the best,' Perpetua said the other night. After a while you get sick of them. Once the season's in full swing, you can't give them away.

The boab trees, which have been bare-branched all dry season, are beginning to sprout their first green leaves, the branches silhouetted against a bright blue sky. Lots of yellow and orange blossoms are out: red flowers on the poinciana; the 'yellow jacarandas'; the rough-barked rain tree sprouting fluffy, pale yellow blossom that falls to the ground like cotton; the cassia fistula, or 'golden shower', a small drab eucalypt that sprouts long bunches of bright yellow flowers.

*

Years ago, when we began to talk about doing a book together on a country town, I had a specific atmosphere in mind. But Broome is something else. Only occasionally does it have the air of dozey self-satisfaction that reverberates somewhere in my memory of how country towns are meant to be. I've caught it sometimes at the bottom end of Walcott Street, where there's little traffic and the gutters are wide and dusty and the houses are hidden behind trees and shrubs. And sometimes at the top end of Forrest Street, where dogs lie about in the dust and Aboriginal kids shout and jostle and race each other on their bikes.

Now, with the town quietening as the Wet approaches, a little more of that country town emerges.

The other night we were imagining the horrors of life up here when women still wore long skirts and petticoats, in the days before 'the air-con' and 'the retic'.

Perpetua said, 'The history of the North is made up of women who give it a go up here, then give up and move down south.'

It's been touch and go for her up here, but at least she has that bit of air-conditioning in her back room.

The Wet is definitely on its way. After ten or eleven in the morning, there's only a few locals left on the streets. But ignorant tourists are out, complaining of the intense humidity, when they should be lounging by their motel pools until the cooler late afternoon.

I was poking around in town this morning for small presents for Annie's forty-second birthday. A shop assistant in one of the half-dozen shops selling skimpy Indonesian and Indian clothes, advised me to wear rayon once the Wet season starts because even the thinnest cotton will feel too thick in the damp heat.

In the co-op craft shop the old gent behind the counter, a Broome resident since 1949, said that during the Wet he gets up at three in the morning to make his jams and chutneys, and finishes work by eight. During the day he spends time quietly in the coolest parts of the house or on the verandah, has a light lunch, a snooze, then begins to stir when the breeze starts coming off the bay in the late afternoon.

'How was it in the old days before air-conditioning?' I asked.

'The whole town shut down at eleven o'clock and adjourned to the pub or went home for a rest and a bite, and only got going again after two. These days I see all these young couples come into town. They buy a house, take on a mortgage, have jobs, kids. They wear themselves out, and the marriage breaks down within five years. It's because they're trying to live a so-called 'normal' life. You can't do that here.'

Dinner at Sheba Lane with the Yus

Peter's face is always alive, seeking eye contact, watching to see if a point he's made has hit home with you or made you smile. Sarah's tanned face is more impassive under the blonde curls, her comments spare. But after a while she connects and wants to talk one-to-one. You get the sense that Sarah has to create her own space, that there is a persistent and quiet competition between them. Peter does try to cede her time, but reluctantly; she just pursues her own conversation when she can.

Sarah came here as an anthropologist in 1979. 'She came to study me,' Peter said with a grin.

I had the impression it was an old joke, but one she doesn't mind.

They're off to Geneva soon for a conference on indigenous rights. They'll be taking two old countrymen from Fitzroy Crossing with them. 'They're used to meat as their staple,' Peter said, 'but meat is expensive over there. So we're getting a serviced apartment so we can cook for the old blokes.'

The conversation swung back and forth from the national and international stage to the nitty-gritty of Kimberley life—the problem of harnessing the creative talent in the Broome community, the competition for the few good jobs around, and Peter's own difficulty in finding and training a replacement for himself at the KLC. 'I've been here a while, I can't stay here forever...'

We talked of the many talented people in Broome, including Jimmy Chi. I mentioned how impressed I was by Jimmy's encyclopaedic musical knowledge; all the echoes and references in his songs. Peter's face lit up. 'It all comes from the radio. As kids we all listened to it all the time. We'd race home from school every day to see if our requests were going to be played on the ABC.'

Broome kids also saw all the Hollywood musicals at Sun Pictures. That helps explain why the music of Jimmy Chi and the Pigram Brothers is so accessible and familiar. It hooks into music one has already heard, but mixes it all up in a very Broome way.

Sarah and Peter both talked about Aunty Bella with respect and affection. The old lady is on everyone's lips at the moment; her death is expected any day.

'Do you think Aunty Bella would want an apology for being sent off to the nuns as a child?' Anne asked Peter.

'No, probably not. I don't think she regrets her life. But that's no reason for the Government not to apologise for the *policy* of removal.'

Every half hour or so, a large, light-skinned open-faced woman called Dot West came over to our table and sat down to smoke a cigarette. Some years ago Dot started what is now Radio Goolarri. Her partner is Kevin Puertollano, chairman of the regional council of ATSIC. The two couples talked fishing—the universal theme in this town.

Just after ten, the Yus excused themselves, saying they had to get up at six next morning...to go fishing.

I've often noticed how the usual predictable political alliances don't quite work in Broome. Peter is undoubtedly Left, yet he thinks that of all the local candidates for the seat of Kalgoorlie, the National Party's was the best.

'In a way, we are the National Party's best constituency, and some of them are beginning to realise it. We've actually got a lot of issues in common.'

Of the Labor Party: 'They haven't done much for us, apart from talk.'

When Peter ran for Shire in the early eighties there was panic among the establishment, Sarah said. 'This town may look good on the surface, but you should see it on Shire election day. Then you see the real ugliness. It divides black and white, literally.'

*

Monday

Broome is starting to turn in on itself. No more announcements on the local radio of the latest tourist figures, no more national and international conferences flying in for a Broome junket. With the wet season approaching, it's just a small town again, in an inhospitable place.

Lying on the bed, staring at the ceiling and listening to the clank of the fan in the little bedroom, I got a glimpse of how to survive here. The guilt-laden rollcall of routine that is our Western work ethic only makes one miserable in a place like Broome. This is why business people go fishing mid-week, why work still finishes by 4 p.m., why not much happens on a Friday.

On the radio this morning, warnings of the probability of more than one cyclone before Christmas. Among the recommended preparations: buy up torch batteries and batteries for radios in case the power goes, stock up on non-perishable foodstuffs and potable water, and the perennial advice: 'Clean up your yard.'

Despite the talk of a shortage of mangoes this year, our trees seem to have plenty—small green ones with bright orange flesh. Every morning we go outside to pick them. Mangoes for breakfast. Mangoes for lunch.

A perfect morning. Quite early, before breakfast, we had a gentle, luxurious swim at Town Beach and, still wet and relatively cool, walked slowly home. We should have thought of doing this before—when the tides permit of course. Here a day must be planned entirely by the tides.

*

Aunty Bella died at nine' o'clock on Saturday night. It was the exact time Peter and Sarah Yu were talking about her so warmly.

I rang Pearl this morning. She said that towards the end she was urging the old lady to die. '"Come on, Aunty Bella," I said, "or we'll all get as sick as you with all this waiting. You go to heaven now."'

Pearl and a small army of Bella's 'nieces' (Pearlie actually is Bella's niece) kept up a twenty-four hour vigil at the hospital. Pearlie enumerated 'Bella's girls'. Among them were Phyllis Bin Bakar and Madge Yu, Peter's mother. The oldest is seventy-four, the younger ones in their late fifties and sixties.

'The nurses were impressed with us, all of us so well behaved, not a rowdy one amongst us. They thought Bella had done a good job bringing us up.'

Pearlie said that we were welcome to come around to her house for the Rosary, 'Any night, between seven and seven-thirty, for the next nine nights.'

Aunty Bella's rosary

There were at least fifty to sixty people in Pearl's back yard and everyone knew each other. The night was still and warm. A large mango tree decked with innumerable green fruit stood to one side of the garden. In front of the seated congregation was a small shrine—a table with a big photo of Bella when young, two lighted candles under glass, a decorative pot plant and a smaller photo of an older Bella.

There was the constant murmur of voices. 'Hail Mary full of grace… fruit of thy womb Jesus… pray for us sinners now and in the hour of our death… blessed art thou among women… lead us not into temptation but deliver us from evil…Hail Mary full of grace.…blessed art thou among women…'

The voices were low and fervent in the night. Most of the women knew the half hour recitation by heart. The men—far fewer of them- joined in. The kids hung solemnly around their parents or played quietly with each other.

Among the younger women, Maxine Chi, and Sarah Yu, who'd brought her three younger children along. The atmosphere was serious and intimate, solemn and informal. Afterwards, with the garden lights up, and people eating, chatting, drifting off, it was like a large family gathering. Lots of food—sandwiches, pizza, damper, chicken.

During supper, Sally's daughter showed us the cover designs she and Sally have been working on for Aunty Bella's Mass book. Four splendid coloured collages—of Ruby Plains where Bella was born, of Beagle Bay and its beautiful church, and scenes from Broome and Gantheaume Point.

Thursday

Two days before we fly home. We're looking forward to it, but there's also the feeling that we're leaving just as we're getting into the thick of things. We'll miss Aunty Bella's funeral. Perpetua promises to send us a description.

We're both suffering from overload. Or as Annie puts it, we're like sponges who can soak up no more.

I called in on Bob Noble, to say goodbye and see how he was. He was subdued, for once, and I think he was in pain. He was just off to the hospital to have his dressings done.

I told him we were going home for a few weeks.

'Oh yes, where's that, to Perth?' he said, in keeping with his never quite registering people. It's all one amiable, anonymous cavalcade with him.

Bob reckons it's hotter now than it will be in the Wet, when the rain cools things down. 'But the real Wet won't start till January the ninth.'

That precise? I asked. Yep, that was the usual date.

Bob had on his best mustard shirt for the visit to the hospital, and he was looking quite handsome, but his eyes had that extra glitter that comes from pain. He squeezed my arm paternally when I left.

Saturday morning

The dogs won't be coming back with us when we return next month, so I went over to Lyn's with leftover dog food and a ball as presents for

Georgie-Girl. Lyn was looking tired and drawn. Her solicitor is now asking the *Advertiser* for a retraction, but she doesn't believe she'll get one.

'The damage has been done, Suze, the damage has been done.'

She's waiting another week or so to see how many advertisers she gets, then she'll probably make a decision. She might well withdraw. She seems resigned—all passion spent.

Seventeen

Developing an eye—Mango medley—A busy morning at the courthouse—Ephemera—Catching up—Lyn in retreat— Phyllis and Aunty Bella

The unbelievable luxury of home! As we stepped out of the car on Saturday night the air was fragrant, laden with cool moisture and blossom scent. The first thing we wanted to do was have a bath. After six months of showers. Lolling in the bath at 1 a.m.—delicious! Then slipping between cool sheets in our own soft bed. The rich scent of jasmine floating in the window. And the silence! I didn't want to go to sleep. I just wanted to savour the quietness and pitch blackness of the farm. A few frogs started croaking. Listening to them, I went off to sleep.

Home is so different from Broome that there is no point in trying to compare them. Each wonderful in their very different ways. The frogs here are brown, invisible but noisy; those in Broome enormous, green and silent. The flowers here are complex and multifarious and heavy scented; those in Broome, strong and strident in colour but only occasionally fragrant.

*

Being at home has made me think a bit differently about Gordon and Damien. From the evening I first met Damien, and after every time I've seen him since, I've started hatching plans for him—how to give this gorgeous, quick-witted boy some purpose in life? I am incurable. And also arrogant—toying with ideas of 'saving Damien', when Damien almost undoubtedly sees no need to be saved. As Gordon says, Damien is happy with his life. He has got what he wanted—a high-status lover who gives him enough money so he can have a good time.

But that's not enough for us white liberals. It doesn't fit with our ideas of a worthwhile life. So we try to intercede. I've seen Gordy watching me once or twice as I've tried to talk to Damien. His look says, 'Don't'.

I used to get angry with Gordy. I used to think he could do more to help Damien 'fulfil his potential'. Now I begin to see that it is not apathy or laziness on Gordy's part, but that he sees that he does not have the *right*. Nor do I.

And Damien does have a good life, materially, far better than most blacks. As for his soul...perhaps, as Mary says: 'We're already there'.

The bishop says that one of the key problems in Broome is a sense of identity. People may celebrate their diverse origins but there is also trauma and a confusion of allegiances. I've seen it time and again in Pearl, whose allegiances swing depending on the context.

But at other times Pearl is very clear about her identity. 'I'm a Kimberley person,' she'll say. 'Sometimes people assume I'm Asian. And I'll say "No". Then I'll say one of my grandmothers was Aboriginal. "Oh, you're an Aborigine are you!?" I'll say, "No, I'm not, I'm of Aboriginal descent, but I am not an Aborigine." That word, that privileged word, is for the full-blood, the true indigenous. I'm not an indigenous person.'

But people with no more Aboriginal blood than Pearl call themselves indigenous. When I said that, Pearl flapped her hands. 'Even less, even less! They're jumping on the bandwagon. Because it's fashionable...They suffered no discrimination and now they want all the benefits. Don't get conned by them. This is from someone who has lived here all my life.'

I once asked Marty Sibosado why it was that people identified as either indigenous or not, despite the extraordinary mix of races in their background.

He said, 'The either/or is, I think, because if you call yourself Aboriginal you have to acknowledge the forms dictated by Aboriginal law and culture, by your clan or tribe. That's the difference. I have wonderful arguments with Kevin Fong and Mark Bin Bakar and Jimmy Chi about this "multiculturalism". They are trying to identify this "Broome culture". Which is fine, everyone has a right to a culture, but not enough prominence is placed on Aboriginality in this Broome culture. That's a legacy from the missions, because their parents were told it was no good to be black, and that attitude is still being perpetrated on young kids now.'

Marty said a lot of people who called themselves Aboriginal were ignorant of their own law and protocols. A generation and more of the brightest kids were sent south for a Western education, so missed those crucial adolescent years of learning in their own culture. Peter Yu likened it, in a limited way, to being a stolen child. 'We had to shine our boots till we could see our black face in them'. Then they came home after four or five years away and had to try to reconnect with their families and culture. Peter managed better than most. The elders understood the broken connections and taught him, and still teach him. But many boys were emotionally crippled.

'What happened to them?' I asked Peter.

'Many of them are dead. Some committed suicide, some died in drunken brawls or of alcoholism or illness.'

Why is he exempt?

'I don't know if I am. I'm pretty mixed up.'

'He's got a lot of anger in him,' Sarah said.

Mark Bin Bakar and his mother are beginning to explore their Aboriginal past. Phyllis was a stolen child, and still carries the scars, while Mark, son of a whitefella, was raised by Ahmat Bin Bakar, a Malay Muslim, his 'Dad'. When Mark visits the country where his mother was born, out near the Margaret River, he is as inexperienced in the bush as any gardiya. Like many others, he is ignorant of the protocols through no fault of his own.

Vanessa is another, with her Muslim–Anglican father and her Jehovah's Witness mother. Now her own kids go to St Mary's Catholic School—but only for the company of their friends—and Vanessa talks of taking them back to live on her mother's country (the mother she is still bitter about). 'We're river people,' she says.

There was a time when it was enough to say you were Aboriginal to be classified as one. That's not good enough for Marty Sibosado. There are responsibilities that go with the right to consider oneself indigenous. But how realistic is that in modern-day Broome? Is it possible to be as Kevin Fong tries to be—Chinese one day, indigenous the next, Malay the next? Most of his siblings have thrown their lot in with one group or another; Kevin tries to bridge them all. And he married white.

You can align yourself with a people simply because you care for them. Archie Weller, whose Aboriginality is now in doubt, has said, 'I wouldn't know what to do with myself if I couldn't write about blackfellas any more.' But does it make you one of them?

November 10

I rang Lyn in Broome to see how she was going with the Shire directory business. There's been an ominous development: some really nasty stuff on the Broome website bulletin board about her being a prostitute, and giving her phone number. Lyn said she wasn't rattled, just angry. 'It's an exercise in intimidation.'

But she sounded tense and overwrought.

ʃ I'm sitting in the lounge room, cardigan on, fire burning, and looking out at a garden full of perennials, rhododendrons and clematis. It can't be the same continent! It's more like flying from Australia to somewhere chilly in Europe.

Back here in the Highlands, less than two hours' drive from Sydney, Broome seems like a small pimple on the vast rump of Australia. The weather on the TV news never mentions Western Australia's vast north-west. There's a blank between Perth and Darwin, as if no-one at all lived in that enormous stretch of land.

It symbolises the lopsidedness of this country, especially its north–south divide, which I'm starting to see as more significant than its east–west divide. Perth, for all its sense of exclusion, echoes Sydney and Melbourne. But Darwin and Broome, even Cairns, are another country, another Australia altogether. An Australia that most of us dream about but don't really want to know about. Too hot, too rough, too wet, too many blackfellas.

*

Doing the shopping in Moss Vale, I look around me and suddenly everyone looks hopelessly Anglo-Saxon and homogenous. I long to see other sorts of faces, hear other lilts in the voices. In Sydney, too, you see all sorts of faces. But in Broome you see how richly mixed in it has become after several generations of interaction.

It seems to me that Broome is almost like a template of what this country could become, if we're lucky, and if Pauline Hanson and her sympathisers don't get their way—a polyglot, robust place where the racial mix merely adds spice and zest rather than unease and distrust.

Developing an eye

Up north we've been slowly 'developing an eye' for Aboriginal art. But there's more to it; it's about learning a language, gaining access to a work by trying to understand its protocols and conventions.

We're also learning about how many forms of Aboriginal art there are. Until recently I'd only really registered two—the acrylic dot painting of Central Australia and the 'X-ray' bark paintings of Arnhemland. In Broome we've found quite different, confronting riches: the spare lines and sombre ochres of the Warmun painters, the anarchic 'childlike' works on paper by the women at Fitzroy, the boldly schematic, brilliantly coloured works from Balgo and the strange ET-like figures that come from Mowanjum.

At first we fell in love with the restrained, elegant work from Warmun. Many Warmun artists such as Rover Thomas, Queenie McKenzie and Jack Britten have long been famous. Their paintings are easy for a Western eye— minimalist in line, using two or three earthy tones. They also seem deceptively easy to understand, especially once you grasp the topographical approach of much Aboriginal art. But their meanings are often encoded, and go beyond the explanation handed out

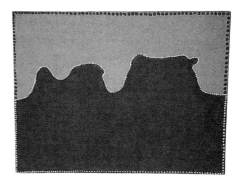

on the official sheets. *Mussel Dreaming*, for example, which we bought during NAIDOC Week, is a very simple painting—a field of ochre yellow, a field of ochre brown, bisected by a wavy white-dotted line. But one dotted hump in the wavy line turns out to be a headland that was the site of a massacre. No amount of looking would have yielded me that knowledge, but it might well have been seen as a matter of course by the painter's fellow countrymen.

It's still easy to forget that each person can only paint the stories of their own country and that they have no right to paint another's. I forgot it when we were watching Jimmy Pike sitting cross-legged on his verandah in Dora Street, doing an elegant dot painting of caramel on a sage green ground.

'Somewhere at Fitzroy?' I asked (Jimmy had just come back from a long visit to relatives there).

'Naah, waterhole in the Great Sandy Desert,' he mumbled.

And only later did I realise that of course he was painting the Great Sandy Desert, because that is his country, where he grew up. And even though Jimmy is a world-renowned artist who has done all kinds of work, including fabric design and illustrations for his wife's books, his inspiration always comes from his own country.

The paintings from Balgo, that settlement remote even from its nearest remote town, Halls Creek, came as a shock to us. At Balgo, many different tribes have been thrown together under difficult conditions. There are drug and alcohol problems, especially with the young. The last of the Jesuits are pulling out of the mission, leaving a spiritual manpower vacuum. Yet out of Balgo is coming an outpouring of vivid, bold, instantly identifiable paintings. Every month the co-ordinator hands out the canvases. The dogs piss on the corners, kids, rain and dust may mess up the paint-work, but month after month the work keeps being produced. Here, too, the names are being made—Helicopter, who rarely uses his second name; Lucy Yukenbarri; and Eubena Nampitijin, who won this year's top Aboriginal art prize in Darwin.

At first we didn't know what to make of the Balgo paintings—the near-psychedelic surfaces that are both intricately designed and a mess of bright orange, blue and red in confronting proximity. But gradually we 'developed an eye'. We looked and looked, then fell in love. Having bought one painting, we bought two more. And we can't stop looking at them.

The Wandjina art from Mowanjum, not far from Derby, remains a mystery to me. Many whites love this stuff, I suspect because it's so 'exotic' but still identifiably figurative. The round-headed, earless figures do exert a fascination, but with them my eye remains obstinately untrained. The figures look monotonous, done to a formula. But I'm open to the possibil-ity that one day I'll learn to look at them differently, that a door will swing open and I'll be able to see something I've never seen before.

*

Saturday, November 28

Back in Broome! The first thing you notice is the body's reaction, and how powerfully it affects the mind. Confronted with a damp wall of impene-trable heat, the body is instantly out of choices—slow down or suffer. And so the mind begins to calm as well. It's still observing and processing, but in a leisurely, automatic way as the body pulls itself slowly through the day.

At night, as if to welcome us back, the first soft heavy drops of rain, a few at first, gathering force briefly, then dripping away to nothing. In the middle of the night, a long and steady rain. Nothing spectacular but enough to give the earth a drink. At 3 a.m. I woke and turned the air-conditioning off so I could listen to the rain on the tin roof, and went back to sleep, content to be back.

It's strange, the quiet contentment of being back. Different from the ambivalent excitements of being home. As my mother said on the phone, sensing my surprised happiness at being here again, 'It's like a second home now,' and in a way it is.

Bruce was at the airport to greet us with our car keys and an invitation to a drink. He was flying out on the plane that flew us in. We sat down in the little courtyard where passengers and hangers-on congregate. Tinselly paper was tied around the wooden posts as a concession to the oncoming Christmas season.

The big news while we were away: a meeting on the proposed development of Gantheaume Point. Over three hundred people, with just about everyone opposed to the proposal. When it was announced that the meeting had been convened by the three Aboriginal councillors, Hunter, Sibosado and Foy, the applause and cheering lasted three minutes. The other councillors were there, too, but they sat mum. Mary Tarran spoke. She was against the proposal generally, but conceded that the racecourse site itself had no particular significance. Later, when Cissy Djiagween got up, she seemed to contradict her daughter, saying that there *were* stories around that site.

We're looking forward to other versions and snippets.

We got into our aqua-blue Rav and drove home through somnolent streets. No sign of the much-vaunted Mango Festival we'd hurried back for, except a couple of blackboard signs with a scrawled 'To the Mango Tasting'. We had no dogs with us and we were talking about how we were going to miss them. When we got to Guy Street, I got out of the car to open the gates and saw Anne gesticulating frantically at something behind me. I turned to see a puppy standing in the driveway, with a where-have-you-been-I've-been-waiting-for-you expression on his face. We fell instantly in love. He belongs to the neighbours but they don't seem to care about him. He spends ninety per cent of his time at our place. He's called Boy, he's as cute as a button and much brighter. Black and white with a white blaze on his face, a white chest and large paws.

This morning we woke without the alarm at six. The air was still damp and coolish. By seven-thirty we were walking to Town Beach for breakfast, amazed that we could do it without sweating. Broome was putting its best foot forward. The streets were quiet—only the occasional tourist now—but Town Beach café was doing brisk business in lattes and waffles and scrambled eggs.

We saw Wendy Albert from the bookshop. She seemed cheerful and relaxed, brown eyes friendly. 'You're back! For the Wet?'

Yes, the Gantheaume Point meeting was big, she confirmed. Sos Johnson, the former Shire President, is calling the Turf Club crowd communists because they don't want the racecourse moved. According to Wendy, he classes anyone a communist who opposes him. 'I'd be happy to start up a branch of the Communist Party here,' she said, grinning slyly, 'and I'd have quite a few takers. After all, the Kuomintang had its headquarters in Sheba Lane in 1922. So what's new?'

She ambled off down Town Beach, dressed in rather tatty long white shorts.

*

Reading Proust in Broome is peculiarly apt; the time it takes, the way you must slow down for the detail to get the essence. When I was at home I had to lay Proust aside. But this place forces one into a greater awareness of the senses, and a greater enjoyment of them. And what else does Proust do, par excellence, but anatomise the sensual and the sensuous? I'm full of awed admiration, fascinated, but then, just as with the heat, every third hour, so with every third page, I get impatient, and say, enough, ugh! Like too rich, too much chocolate. But a few minutes later I'm beguiled again by the layered sophistication of his language.

Mango medley

Sunday, and the Mango Harvest Ecumenical Service is being conducted in the courthouse grounds, under the giant tamarind tree. I see Jimmy Chi at the back of the small congregation. Jimmy is a believer and many of his songs have a religious theme...*Fill me with love my Lord/ That flows from thee/ Heal me O risen Lord, lay healing on me...*

He joins in with a couple of the songs but he can't stand still; his movements are jerky, his eyes dart about. No-one takes the slightest notice of him—he's just a local come out for the service. I wonder, from his restlessness, if he's going through a bad patch.

Then it's on to Matso's for 'Mango Medley and Other Fruity Poems'. This is now the fourth poetry event since Perpetua instigated a National Poetry Day do in September. The mango theme has inspired the local poets, and there is some good stuff. Others have gone to their poetry books to find fruity poems—Robert Graves, Phillip Salom, *The Song of Solomon*.

Nolan Hunter arrives late, looking handsome in a dark singlet. He's embarrassed about reading his 'Bloody Mangoes' poem, but then reads it with great verve. He wins Most Popular Poem.

We've booked for the *Matso's Dinner with a Mango Theme* afterwards. It's a hot sticky night, even though Matso's large central room has all doors open to the verandah and the fans going. We sit down with Lyn and her friend Jeanie, who is still staying at Lyn's place. Without thinking, I ask Lyn about the Gantheaume Point meeting. Well, it was *not* the right question. She begins to rant about how emotion-ridden it was, how people didn't know what they were talking about, that they didn't seem to realise that the development was a State Government initiative, nothing to do with Shire. That the Government was just calling for expressions of interest at this stage; it was premature, selfish, childish for people to start making demands now.

A raging argument begins, Lyn gesticulating and aggressive. When Anne says that the council has a responsibility to listen to the concerns of electors, Lyn calls her 'idealistic'.

Anne retorts, 'It's not a matter of ideals but of principles. If you pretend to represent people...'

'I do represent people!' Lyn is starting to shout. 'I'm sick of being told I don't represent people.'

'Then you have a responsibility to listen to them. That's what representative government is about.' Anne is starting to shout, too.

'Oh you're just one of those greenies,' Lyn says.

'Don't try and lump me in with them,' Anne says, 'There's something in the view that the extreme end of the greens are really the new conservatives.'

'You can't turn things back to how they were,' Lyn says, half-conciliatory.

We try talking of other things. But ten minutes later it's Lyn and Jeanie at each others' throats. Lyn suddenly jumps from her chair. 'I've had enough of you, Jeanie!' she cries, and stalks out of the restaurant.

After a couple of minutes I go out after her. She's in her car, fumbling for her cigarettes and crying. 'It's ten years since Lyn Page has cried,' she says, wiping the tears away. 'You won't see me crying too often.' Out pour incoherent words about how difficult Jeanie has been, and how depressed she's been after the Gantheaume Point meeting. 'They just won't see how conservation and development can go hand in hand; they're just ignorant of the processes, so selfish...so selfish...I've just got to look after Lyn Page for a change...I've had enough of this town, I've got to get out.'

I point out that her distress is as much to do with the tension and uncertainty over the Shire Directory. Anne comes out and says she's sorry, she didn't realise how stressed Lyn was. But Lyn's not really listening.

'Go to bed,' we say. 'Have a good sleep.'

She blows her nose again, gives a watery smile and drives off.

A busy morning at the courthouse

Gordon is looking pale and a bit more portly but otherwise well. 'Aah, you're back!' he grins at me. 'I was beginning to wonder whether you'd chickened out.' I give him a kiss. He asks after our new calves back home. He has an extraordinary memory for a man who drinks so much.

In the courthouse grounds there are lots of people, mostly Aboriginal, standing around in small groups or alone in the shade. 'There's hundreds out there!' I say, and he shakes his head ruefully. 'I know, and it'll be like this all week.' But he's looking relaxed and alert, as if anticipating having a good time.

How's Damien? The domestic dramas continue. He recounts how the other day he brought his own troubles into the courtroom, to the magistrate's disgust. 'This sort of thing happens all the time, sir, in heated moments,' Gordy said, referring to an assault charge. 'A lover's tiff. Why, only last week I had a full can of beer thrown at my head and Damien—'

'Yes yes, Mr Bauman, that'll do,' said the magistrate. 'We know all about that.'

One night Gordy and Damien had a domestic in the taxi home. 'I'm getting out of the taxi in front of the restaurant below my place, you know, Sheba Lane. I've got my back to the street and I'm yelling at him, "You just sit on your arse all day while I work my butt off!" and then I turn around and this hush has fallen over all the patrons! So I just bolted upstairs.'

I see Angela in court and we arrange to have lunch together.

Angela's adjective for the Gantheaume Point meeting is 'hilarious'. Why? Because it was so partisan; the white councillors determined to say nothing and push it all onto the State Government, the rest of the meeting so passionately opposed to the development. One man abused Angus Murray, accusing him of getting some sort of kickback out of it all, and a woman read something from Hansard that seemed to implicate Murray. Then a large ponderous old man attacked Angus's attacker. 'I've lived here for over forty years. You know nothing about this place, son! You're full of shit.'

Sounds awfully like Bob.

Jimmy Chi was also at the meeting, saying strange things from time to time. Different people would quietly lead him out of the room, but after a while he'd wander back in.

Wednesday

The ta-ta lizards have grown enormous, now truly 'Gilbert's Dragons'. I saw one this morning, almost upright on its agile back legs, a broad black streak on its otherwise white face. They sprint around at great speed in the heat.

Boy, the puppy, is lying in his favourite cool corner under the dining table. He was in trouble this morning for not getting to the door on time and widdling on the tiles. Just now I took him out and he weed obediently on the grass, then raced back to the door, waiting to be let into the cool. He isn't the least ambivalent about air-conditioning, unlike us.

We decided to brave the lumpen proles next door and ask if we could take Boy for a walk, rather than sneaking around them. It's a mysterious household—the constant comings and goings, the three or four cars at a time parked outside, yet the quiet of the place! Drugs, goes the rumour, hard drugs. Raelene said she didn't mind if we walked Boy and promptly produced a natty little lead, probably never used.

When we got back just before dark we sat outside for a while, watching the thunderstorm approach. An eerie yellow light behind fat black clouds.

Ephemera

The little butterflies that look green or white, depending on the light, are everywhere. Many trees are in spectacular flower—reds, yellows and oranges in fantastic and graceful configurations. The boabs seem to follow an individual path; some flowering, others sporting fresh brightly green leaves. The flowers are big; a creamy white, with feathery long stamens, the petals folded back like Christmas-wrapping rosettes.

It's the same town, but subtly different, too, and changing more each day as the Wet encroaches. No longer the differentiation between the dryish hot days and cooler evenings. Just a lowering constant yearning for rain.

At night, from Gordy's verandah, the lit-up oval is a surreal bright green. The town looks quiet and deserted, yet there are little pockets of activity. All the restaurants have half-a-dozen diners at their pavement tables. As the tourists become fewer, the locals emerge. They are making us feel more welcome. We're being acknowledged as 'stayers', if short-term stayers, so are included more in what is going on.

Gordy's flat is looking positively homey now and he is quite proud of it, in a self-parodying way. There's a decorative quilt on the wall, two pot plants, a print of an old-world map. All quite neat and tidy, if it weren't for the swag with the pink pillows permanently on the floor in front of the telly. That remains Damien's preferred spot.

A The air smells of mangoes after rain. Lying stretched out on the bed after cutting up mangoes, arms above my head for coolness, I go to sleep smelling my mangoey fingers.

How different the style of life is 'back east'. There, homes are nests and havens, particularly in the Highlands where it's often so cold. Curtains and carpets and soft fabrics cosset people from the external world. In Broome there's not a single interior decorating shop. Even people with money don't take so much notice of their homes. The combined depredations of humidity and white ants deter them from buying expensive furniture. Curtains are almost unheard of, probably because they turn red from the dust in the Dry and green from mildew during the Wet.

The life lived here is viewed by people elsewhere as exotic—weird, out of sync with modern life. But the truth is that *this* is normal life. A place where people work, yes, but not so hard as to exhaust themselves; where a large part of the day is spent sociably—talking over coffee, under a tree, on someone's front porch; where people know each other and know what is happening in their area, and talk about it and go to meetings about things that concern them. Or go to the pub with their relatives or fishing with their friends, and where all these things are as important as anything else in life. This sounds like normal to me.

It strikes me that those 'mythical' characteristics of Australianness— informality, friendliness, lack of pretension—do actually exist here. Ironic that these 'Aussie virtues' are so much in evidence in Broome, where white Australia's grip has been least certain.

Catching up

The Gantheaume Point meeting has stirred a lot of people up. But Dave Lavery remains his usual calm, lawyerly self. 'The meeting was good because it showed the strength of the opposition,' he says. He doubts if a proposal for development would get Shire support at the moment.

'I hear Angus copped a lot of abuse at that meeting,' I say.

'Yeah, and maybe that was appropriate, because he has avoided saying what his interests are. He has admitted now that he does have an interest.'

Dave thinks Angus has been trying to get as much as possible through the Shire before the elections in May.

*

Angela had the impression that Rubibi may have done some sort of deal with the Shire. But at the meeting Cissy Djiagween went up to the mike in her quiet, dignified way and said: 'I am the custodian for that land. I am the last one who knows that country. Believe me, it is special country, there are special places there. So listen to me. I know that place. We must protect this land.'

Thunderous applause.

It was noted that Cissy and Mary seemed to be saying different things.

After dropping Susan at the courthouse, I went over to Goolarri to see Mary. At the recent Goolarri annual general meeting, she was nominated as chairperson but she declined. She took the deputy chair's job. There are four men on the new board, including Jimmy Chi, Baamba and Marty Sibosado. 'But it'll be you women who do the work!' Jimmy told her.

Mary was sitting on an old metal chair just inside the shed, talking to a spongy Englishman called Hal.

Marty Sibosado turned up, so I grabbed him for a chat about last week's Gantheaume Point meeting. Marty looked like he needed a shave. He wore his habitual cheerful big grin. He has a very expressive mouth and twists it around a lot as he speaks.

'There were motions moved at the meeting which the Shire elite think they can just ignore. But they can't do that, not under the new Local Government Act. I'll wait and see if they do anything about them—if they don't, I'll force their hand.'

Marty thinks the whole process has been organised so that the Shire can avoid responsibility for what happens to Gantheaume, while facilitating it happening.

When the others had gone, I asked Mary about the meeting. I'd heard that there were differences between her and Cissy, and that Rubibi was going along with the council. She said neither was true. 'People say these things; I don't know where they get it from.'

She gave me a copy of the expression of interest she had lodged on behalf of the culture centre, which said that the culture centre would withdraw if Rubibi decided there should be no development. Her mother wants the racecourse to revert to natural country. Mary spent some time searching through the submission because she thought she had put that in it. But it was not there. She appeared nervous about being even slightly at odds with her mum.

*

'At least the Aborigines get consulted,' Dave Dureau said. 'We white conservationists get ignored.'

Dave had come around to inspect our yard, to see what needed to be cleaned up in case of cyclones—the cyclone season is creeping closer. But for the first hour we didn't get any further than the chairs on the front verandah. Dave was in his standard work gear—long scarlet socks and work boots, an ancient yellow T-shirt with a giraffe on it, long grey hair in a pony tail, a floppy-brimmed hat jammed on top.

He's disgusted with the Shire and the State Government. There's no environmental strategy for Broome, no planning, he said. He wants the whole Gantheaume Point area to stay as it is. He's not impressed with Rubibi, either. 'They're getting what they want and they seem satisfied by that. But what are they getting? Thin strips of land for cultural corridors—which aren't even in place yet. And have you seen where those corridors go? They just follow the roads and easements. Huh, very convenient.'

We finally got up from the verandah and got as far as the tree at the front. Dave stopped. 'Now you know about this tree?' he asked. 'It's a Neem tree, a wonderful tree. Its gum is a natural insect repellent, the potash from it makes a wonderful fertiliser...' and he was away.

Lyn in retreat

It looks like the Shire Directory wars are over, and Lyn is not the victor.

On Sunday evening we walked down to her place with Boy. Greg Powell was there, with his wife Cathy. Lyn was sitting at the table doing paperwork, her reading glasses pushed halfway down her nose. She would look over them from time to time to take part in the conversation. Everyone was relaxed, drinking champagne, although Lyn kept on working throughout.

Eventually Susan asked her what she was doing. She was returning cheques to people who had signed up for her directory, together with a covering letter explaining to clients that she was not going ahead. And there was Greg, the Shire CEO, sitting next to her pretending not to notice, or at least not mentioning it!

Was Greg feeling smug that his prediction had come true—that whoever received the most cheques in the mail would produce the directory? In any case, none of us raised the matter. We all studiously talked of other things. Lyn seemed composed, if slightly subdued.

After Greg and Cathy went home, I asked to see the letter Lyn was sending with the cheques. 'Read it out for Suze,' she said, handing it to me. It was a dignified letter, explaining why she'd decided to leave the field and thanking advertisers for their support.

We ordered fish and chips from Maccas. Lyn went to get it, wearing nothing but a faded black Chanel T-shirt and knickers.

Phyllis and Aunty Bella

Phyllis Bin Bakar and her husband live in a true old Broome house down near the airport—push-out shutters, no glass or flyscreens, most of daily life lived on the verandah. The front door is painted bright yellow and there are wooden floors and a charming French window from the 'inside' room.

I wanted to talk to Phyllis about Aunty Bella. She told me that she was at Bella's bedside when she died, with Sally and Sally's partner Ahmat. The others had gone outside to have a cigarette.

Earlier, Phyllis and Sally had been sitting on the edge of the bed laughing and talking about Aunty Bella and the old days. 'I think she heard us and thought to herself, "they're okay now", and just passed away.'

A few months before she died, when she was still living at Pearlie's, Aunty Bella saw an apparition. 'Our Lady appeared to her. She was getting into bed when she saw a blue cloak coming out of the wall, then a face.' Bishop Chris announced the event in church.

Aunty Bella was nice looking, gentle and honest. 'Quiet, quietly spoken,' says Phyllis. 'A lovely, gentle person. All loving and caring; a saint. She dedicated her life to looking after us. She said many times, "I'll work with the nuns for the sake of God." And other times, "Thank God I never got married."'

Was she happy?

'Yes, she was happy, because she had all of us, see? We'd sit around with her and she'd tuck us into bed and see that we were warm in winter. If we were going out to the movies she'd make sure that we were covered properly.'

The day of the funeral there was an enormous dust storm, a cloud like heavy rain coming. It reappeared the day of the big Stolen Children's meeting at Halls Creek.

'That was a sad meeting,' Phyllis says. 'A woman from the language centre, she got up and she said, "Before I say anything I want to welcome all my sisters. It's good to see you all, we're all one big family." That brought tears to all our eyes. She was one of the girls from the orphanage.'

As she speaks, Phyllis smooths the white tablecloth with big yellow flowers on it, passing her hand slowly over the cloth time and again.

I ask her about the Stolen Generation, what should happen now.

She says, 'I don't know what the Government will do.' Then, suddenly feisty, 'We're not animals and we should be recognised. I mean, this is our country. It's not for us; we'd like to help our children, too, for their future. The others got compensation from the British Government...

'There were bad times here, too, on the pearling luggers. They used to chain people up. People say it didn't happen, white people, but it happened. They were just shootin' them like animals, like flies. There are so many bodies, all around the Kimberley, there in caves. Those old people can show you. It's not just a story. It happened.'

the Wet

Eighteen

*Lyn's party—A barbecue at Town Beach—Stayers—
'A Pearl named Desire'—Cyclone season—One million
dollars worth of pearls—Thelma watch*

We hear that Bishop Chris is a good cook. He's invited us to dinner before he leaves for the Synod of Oceania bishops in Rome. We arrive at seven but dinner is still some way off. He's had 'a bugger of a day', he says, and is running behind. But there's a bottle of wine open and a dish of oil with a drizzle of balsamic, and a stack of fresh bread beside it. So we sit and dunk bread in oil and talk to him while he cooks.

He's looking forward to Rome—he's just received a list of instructions as to what he is and is not to wear. He tells us about a favourite little restaurant that he's hoping to get back to; it's there he picked up the oil and balsamic idea.

We're having fish for dinner, and pasta and sauce. Finally the fish goes into the oven. He sits down and talks and smokes a couple of cigarettes while the fish is cooking. We're all getting peckish so we guzzle the bread and oil, and wine. About twenty minutes later there's a loud 'Crack!' from the oven. The dish with the fish in it has broken. He's upset—the dish was given to him by his parents on his ordination. We have to wait till the oven cools enough to remove it, then I help him transfer the fish to another dish, then back into the oven. It's well after nine by now. We open another bottle.

I go for a walk in the garden. There's a lovely big old lemon tree in the centre and the controversial fence has bougainvillea growing over it, giving the whole place the feel of a walled garden.

Back inside, dinner is almost ready. We're all getting a bit tired and pissy by now. Chris shows us through to the dining room. The table is covered in a lace tablecloth and there's a bowl of carved boab nuts in the centre. The housekeeper has set three cups and saucers at one end for after-dinner coffee.

Chris brings in the bolognese sauce. Then disaster. The bowl is very hot and as he picks it up with a cloth to move it to the centre of the table it flies out of his hands. Bolognese sauce everywhere! It misses Susan and me but gets just about everything else, including Chris's hand.

'Get it under water!' we yell.

He's dashing out to the kitchen but careers to a halt in the doorway to say a hasty grace so we can begin eating, then runs to the tap. We clean up a bit. When he comes back we sit and eat amongst the splodges. The food is delicious.

On the dining room wall there's a rather good drawing of an elderly Aboriginal man from Kalumburu, who Chris says was described to him as one of the last of the cannibals. 'A great old chap. He took to his wife with an axe once. Yet they were inseparable. He cried when she was taken away to hospital.'

The old chap had prodigious eating habits, it seems. Chris once gave him three fruit bats he'd just shot. The old man sat down there and then and ate the lot. Another time he found a consignment of bully beef and methodically ate his way through it until all the cans were gone. He couldn't move for five days afterwards.

'We baptised him not long before he died,' Chris says.

'You got him in the end,' I say.

He grins a bit uncertainly. 'That's a cynical way of putting it, but I suppose that's right.'

A couple of young men from Kalumburu are staying in the house. Chris has sent them out for chicken and chips, 'because they wouldn't feel comfortable'. When they come in, he formally introduces them. They are terse with him and he with them, yet they clearly feel easy making demands on him. He deals with them with a mixture of paternal gruffness and helpless acquiescence.

'Blankets!' calls out one of the young men, and Chris goes obediently to find them. Then they wander upstairs to watch boxing videos.

It turns out that one of the young men, Magnum, is Chris's 'brother'. When Chris was a priest at Kalumburu, he used to go fishing with Magnum's older brothers, and was made one of them. Once you've been around a while in an Aboriginal community and are accepted, you have to be 'related' to someone to fit into the kinship scheme.

It's getting late. Chris lights our way out, walking with us to the footpath. He farewells us cheerily, calling to us through the darkness: 'God Bless. Happy Christmas, so to speak.' We won't see him again till January.

Broome's particular atmosphere is still rooted in its deeply-felt Catholicism. As Bishop Chris said last night of Broome's indigenous Catholics, 'They mightn't be strong on practice, but they're still Catholic to their bootstraps.'

Those who are not part of the Catholic tradition feel themselves to be in some ways outsiders. Vanessa, for instance, feels excluded from a certain elite. 'My mother always believed that between the Government and the Catholics, they worked hand in hand to undermine the Aboriginal people...We have our own cultural beliefs and spirituality, and the Catholics are still coming down and saying, "Here is God".'

Many of the town's elite, the offspring of mission-trained mothers, are ambivalent about the Church. They may practise infrequently or have lost their belief altogether, but the Church is interwoven with their lives and with the fabric of Broome.

I remarked on this to Baamba once. 'None of you are really bitter about the Catholics,' I said.

'Peter Yu is,' he replied.

But not really, not once you get Peter going on the subject. He might be more outspoken than most, particularly about the cruelties of the far-away boarding school in Perth, but he acknowledges Bishop Chris's record on native title issues. And his kids are still getting a Catholic education.

Sarah Yu says that Chris is a bit of an autocrat. When he was at Lombadina no-one was allowed to go in there without his specific permission. Yet Sarah likes the rituals of the Church. All her children have been christened. 'Church ceremonial has a unifying effect,' she says. 'Beagle Bay is a wild community but when there's a feast day they're all there, weaving their garlands, making it beautiful. The church is full on those days. It's really something. They might be bad Catholics but they're Catholics.'

Lyn's Party

At Lyn's, the louvred shutters around the living room are pushed right back to catch the slightest breeze and the fans are going full tilt. But it's still so hot that the guests stand under the fans to cool the sweat from their faces. Tony Hutchinson's girlfriend tells me that all the break-ups, rows, bashings and flights from town always happen in November and December when the weather gets to people.

Just about everyone at Lyn's party is white, middle-class and nouveau. Business types, a few professionals. The only non-whites are Beverley Kinney and her sister Corrie, and Shama of course.

Beverley, herself hardly an enemy of commerce, claims that Lyn and Sos Johnston are largely responsible for the suburbanisation of Broome because they both pushed hard for the huge Paspaley and Boulevard shopping centres, which have completely changed the character of the town. But the real death knell of old Broome, according to Bev, was the first beauty parlour. Up till then women had to live with the stripping away effect that Broome has. They didn't bother with hairdos and make-up—make-up just runs in the Wet, and hair turns lank or frizzy.

Bev is looking spunky in a little rust-red shot-silk dress and black evening shoes. No make-up.

A barbecue at Town Beach

Down at Town Beach there was a send-off for a young English anthropologist who's been working with the KLC. A gathering of not much more than a dozen people, among them the cream of indigenous Broome: Baamba, Nolan Hunter, Mary, Kevin, Marty Sibosado, Maxine Chi.

'Hello, brother,' Mary said softly to Kevin as he came up, and chucked him gently under the chin.

Mary is pleased about the article Annie has written on the culture centre. She wants to keep in touch when we leave for home. I thought she was going to say something affectionate, but instead she said, 'It will be good to have a journalist I can trust over in the eastern states', (which doesn't necessarily preclude the affection). That's what I like about Mary. She uses people in such a straightforward way that it's impossible to take offence.

It was a gentle, easy night. People picked at the generous salads (it was 'bring a plate'), chatted and sang. We talked a bit about cyclones. There's a couple hovering off the coast. It's a long time since a cyclone came really dangerously close to Broome—something to do with it being on a peninsula.

We teased Baamba about joining the Chamber of Commerce. He said he'd done it to heighten the profile of Baamba's Chinatown Tours.

Marty, Nolan and Baamba took it in turns to play the guitar while Baamba sang; mostly seventies hits. Baamba had brought Uncle Kiddo along. He's a thin, white-haired, white-bearded old fellow who plays a wild piercing harmonica. He had three harmonicas in different keys in his shirt pocket and kept switching between them. 'He's the boss man of the harmonica,' Baamba said, beaming at him. 'He's been dying for me to get home from the *Corrugation Road* tour so he could go to a party!'

Uncle Kiddo was lapping up the attention. He couldn't make up his mind what he wanted to do more: talk, drink, smoke or play. 'My dad was from Trinidad, my mother was a half-cast Chinese-Aboriginal,' he said. 'I don't know what to call myself, so if anyone asks me I say, "I'm just an old Australian Abo!"'

Everyone laughed and it set off a string of jokes. Baamba's joke: 'Why is it certain that Adam was a white man?' Answer: 'Because if he'd been black he would have eaten that snake!'

Kevin told a 'Jacky Jacky' joke, slipping perfectly into the Broome dialect they all grew up with. The joke was an affectionate self send-up—but there was an edge of anger, too, about a colonialism that is by no means dead.

Mary told another 'Jacky Jacky' joke about Jacky catching a white man with his missus. Jacky shoots the white man dead. At his trial the judge asks Jacky, 'Would you say you shot him in self-defence?'

'Naah, boss,' says Jacky, 'I shot him before the fence!'

Stayers

Yesterday we looked for Christmas presents at the courthouse markets and got some more local honey. 'Kimberley Gold' was the bulk honey this week.

The markets have shrunk. All the crappy tourist stalls have gone, but the regulars were still there: Roy the Lantern Man, and Angela the potter, valiantly manning her marvellous stall, even though she was pink and damp from the heat, strands of hair sticking to her fair face. There was food in abundance. (I don't know how Peter Ghouse can cook hot dishes in this steam-bath weather!)

We're thinking about buying another lantern from Roy—a big one with reeds and bird shapes made from the distinctive parrot bush worked into the paper. Roy was in full selling mode. Only one-seventy-five for us, he said.

Lots of people are starting to head south for holidays. It seems to be the thing here, particularly for school teachers or families with children. It's meant to keep them sane, give them a break from the Wet. I thought of the little Turkish guy I'd seen at the Nippon the other night, wandering around, beer in his hand, sweating profusely, muttering, 'I've been here too long.'

Roy, too, is thinking of leaving, maybe heading east to Port Douglas. 'Seven years, I think it's enough, don't you?' he said, as if giving oneself to Broome for a longish stint merits a special badge of courage. We too are getting nods of approval for our paltry little effort of staying on for the Wet. Talking to the artist Kerry Stokes last night, she said, 'If you stay on in the quiet time, you get the real story.'

'A Pearl Named Desire'

There was play on at Matso's last night, a take-off of Tennessee Williams transposed to Broome. It worked surprisingly well. Kerry Stokes was directing it and she was on lights as well.

Kerry was elated because she'd sold a painting that day at the Pearlers' Row Gallery. She was wearing one of those gauzy black little outfits in which she always manages to look both classy and vampish. She'd clearly had a drink or two, which made her rather cavalier with the lighting. She disappeared for minutes at a time; at one point one of the actors switched on a stagelight in vain.

Just about everyone in the audience seemed to be pissed. There were a couple of women on their own. One young woman wept through much of the first act, for reasons not directly due to the play, I suspect. It was Broome in a state of undress that night, as if it didn't have to put on a good face for visitors any more.

Jimmy Chi was there, and in the second act he leapt into the action with a few bars of an old Slim Dusty number: 'No matter the wrong that's done, you'll always be your mother's son.' He told us later that the tragedy of the main character was that he drank because of all the things he couldn't handle in his life. That was very true to life, something he could relate to, although he himself doesn't drink.

A drunken woman passing us on the verandah lunged at Jimmy and grabbed his arm. He reacted instantly and violently.

'Get off me, you're not my boss! You have no right to do that, you're not my boss.' She tried to placate him, but he was riled. 'Excuse me,' he said to us, and disappeared into the bar. As we left, we heard him loudly singing the Slim Dusty song.

*

Perpetua has just returned from a whirlwind trip overseas, part spent in London organising an exhibition of her mother's recent Burrup paintings.

On our verandah she and Lyn discuss the Shire Directory. In that hesitant yet forthright manner of hers, Perpetua tells Lyn that having to decide between rival directories had put her in an impossible position. So she didn't send Lyn a cheque, but she didn't send one to her rival either.

Lyn says Ian Moore is still slandering and threatening her and getting off scot-free. She's convinced that Moore is associated with the Coffin Cheaters. She is consulting solicitors in Perth.

Perpetua is eager to know who the solicitors are. She's reassured when they are a familiar 'top' firm.

Cyclone season

It's years since Broome had a direct hit from a cyclone but they often swirl past in the vicinity, bringing wind and rain. December is usually the worst month for them. The Shire has already done its yearly pre-cyclone clean-up, urging everyone to throw out any rubbish around their yards, anything that could become a flying object in high winds.

These days the town gets plenty of warning if there's a cyclone approaching, but in the early pearling days the only warning people had was if the barometer started falling alarmingly. And in any case, there wasn't much they could do. The small luggers might seek shelter up a creek and the bigger boats could try heading out to sea to ride the worst of it out. Sometimes they survived, sometimes they didn't. There was a string of bad cyclones in the early 1900s. Dozens and dozens of boats and hundreds of lives lost.

Often the cyclones skirt the town to the north and west; sometimes they cross the coast further north, sometimes further south. Even though the pre-cyclone clean-up is an annual ritual, no-one actually talks about the odds of a cyclone crossing the coast right here. But perhaps the threat of cyclones is one reason for the air of impermanence in this town.

At the markets this morning we ran into Alison Lawrence, plump and cheerful in a sleeveless dress and big hat. School finishes this week and a day later she'll be leaving town. 'In sixteen years of living here I've never spent Christmas or New Year in Broome.' The Department of Education 'virtually pays us to get out of town', which she thinks is a good idea. She needs the break away from the pressures of small town life.

Alison had intended going to Karratha for an electorate council meeting today but it was cancelled because Cyclone Billy was heading that way. Billy has now been downgraded to Category One, but the weather bureau is predicting more cyclones before Christmas.

There were motorbikes everywhere at the markets—everything from innocent little numbers with dad and the kids to monster bikes with gang members in leathers, shaved heads and beards. It was the annual pre-Christmas Toy Run and the 'outlawed bikie gangs' were doing their bit for the community.

We bought some vegies and a five-dollar bunch of haliconias—long stems, spiky pink, orange and yellow petals—and afterwards went into town to have a coffee. Lyn and Jeanie joined us at Blooms. Lyn's ex-husband, Carl, was at another table, talking to Shama's boyfriend and Ralton Benn, the good-looking young Aboriginal guy who was Kevin's offsider during Shinju. Ralton is now working for Carl on promoting Eco Beach. Cross-connections! The town has so shrunk that everywhere you go you run into friends.

When we came out of Blooms it was teeming with rain, a real monsoonal downpour. As if the Almighty had upended a giant bucket of water on the town. None of the buildings in Broome have gutters, and after seeing the way it rains here I understand why—they would overflow in seconds. Instead, the water falls straight to the ground and disappears into the pindan. Half an hour later, the sun out again, the pindan looks almost dry.

With the Wet upon us, the dry season is like a distant paradise of calm days and perfect nights. There were virtually no insects in the Dry. You could sit outside at night with a light burning and not a single moth or bug would be caught within its glare. Now that is changing and I am reminded of my various fears about life in the tropics—scorpions, mosquitoes and other nasties. But so far the only problem insects have been sandflies—the dreaded 'midges', which rise from the shores of the bay in invisible hordes, flushed from the sand by incoming spring tides.

Last night we watched the sunset from the point at Town Beach. The sun was setting almost behind the new jetty—south-west. I said how odd it was to see the sun in the south. You looked at me blankly. The points of the compass are a mystery to you.

Since we've been back I've noticed that the sun shines into our south-facing kitchen. It makes me feel upside down; as if we are not in Australia at all.

*

For months now I've been talking to Mary about trying to raise the profile of the culture centre by getting a feature article in the *Advertiser*. She finally agreed, as long as I wrote it. So I did it and it was published yesterday. I've never before written a newspaper piece basically as publicity for someone I know. But here I have no qualms about it. Rules that I would be strict about 'down south' don't seem relevant here; objectivity looks like indifference.

'People here still have story, history,' Mary said. 'They experienced Broome being built, people taken away. We've all been down that track. Nobody should be blamed for their past.'

She said her younger children are proud of their Aboriginality. It makes her smile. Her children have had so many different influences, which is good in its way, but she wants them to also have their culture and their language.

'Why shouldn't they be able to have a glass of wine around a dinner table and still speak their own language? Other people do.'

We were out at Minyirr and Mary was fishing among rocks just north of the point. The tide was right out and she found some good oysters for us, knocking them off with a rock. As we were leaving the beach along the narrow track that joins Gubinge Road, she asked me to stop the car so she could check out some bush tucker.

'That tree there—should be just about ready.' It was a low spreading tree with largish leaves and small green fruit—the Gubinge fruit that gave the road its name. She got out to pick a few. 'Not quite ready,' she said when she came back. 'Needs another bit of rain.'

One million dollars worth of pearls

Five men who have been charged with stealing pearls are up in court this week. They are all locals. Two of them, Charles Connolly and William Pike, look like they might be divers.

There is a handsome Maori woman in the public gallery. She keeps her eyes on Connolly. She is carrying expensive sunglasses and has red-painted toenails.

Pike and Connolly are first up in court, holding rolled-up copies of 'Application for Legal Representation' in their hands.

The charge is that on the 1st and 30th of March they stole 1700 pearls worth $500 000 from Broome Pearls up in Yampi Sound. More charges may be laid because more than one million dollars worth of pearls are said to have been stolen.

Bev Kinney had pearls stolen from her farm around the same time.

Each of the defendants is bailed for $50 000 with $50 000 surety. They have to surrender their passports and report to Broome police on Mondays, Wednesdays and Fridays.

Peter Bibby is there observing, too, and sitting next to me. He leans his body slightly in my direction and says quietly, 'The bench and the dock are like mini-fortresses, confronting each other.' His pale blue eyes hold mine. 'It's the place where battle begins, where confrontation begins. Also curiosity, jealousy, dishonesty.'

*

The quiet of the streets in the evenings now, the air like warm silk against my skin. The screech of cicadas, so loud it's like the high-pitched zinging from power lines, only more intense. The poinciana tree in our yard is flowering at last—big bunches of orange flowers and fresh green leaves.

We're keeping an eye on Cyclone Thelma. So is the national media— it's near Darwin. Everyone is remembering Cyclone Tracy. Gordon was in Darwin during Tracy and has horrific stories.

Cyclone Thelma is moving south-west. Category Four at the moment. Cyclone Billy passed by at the weekend and weakened over the Pilbara. Brought us rain, though.

Wednesday

This morning has been occupied largely by following developments with Cyclone Thelma and checking our preparations. Darwin has escaped this time but now the cyclone is threatening the Tiwi Islands. Gordy is worried; his wife and three kids are there. Kevin says that if one wanted to get away from the cyclone as it approached Broome, it would be best to go north rather than south, for reasons I can't quite fathom.

Thelma is moving very slowly but is heading straight for us. At its current pace it will not reach us for at least another two or three days.

We're trying to listen to the cyclone updates, which are on the radio every three hours at a quarter past the hour.

Thelma watch

Thursday

The last couple of days it's been nothing but Cyclone Thelma. It's been upgraded to Category Five—the worst for over a century.

It is driving south, coming closer and closer to places that a few months ago were tiny marks on a map, never heard of. Now we know these places. We've visited them, or know people born and raised in them. That's why we can't leave, despite the urgings of our friends over east. In some small way we belong here now and can't contemplate deserting.

Kalumburu, the most far-flung community in the bishop's diocese, is threatened. People are gathering for shelter at the school and the mission. They're being lashed by strong winds and rain. If Thelma maintains the same course, Derby will be threatened next—that unfortunate town so poorly situated on the mudflats of King Sound, with the biggest tides in the world. Today Cape Leveque and Lombadina are being evacuated down to Broome. Several buses have been commandeered; some six hundred people are to be moved. Cape Leveque has a small Aboriginal community, plus an award-winning resort, Kooljaman, which the community owns. It's a small unpretentious place in an idyllic setting.

We saw Lombadina and Beagle Bay with the bishop. How will their two very different but lovely churches fare? Everyone is being urged to evacuate but we've heard that some of the old people refuse to leave, so others are staying on with them. Those who are leaving are being housed in a 'designated place' in Broome. It won't be announced where the Broome population is to find shelter until a Yellow Alert.

There are three graduated alerts—Blue, Yellow and Red, each with their own protocols. At this stage the radio is broadcasting updates every three hours. When it comes to Red Alert, broadcasts will be continuous.

We are working through things that need to be done: check our food, stash a bottle of scotch in the food box, put the outside chairs and tables away, take down the hanging baskets. Roy the Lantern Man will be coming to help us take the UV sails down from the carport and back terrace. They would be torn to shreds in the wind. He'll also help us move the pile of fence posts to a safer place in the covered greenhouse.

If the cyclone hits, Lyn and Jeanie propose to see it out under Lyn's big heavy dining room table with plenty of grog. Because of her house's open-plan no-glass design, Lyn reckons it would survive a cyclone better than most. God knows how our low-roofed little house, basically just a renovated tin shed, would fare.

No-one is quite sure whether the town will survive a Category Five cyclone. The more recent buildings in Broome are rated only to Category Four.

Thursday night

A blue alert is declared in the early evening. We're storing everything that's outside and listening obsessively to the three-hourly bulletins.

George Manning, the local ABC man, was telling the afternoon host of the State-wide program that in 1910 there was a cyclone that developed in the Arafura Sea in mid-December, same as this one. It came down and crossed the coast south of Broome. George said cheerfully that if it does hit Broome, it will not only wipe out the town but change the landscape forever—a combination of high winds and high tides.

So far no-one seems to be taking this cyclone very seriously. There are some jokes, but on the whole the town seems to be in denial. 'It can't happen to us...'

I start organising some of our papers, putting things in plastic bags.

Perpetua comes around at five-thirty and Lyn and Jeanie call by, too. We all sit on the front verandah drinking wine and discussing what we'll do, where we'll go. Perpetua doesn't want to talk about it. Says we're making her nervous; she hasn't been worrying about it but now she will.

Lyn and Jeanie say they are staying put. Lyn won't leave her dog.

Perpetua asks, 'Well where are the evacuation shelters?'

She's been in Broome ten years and asks this! No-one knows. She says she might go to the Conti. I say it's very low-lying at the Conti—might flood. I suggest the Mangrove because it's higher, but everyone says it's too exposed. Perpetua thinks the Civic Centre might be the place to go. Although it's only got storm shutters for walls, it appears solid.

We worry about our little house. I expect it will flood, it is so low-lying. The houses next door are on a good forty centimetres of land fill.

Our friends Petrea and Wendie ring from home. 'I don't have a good feeling about this,' Petrea the white witch says.

Wendie says, 'I've been through a cyclone in New Guinea. It was only Category Two but it wasn't pretty. Secure the place as best you can and get on a plane to Perth.'

I try to laugh it off. I can't imagine going to Perth. It would be unbearable to not know what was happening here.

But when I go back out to the verandah I say to Susan and Perpetua, 'I don't want to be a panic merchant but I also don't want to be one of those people who say, "It can't happen to me".'

They agree. We discuss decamping to Fitzroy Crossing. 'Some people have already gone,' Perpetua says.

We're about to head down to Chinatown for the town Christmas party. Before we go, I ring the Fitzroy Crossing Lodge and book a room for Saturday and Sunday nights. No-one expects it to get here before Saturday night.

∫ The main street in Chinatown has been closed off for the Christmas party. There is hardly a tourist to be seen. They've all fled because of Thelma—still Category Five, still coming directly at us.

Broome is almost back to being a black town tonight. Kids are running around with balloons, the food stalls—particularly the Thai—are doing good business, and a few traders (fewer than usual) are trying to get some Christmas sales. With Chinatown cordoned off, the main street is one big comfortable promenade.

We run into our friend Angela, who has brought her camera, 'to catch the pre-cyclone panic'. Angela is in her high ironic mode, because there is remarkably little such panic, at least among the crowds out for the night. There is enormous cheeriness and camaraderie, but also a special atmosphere, an eerie apocalyptic edge, as if people are farewelling the place they know and love—just in case.

We catch the tail end of the Christmas carols, then the Pigram Brothers come on. They announce that by negotiation with Sun Pictures the movies will begin late so that the concert can continue till nine o'clock. Their first number is 'Corrugation Road', followed by a melancholy song about a cyclone.

A few countrymen are dancing in front of the stage. Others are standing around or sitting in the gutters, sipping coke and beer and mineral water. Jimmy Chi is on the sidelines, wearing a T-shirt with the Aboriginal flag on the back and a redheaded Hanson lookalike on the front. He's very high, only just in control. He can't wait to get on stage and is organising various mates and co-singers to go with him.

Once on stage, Jimmy is the boss of the show, maniacally directing the action, shouting commentary: 'Broome should be an example to Australia!

This is a multicultural society!' He introduces a religious song, yelling 'black-fellas believe in Christmas too!'

He and Peter Bibby are singing together at one microphone; Baamba and Gavin Pigram at the other, the other Pigrams accompanying. 'We'll do a song for all the people we've lost this year,' Jimmy says.

They sing their hearts out, united in the music. They sing full-throated and full-hearted with the unpretentious musicality that is the hallmark of the Broome sound.

And the songs they sing! All composed here, for and around this little town.

> Just one step closer, don't throw me away
> and carry me back to my town by the bay
> When the darkness is falling at passing of days
> won't you cherish the memory of my town by the bay?

The crowd stills. The unspoken hangs in the air—that this could be our last night together in this beloved place.

When it's over, people crowd around Baamba and Jimmy, kissing and congratulating them. I hug Baamba and say, 'If we die after that, what the hell!'

'Exactly,' he says, beaming.

We join Angela on the terrace in front of Chinatown Music. A motley little group of revellers has assembled around a huge esky packed with drinks, both alcoholic and soft. Baamba is there, and Jimmy, drinking tons of coke and engaging an American woman in feverish conversation.

Susan and Anne at the Christmas party

A guy in a red Santa cap with a mordant sense of humour sings a few impromptu ditties about Thelma. He's not waiting around to die, he says; he's off to Perth tomorrow on the morning plane.

We could stay all night within this peculiar Broome magic, talking and singing in the open air, the usual hierarchies and protocols quite vanished, relaxed, yet with that particular Broome intensity in the air.

Walking back to the car we meet slim black gorgeous Sharon, hanging on the arm of 'the new love of my life', a tall white guy who looks bemused and fascinated by her. They wander off into the dark, their arms around each others' waists.

Friday morning

I walk around to Seaview to see what's going on. The streets are ominously quiet. A car goes past pulling a trailer piled high with enormous branches of bougainvillea. Someone has obviously been doing a frantic last-minute clean-up of their yard. The next sign of cyclone preparations are a man and woman dismantling the big sign advertising The Catalinas for sale.

It's a beautiful day—sunny, hot, a light breeze. The birds are singing in the trees. Nothing to indicate that in twenty-four hours it could all be blown away.

Roy comes around early to help us get down the sails. It's hot work and he's drenched in sweat by the time he's finished. He brings our new cane lantern. It feels so weird to be on the one hand preparing for destruction, and on the other acquiring flimsy possessions. Roy says we should take the paintings down and wrap them in plastic. He saw Lyn in the hardware shop earlier, getting bubble wrap for her paintings.

I go into town to get some rope to tie down the spare wood. The hardware shop is full of people buying rope and masking tape to tape up their windows. Chinatown is busy. A lot of people are in town from the communities. Six hundred have been evacuated from up the peninsula. Most of them travelled in their own vehicles, judging by the traffic on the streets.

A carpenter is fixing sheets of wood over the windows at Hutchinson's Real Estate. Tony has only just moved into the new building and doesn't want his brand new windows broken.

The waitress in Blooms says it's been very quiet today. All the tourists have gone and a lot of local people as well. It's impossible to get on a plane. The lady in the giftware shop near Paspaleys says her son has left town with his three children, heading by car towards Port Hedland, because 'he doesn't want to put the kids through the terror'.

'I used to work at the Seaview supermarket when I first came to Broome,' she says. 'Do you know what people stocked up on most in cyclone season?'

I shake my head.

'Baked beans, sardines and toilet paper.'

Nineteen

*Cyclone Bob—At the Bucknalls—Two days in Derby—
Aboriginal affairs—Mark Bin Bakar's guide to Broome
English—Party hats—Christmas Eve—Christmas Day*

I just listened to the 10.15 a.m. bulletin. An hour ago, without warning, Thelma changed direction and crossed the coast north-east of here. It seems that as soon as a cyclone crosses onto land its intensity starts to decrease. Thelma's been downgraded to Category Four—but that's still Cyclone Tracy strength, still capable of wreaking enormous havoc.

The 1.15 p.m. bulletin. Thelma now down to Category Three. People are starting to breathe more easily. Silly, really. If two weeks ago they'd been told that a Category Three cyclone was coming right at them they would have been panicking. The SES has issued a warning that the situation is still very dangerous, that people shouldn't be complacent.

4.15 p.m. Thelma is down to Category Two and heading in the direction of Fitzroy Crossing. Good thing we didn't go there! In the space of ten hours the winds have decreased from 320 km/h at the centre to 120 km/h. I've just rung the Fitzroy Crossing Lodge and cancelled our booking.

Friday evening

By dinner time she's down to Category One. The danger is over.

I ring Angela. She says she's just started eating her way through her store of cyclone food—tins of tuna and boxes of boiled fruit cake.

Saturday

So habituated have we become to the three-hourly cyclone bulletins that we rush to listen to the 7.15 a.m. report. But it's so abbreviated we almost miss it. The cyclone has dispersed. The announcer says there won't be any more bulletins unless Thelma heads back out to sea and gathers momentum again. We haven't even had any rain out of it yet.

Now that the danger is over, more stories emerge of people leaving town, or having planned to leave. Bev Kinney had the car packed and ready to drive down to Hedland. She'd also booked a seat on flights to Perth on three consecutive days.

The SES has admitted that the present contingency planning is totally inadequate for a Category Five cyclone. But the question on everyone's mind—is there any plan that could properly prepare for something of that force? A 'Broomour' is doing the rounds that when Thelma was threatening, the hospital ordered in eleven hundred body bags.

Sunday

The Anglican church was not looking its best this morning. The back pews were full of paraphernalia stored inside the church for protection from the cyclone. The Very Reverend Raymond Molyneux's sermon was, of course, built around Thelma. Like many other locals, Reverend Molyneux had put off doing his pre-cyclone clean-up until it was almost too late, so he had to join a long long queue of people waiting to dump their rubbish at the tip. Ergo, we mustn't be tardy, we must be ready when our Saviour comes.

At morning tea there was more cyclone talk. There were a couple of semi-joking references to Thelma having been 'prayed away', and indeed this town would have seen more praying than most.

The Very Rev Molyneux, for all his hearty sincerity, is in danger of losing his already small female flock. He is still holding out against the ordination of women. Alison has told him she is not willing to be on the church cleaning roster until he changes his mind. She is a stalwart nonetheless, as she's a stalwart of other institutions around town—the ALP, the museum, the arts generally. And she does it without a skerrick of sanctimoniousness or pretension. There should be a monument to Alisons in small towns.

Everyone asked Alison when she's going south. She'll be driving to Perth in her jaunty little four-wheel-drive Suzuki, much favoured by the single women around town (although Lyn has a burgundy Rocsta, instantly recognisable.) Alison said she might leave this afternoon, but then again, maybe tomorrow. She's having trouble tearing herself away. She's told me more than once that after sixteen years in this town she's yet to have a dull day.

Cyclone Bob

'Naah,' Bob says, 'there was never going to be a cyclone. If anyone had thought for a second, they would have known that cyclones never happen at neap tides.'

One of the blokes sitting on the verandah agrees that it was all a media beat-up. A lot of people left Broome in a panic, and that's never happened before. Still, if the cyclone had hit, Bob concedes, his place would have been badly flooded, and as for the infamous Catalinas next door, they would have been gone for sure.

'What would have happened to the drop-in centre?' I asked, indicating the coterie on the verandah.

'We call it the rehab centre,' one of the young blokes said drily.

Coralie, Bob's daughter, is talking of buying his house. She wants it for her kids, for their future. 'You could still live there, Dad,' she's told him. He's thinking of it, despite the inducements of the magnate next door to sell or go into a development deal with him. Coralie is loyal to him, and he appreciates it.

Bob is looking a lot better. His leg's improved so he won't have to go to Derby for a skin graft.

At the Bucknalls

A birthday party for John Bucknall. A pleasant evening, people spilling between the wide verandah and the large shady back garden full of palms.

The Bucknalls are Labor Party diehards, ex-teachers, pro-Aboriginal activists; gentle, right-thinking people. Yet such is the divide in this community that there was hardly a non-white face at the gathering, apart from the Bucknall's daughter-in-law, Selena, and their neighbour, Bev Kinney.

Not that the Queen of Broome, as some call Bev, has necessarily crossed the line to align herself with the whites. She talks freely about her mother Joyce's rediscovery of her aboriginality since the death of her Chinese husband.

Bev Kinney is well-travelled, sophisticated. She's been to Vietnam, Africa, Europe. She is quite unpredictable in the normal right–left divide. I think she enjoys that. She is very pragmatic about the frequent deaths in the old pearling days. 'People had to die somehow,' she says. She regrets the passing of the pearling luggers. The new industry involves too much bureaucracy, constant battles with the Government over rules and regulations.

Bev likes to run a tight ship on her pearl farm. Nearly all her employees are young blokes. After a stint in her regime, their table manners improve, along with other life skills. She personally ransacks their rooms for drugs. She likes to see them gradually take pride in their rooms, start saving for a TV or a CD player. They get presents for their birthdays—cheap, attractive bedspreads, or other decorative items she buys in Indonesia.

Peter Walsh, Bruce's friend, arrived in a jovial mood, but it wasn't long before the edge came out. I said, jokingly, that no-one yet had taken us fishing. 'And no-one will,' he said, 'while you continue to associate with Perpetua.' He can't forgive her the Burrup business. I reiterated where we stood; that the entry to the Aboriginal art prize was inexcusable, but it didn't help.

Yet many of the real locals are far more forgiving and tolerant than Peter, who didn't grow up in Broome. Maybe the Catholic connection, and the shared sense of history with the Duracks ameliorates the anger.

Monday, December 21

I'm reading *The Forest River Massacre* by Neville Green, in which there's mention of the Duracks' involvement in the savageries of frontier-pushing. The Duracks were no worse than some, and much better than others, but of course they were implicated. Why should Perpetua be trying to whitewash them, with letters to the paper etc?

Lyn says Perpetua's relatives thought she wouldn't last more than a week up here and could never manage a business, that she had to be looked after. She's proved them all very wrong. Perpetua is a lot tougher than she looks.

Chi left town a week ago, out of the blue! She's gone to live with some bloke on a farm near Mudgee or somewhere.

Two days in Derby

After spending a couple of days in Derby on circuit with Gordon, I became almost fond of it. The town is stinking hot, dull, and much of it is unsightly. But there's an openness among people, and a sense of battling life together, keeping a community going. There's a rude honesty to the town. No frills. I'm glad the cyclone passed it by.

As I said to Angela, two and a half days with Gordy can be like two and a half years with anyone else. She knew what I meant...

He picks me up from Guy Street just after 6 a.m. It's a grey morning, already steamy. He stops to get some cash and a flavoured milk, then stops again outside his flat. 'Just got to give Priscilla some money.'

'How much are you giving him?'

'Forty bucks. Not quite enough to keep him for two days.'

On the long straight stretch to Derby the car bears down on two eagles feasting on a dead animal. They won't budge till it's too late and one of them thuds against Gordon's side mirror.

'Fuck,' he says, pointing to the damage to the car. 'But I learned early, you must never swerve when driving in the bush.'

He sounds tough and matter-of-fact, but fifteen minutes later he's still brooding on it: what infinite chance has made him the instrument of the eagle's fate?

We book in at the King Sound Motel, a large ugly red-brick 'resort', then drive the long main street to the courthouse. It's a mean little sixties building with cement squares on one exterior wall. A metal pergola, unpleasantly suggestive of iron bars, leads to the entrance, made of cheap wood and glass. Inside, the police station on the left, the court on the right.

We go down to the cells before court begins. They are small and airless and smell like dog cages. Two guys are sitting on the floor of one, sharing an orange. 'Your case is straightforward,' says Gordy to the younger one, 'but you have to think about how you'll plead.' The young man shrugs, an obtuse look on his face, and bites into his orange.

In the other cell is Peter Djuguna, who is to be tried tomorrow. The young copper on duty warns that Peter is very excitable this morning, resentful at having been locked up for six months awaiting trial, resentful, too, about being forbidden the exercise yard.

'Explain to him,' says the young copper, 'it's nothing to do with him. We had two guys escape last week.'

Gordy is patient, calming. He is like this with all his clients, patient and plain, never patronising. The cops often use him to quieten a situation down. He has a technique passed on to him many years ago: if a black person is becoming aggressive, say nothing and look at the ground and they will almost always back off, because 'they don't like to hurt your feelings. They might think, "I've said something to offend Gordy", and they'll quieten down.'

Gordy tells Peter Djuguna that the six months he's already spent in gaol will count for two years if he's found guilty. Peter gets a smoke off him and a rollie off the cop and begins excitedly to tell his version of events. Gordy says, 'This is your chance to tell your story in the witness box, but you have to stay calm.'

The young prosecutor from Perth arrives. He is tall and handsome in a pale namby-pamby way. He carries his files in a series of clear plastic folders. 'He looks thirteen,' Gordy says gloomily.

The court is ready for the day's work. Mostly guilty pleas. It's all a sad little farce: the judge seems soft-hearted and unconvinced of the efficacy of prison, the sympathies of the young prosecutor from Perth are clearly not with long prison sentences, and Gordy is being paid to keep 'em out of gaol. But then there are the requirements of the law. The judge keeps saying, 'What a waste and pity, a young man who's only nineteen. What's the minimum I can do?' and the two lawyers play along, although the prosecutor makes token attempts to be more severe. And yet the sentences keep rolling out, meaningless and unproductive.

'A few family problems, sir,' says Gordy in defence of one young man.

'That seems to be a Kimberley feature,' says the judge plaintively.

'Derby is always a highlight of the circuit, sir,' says Gordy with a sly grin.

Gordy and I are both weary and jumpy by the lunch break. Back in the car and down the broad, somnolent main street. At the motel we eat one 'barra burger' between us. We get into the habit over the two days of me ordering a meal and he eating half of it. He dreads getting fat; he's put on half a stone in the past two months.

In the vast motel dining room the judge, his associate and the usher are eating together at the next table; the judge in shorts and a discreetly Hawaiian-style shirt, the associate in trim jeans and neatly pressed shirt, the usher in long shorts and long socks. They are always together; a tight little phalanx. The young prosecutor wanders through. Out of his well-cut court gear he looks even younger, and very vulnerable.

In the afternoon Gordy ambles off in shorts and a ragged sleeveless shirt to take a statement from Peter Djuguna for tomorrow's trial. I swim in the lukewarm pool. The surrounding pavers are burning hot in the afternoon sun.

In the evening Gordy and I are resolved not to stay up drinking. But we get into a long, meandering conversation nonetheless.

Gordon deeply believes that homosexuals are not 'normal' because they don't procreate the race. And I wonder, given this deep-seated conviction, if he's not punishing himself by going to the full bounds of his sexuality—exploring all the permutations, needing to express what others only fantasise about. Whether it's a journey, once begun at forty, that he is compelled to keep taking, with all its dangers and risks. All his life he's done things he's been afraid of, including being in the front line in Vietnam. So this is again living out the danger, facing what you are afraid of. Another paradox: he is afraid of being ridiculed, yet he courts it, with the long fingernails, the dyed long hair, the in-jokes about himself to all those in the know. And another: Damien is very comfortable in a roomful of men, while he is not. Why? 'Maybe it's the homosexuality I used to repress. Funny, it's the first time I've said that.'

He talks nostalgically of Europe. We share this, the peculiar feeling of being comfortable on a European street, in some way spiritually at home. Take Damien to Europe with you, I urge. But no, he's convinced Damien wouldn't cope. If he'd met Damien earlier, he could have trained him, but it's too late now; the mood swings are too great. But he loves him, will stay with him, they are essentially suited. And things have calmed down since they've been in the flat and since Peggy's been away in hospital.

'Sometimes I smile at us,' Gordon says. 'It's a peck on the cheek as I go to work: "Have you had breakfast? See ya."

'I'll probably grow old with Damien—if he doesn't kill me. Sometimes I'm afraid of him. I think he is psychotic; at least, he has periods of psychosis.'

'Yet he has his own sort of morality,' I say.

'Oh, he's very moral.'

The whole of the next day is taken up with Peter Djuguna's trial. Gordy has an uphill job with this defendant; he's truculent and aggressive and the jury is not impressed with him. The judge will give his summing up in the morning.

We adjourn to the hotel for a long last evening. We have a couple of drinks with the prosecutor, who's got a third child on the way, despite his youthful looks. He talks wistfully of joining the ALS, but wonders if he could cope with the drop in salary and career prospects. He ponders all this out aloud, which I find rather endearing. He seems without guile. Gordy says to him, 'If you come into the ALS, always remember that you're trying to help the hopeless ones. And keep in mind that it's not about ordinary legal battles.'

Tonight the whole legal troupe has dinner together—no-one can be seen to be influencing the judge if they're all sitting at one table. They remind me of a group of strolling players, wandering from town to town with their wares, bonded for the time they are together.

Once everyone else has dispersed to bed, Gordon and I go out to the outside bar where the pool tables are. The night is steamy and still; mostly countrymen clustered around the tables. They keep coming up to Gordon. He's a magnet. With those who don't know him he establishes his credentials through Damien. Once or twice he says, 'I'm Damien's partner,' and waits for it to sink in.

He deflects a lot of aggression, but he can also be aggressive and hard back to the men, especially to a white man who is trying to one-up him on his knowledge of Aboriginal people. This man has a rather beautiful, plump Aboriginal wife with sad eyes, who whispers confidentially into Gordon's ear. Gordon contemptuously calls her husband 'a failed teacher'. They spar in that bleak way men do.

Gordon and I are the last ones left in the bar. I don't have the heart to leave him there alone. He says to the barman, 'Open one of your better reds, Graham.' The barman obeys with an air of routine, then closes the bar.

Up in Gordon's room with the bottle of red, I briefly try the routine question-and-answer probe: just why and when did he leave his wife? But that's exactly when he won't answer me. That's not how he wants it. It's got to happen at its own speed. That's why he never turned up for a taping session. He wants it all to unfold organically.

How am I going to write about him? he wants to know. He wants it straight, no embellishments, but not too clinical either.

'With affection,' I supply.

'I just want you to put in the despair. The despair. You see the despair.'

I see the despair more, he thinks, because I was born in Europe, and so carry some legacy of suffering and extra knowledge in my bones.

He's pleased with me that I've stayed the distance tonight. He calls me 'sister', and asks if I love him. I do, in a way. He's one of a long line of on-the-edge, full-tilt people I've always been drawn to, loved and identified with, but eventually had to withdraw from. Now I just write about them.

He looks at himself in the mirror for a long time, as if trying to penetrate the secret of himself. He watches as his face changes, or he makes it change, from a ruddy male face to one where his green eyes narrow and a sphinx-like impassivity comes into them, and his lips thin. This is his brooding witch face, the one that's almost fearful of its own knowledge. (The witch is another theme with him; Damien and some of Damien's friends believe him to be one.) Then the face changes again, to a little girl face: the eyes soften, a bit of a pout, hair pulled caressingly over his mouth. Then back again to his everyday hard man-of the-world face.

Mirrors never fully reflect us back, he says, never give us the glimpse of ourselves that could be the true 'us'.

He'd really like to be a girl, he says later, in sexual fantasy mode, who cooks and cleans and keeps the house pretty and waits for her man to come home. Maybe a dominating woman would even be better. Someone who would beat him if things weren't right, but who would, ultimately, love him.

'Anne's a little girl,' he'd said earlier. I realise that this is possibly a jealous statement. He would like to be a little girl, but can't be.

He loves playing the wife to Damien and Damien enjoys being a fifties-style male—'get me my drink, get my dinner'. He and Damien are the reverse of each other—he macho yet passive, Damien effeminate yet aggressive. Gordy finds keeping house, being a good little wife 'relaxing'. That's the word he uses. Plays the husband, the breadwinner by day, the wife at night, but either way, in servitude.

Then comes the self-questioning, the whys. Why, why is he like this? I try to tell him it doesn't matter really. He's functioning, more or less.

His last ambition, since he's done everything else, he says, is to be a long-haired old man hanging around the fountain at the Cross, telling stories. As if there would be no shame in this, just a logical end.

He swears he doesn't care what we write about him. 'It's not as if you could hurt my burgeoning career as a leading QC or judge.'

But that's exactly what he could have been, and he knows it; it's implicit in what he's just said. Everyone around him, especially the judges, recognise his ability. And his caring. That's what comes over to a jury. He cares about his clients.

Aboriginal affairs

'You know the meaning of Aboriginal Affairs?' Mark Bin Bakar asks, shaking his mop of hair at me. 'When the black fat cats roll into town and expect you to fix them up with a woman.'

Mark is bitter about ATSIC. 'Just little bureaucrats. And the commissioners, huh, they're only interested in doing favours for their friends.' Goolarri has training programs ready to go, he says, they only need some funding from ATSIC to get underway. But there are the usual bureaucratic hassles.

We're having lunch together at Blooms. In this quiet time you see Mark's large loping untidy figure around town more often. But he's as busy as ever, working on four different documentaries at the moment, plus a couple of music albums.

He has started filming a documentary about his mother Phyllis, to be called *Peeping Through the Louvres*, the story of her life as a Stolen Child. He's filming Phyllis going back to her people's country on the Margaret River, meeting her uncles, seeing the place where she was born, interspersed with black-and-white re-enactments of key times in her life.

All Phyllis's friends are talking about it, and are dying to see it. Phyllis is nervous.

'I don't know yet whether it will turn out to be a good thing for her or a bad thing,' Mark says. 'I'm not sure if I've done the right thing. It's stirred her up.'

I tell him about Susan's experience with her mother. Heddy was nervous of talking about the hard things in her life, but after *Heddy and Me* was published it proved to be a terrific thing for her. He was interested in that.

Mark has lots of ideas on the go. On top of the films and albums, he's writing a black musical—a rock opera. But it was a surprise to hear that he's also interested in setting up a tourist operation out on his people's country, beyond the Margaret River.

'In two or three years,' he says, 'after Goolarri.'

Vanessa, too, has talked of going to live on her people's country. It's almost as if, for sophisticated part-Aborigines like them, it is a rite of passage.

Mark Bin Bakar's guide to Broome English

Mark is a sophisticated man, but the Broome dialect comes out in him once he starts telling stories. When he was living in Perth, he says, people loved to hear him talk because of his Broome accent. And when he's doing his Mary Geddardyu program, he really lets it rip. He's a past master of innuendo and double meanings. Many Broome words have two, even three meanings. For example, 'kuckles' means cockles, but also female genitalia. Feeling 'itchy' means randy. 'Mrs Moon' might refer to a pregnancy or a full moon or a pearl, depending on the context. 'Smoke' can be a cloud, or weather changing, or things blowing away in the wind. And only Mark (and only then as Mary Geddardyu) could get away with calling Kevin a 'Thai-coon'.

There's no embarrassment about sexuality or sexual terms or innuendo among Broome people. A woman saying fondly 'Come over here and let me feel ya balls' is just the Broome way of saying 'hello'.

*

At the Shinju Annual General Meeting in one of the big rooms upstairs at the Mangrove, there are only five committee members at the top table and about a dozen people in the audience. Perpetua is there, which surprises me a little. I haven't seen her at a Shinju meeting before. There's only one person there from the Shire—Lyn Devereaux, the community development officer. She asks a question of Kevin. He responds with that slight tilt of the head and half-smile that indicates he's displeased.

Kevin is re-elected unopposed as Shinju President. People are asked to volunteer for the committee. Perpetua sits mute. When Kevin asks her if she would like to join the committee, she alternates hesitancy and eagerness: 'Oh, oh, well...ah, yes. Yes I would, if you'll have me.'

The business is all over pretty quickly, then it's drinks at the bar. Kevin says to Perpetua, 'I know what portfolio we'll give you!' Meaning the Shinju art prize. Perpetua looks uncertain, but then Perpetua often looks uncertain. At first I think she's uncomfortable about the prospect of running the prize. Then I wonder if that's exactly why she came.

Kevin seems to be in better spirits than he was a while back. He tells me that 'people in the community' have urged him to stand for the Shire Council at the May elections. He has spoken once before about perhaps going into politics one day. The Shire may be the first step.

Goolarri's problems with ATSIC are still not resolved. He's angry about them giving $1.6 million to Imparja in Alice Springs while Goolarri is still penniless. 'We're still hanging on by our teeth.'

Party Hats

We found Gordy on the mattress watching TV. No sign of Damien. Peggy is back in town and has summoned him home.

Damien and Gordy are getting on very well at the moment. 'I don't understand it,' Gordy said. 'He says he's in love with me again. He's been so affectionate and sweet I can't believe it. He's been coming home late and waking me up. I'm begging to get some sleep!'

'We seem to have really settled into these roles now [Damien as the boss, Gordon as the "wife"]. It's not what he expected but he's found he likes it.'

Legal Aid was having their combined Christmas party and farewell for Angela at the Sheba Lane restaurant and Gordon was meant to be joining them. 'For Angela's sake. Otherwise I wouldn't go. The rest of them don't really like me, nor I them.'

Susan and I went down to have a laksa. The Legal Aid mob were at one big table, all wearing party hats made from tissue paper. When Gordy came down he donned a pink and mauve one. His blond locks suit pastels—he looked like the fairy queen. From time to time Angela and Gordy came over to our table. Then Gordon joined us permanently, looking relieved. He ordered another bottle of champagne.

He was in a talkative mood. We heard more outrageous stories of his improbable life; from being a 'tunnel rat' in Vietnam (where his best mate was killed) to the horror of being in Darwin during Cyclone Tracy. While Tracy was raging, a baby was torn from his arms. 'The neighbours were sheltering in our place and I was holding their baby. The window blew in and the baby was just blown out through the louvres.'

Susan and I stare at him. Is he serious?

He was so traumatised that as soon as it was over he and his wife just got in his old Valiant and drove to Melbourne. But that was no solution. A few days later he drove back again, 'with the missus and the dog', wangling his way back into the city through quarantine restrictions.

'The thing I remember most after Tracy was the stench of rotting food.'

∫ Gordon is bemused, but pleased too, that life is actually getting better. He now has a three-year contract with the ALS. And he knows the Aboriginal community wouldn't let him leave anyway. He and Damien are both enjoying the flat, and making it nicer and nicer. There were even copies of the Weekend Australian's colour magazine artistically arranged on the coffee table!

As we leave the flat, we reflect that all that's desirable in Gordon and Damien's world is within walking distance: the handybank, the Pearler's Bar and the Nippon, Murray's Seafood and Asian Restaurant and the bottleshop.

Gordon is not as much of a reprobate as he seems, really. He sent the wife and kids a Christmas card, as he has done for some years, but they never reply. He's still hoping one of the kids will turn up one day—'and they'll see this fat silly old man with dyed blond hair!' He laughs uproariously. (He's not fat but the stomach has got bigger the last couple of months).

Later in the night, at the devil's nightmare that is the Nippon night-club after midnight, he sees my dilemma with a drunken Aboriginal man who keeps gesturing and mouthing at me. I can't hear a word in the din or make out what he wants. Gordon is very used to this. He just puts on an impassive air—not unkindly, soothing in effect somehow—or is it his witch's look?—and rides it through. He can see I'm struggling, so he says, 'Look I'll get you out of this. Let's dance.' The guy follows us and dances with us, but the tension is diffused.

Mary is at the Nippon, looking rather luscious, a little drunk (happily so) and getting into the dancing. She and Anne dance. It's about sixty per cent black locals tonight, a couple of older white women wandering through. It's all din and lost souls to me. The only good sight is Mary swaying to the music, enjoying herself.

Christmas Eve

On Christmas Eve we visit Pearl to give her a little present we've bought her. We're welcome. Sometimes when we've turned up she's been a bit equivocal, but we're her first visitors today, and she is pleased with her present. Sally is there, too. They've just been to visit Aunty Bella's grave.

They tell us their plans for Christmas Day: thirty people will be coming over to Pearl's for lunch. Hama already has his Christmas present—a special TV set and satellite dish that can pick up Japanese television. Pearl shows us the lounge room, which she has rearranged so two armchairs are set up in front of the big new TV. Then she makes a cup of tea, gets out some cakes from the fridge and we sit at the table just beyond the kitchen.

The whole house is so open plan that it's hard to define the rooms. Large spaces, gleaming floors. Various people wander quietly through: two of her sons, then Hama. Ahmat arrives and is quickly dispatched to go and watch TV with Hama. Ahmat likes to watch it with him because he understands a bit of Japanese. On the luggers, they all learned a little of each others' languages.

Back then, Pearl says, everyone mixed with everyone else. Now the kids stick in their own little grooves. She is critical of the lack of initiative in the young, the lack of adventure. When people point out the exceptions to her she says 'I don't want to hear about *them*. I know all their names. I want to hear about the other ninety per cent, I want to hear that they're getting off their backsides.'

Pearlie doesn't just criticise, she puts her money where her mouth is, and for that she has a lot of respect around town. She supports various endeavours, like the *Little Piggies* album—music and songs by the Pigram offspring—which has a big thank you to 'Aunty Pearlie' in the acknowledgements.

Pearl and Sally are going to midnight Mass tonight. We say we are, too. The bishop won't be officiating—he's still away. 'We're going to miss the bishop,' Pearl says. 'He usually does a beauty on Christmas Eve. He socks it to us.'

In the evening Perpetua comes over for a barbecue, to help keep us awake until midnight Mass. We arrive at Our Lady Queen of Peace early but it's already filling rapidly.

The sermon is given by Father Paul. He loses the plot a few times. Nerves or too much Christmas cheer? Father Matt is assisting, wearing spectacular robes with bright orange, red and black stripes down the front and on the back a black tree silhouetted against red earth and an orange sun.

A couple of rows in front of us is a large family—white dad at one end, Aboriginal mum at the other and seven children in a row between them. The ideal Broome Catholic family. The two oldest go up to take communion with their parents. All the littlies stay quietly in the pew, perfectly behaved. In their hands they clutch their coins for the plate.

Alan Gronow, the police chief who is just about to leave Broome, is being formally accepted into the church. One of his sponsors is an old Aboriginal lady, Vera Dann, a church stalwart. They walk down the aisle with their arms around each other: she slight, bent and grey-haired, wearing pink; he tall and soberly dressed. (Gordy thinks Gronow's religiosity might be the reason there was no police piss-up this Christmas, just a sedate affair for cops and spouses only.)

We walk home through the quiet streets, feeling safe, a small breeze blowing, the sweatiness finally gone from the air. It's 2 a.m. by the time we get to bed, so Christmas Day is cruised on one engine.

Christmas Day

The quiet drone of the air-conditioner, the constant whirr of the fans. Jimmy Chi standing on the edge of Clementson Street, arms wide, face desperate, bare chest, long shorts, looking as if he's about to launch himself into the traffic. Glenys and the kids have gone south; they can't cope with him any longer. No-one has yet bitten the bullet and had him committed. Everyone thinks it has to happen, though. He's been off his medication for weeks.

At Shama's on Christmas morning, in the small lounge room off the kitchen, a few guests are chilling out. The smell of dead joints, fag-ends lying about. Beer and champagne and the ubiquitous nori rolls. Most people are outside under a tree, a few chairs drawn up, a couple of eskies used for seats. Staff from Blooms, a few semi-permanent residents just entering parenthood, plus a couple of itinerants talking of home. All swathed in the special intimacy of people who haven't been together very long or don't expect to be.

To Gordy's after midday. The flat is neat, the swags off the floor for once. Gordy is sitting decorously at the table with his mother-in-law, Peggy, and a young chap. He's contemplating a packet of instant gravy. He's got the chook in the oven and he cooked the pork last night. It's all domestic decorum, except that Damien is nowhere to be seen and hasn't been sighted in hours. No-one is surprised. Gordy seems philosophic.

He's pleased with our Christmas present of a black wrought-iron lamp. Says it will go with the black cast-iron bed. He reminds us that in one of his many past lives, he and his wife renovated old houses and sold them on.

A youngish couple drop by, carrying grog and nibblies. She calls Peggy 'Mum', but is probably her niece. He is a white guy who runs some Aboriginal economic corporation. (So many corporations around town with impressive names!) They look married. As the town gets back to its quiet post-tourist self you notice how many mixed marriages there are—both ways, but more often black women married to white men. But with the high-profile black men it's usually the other way—Peter Yu and Sarah, Baamba and Pam, Jimmy and Pat, Jimmy Chi and Glenys.

Peggy is a slight woman in her fifties, still rather pretty. She must have been a real looker in her time. I think of her as much older than me, but she's probably my age. She looks a bit sad, doesn't say much, but livens up every now and again. She laughs uproariously when I describe Peter Djuguna's behaviour in Derby court—how he swore that the cops fuckin' hated him, he'd fuckin' been in gaol for fuckin' nothing, etc. I'm not sure if she's laughing in delight because this respectable-looking white woman is saying 'fucking' a lot, or whether she can picture the scene in court.

It's tempting to stay for lunch, but we have a Bloom's hamper waiting in the fridge. Later, Bruce comes around to help us eat it.

We read and sleep the afternoon away. Walk the quiet streets at night. A disjointed, disembodied sort of Christmas Day, but a good one.

Twenty

*A New Year party at our place—Trouble at Goolarri—
Vanessa's dream—Last night at the movies—Mary's
farewell—Last morning*

Monday, December 28

It's that dead time between Christmas and New Year. Broome has shut down and there's not much to do that doesn't trespass on people's private lives. We feel intruders again, and redundant.

You've got your nose in the Barbara Vine I bought you for Christmas and you've got that spaced-out look of someone reading too fast. And you won't talk to me! I knew this would happen when I bought it. I'm *bored*. I'm sick of reading. I want to go home early. The next month stretches interminable.

Tuesday

You've gone out somewhere, leaving me with instructions to go to the computer. But I'm sick to death of Broome, or not Broome so much as having to write about it.

You've just come home. I've been impossible. We've had a fight. I'm like a child who knows I'm having a silly tantrum but can't stop.

But there are still nice moments! Last night, for example, sitting on the grass above Town Beach, the light from the café casting our shadows across the sand—although you were still hot—then wandering home along the back streets. Everything looks a bit more ramshackle in the Wet, as though in this weather no-one bothers being neat.

There was a big storm on Boxing Day night—a clap of thunder directly above us and the power went off. Torrential rain, enough to make the roof leak. The town is green and lush now. Clumps of tall grass on the spare blocks, more trees in blossom.

Along the sides of the unkerbed streets are wide stretches of water. Perpetua says that when all the streets were unkerbed, kids used to play in these huge puddles, black and white emerging red from the muddy water.

I've just repaired the retic for the third time, the pup having dug it up again. It's as hot as Hades today; the humidity is incredible. Five minutes outside and I'm dripping.

Wednesday

There was some cloud cover this morning and a slight breeze, so I took Boy to the small park near the mangroves. It was very quiet and Boy was good. Plans are underway to take him home with us. I wonder what Scruff and Jack will think of that!

A fairly boring day. Everyone is inside in the air-con, still recovering from Christmas, either lying around reading or watching videos. We walked over to Lyn's around six. The house was in darkness. Lyn, too, was on her bed reading. But she got up, lit a fag, opened a bottle of wine and we were away.

The news:

* Jeanie has arrived safely in London and is sounding much better.
* No word from Chi since she left.
* Lyn thinks she might turn up at her son's engagement party in Sydney with a black man ('well, actually, he's not that dark') just to infuriate her first husband's second wife. The kids won't mind—'they're not bigots'—but the current wife would be appalled.

Lyn says the house is nice and quiet now she has the place to herself. But she's obviously a little lonely, too, what with the Powells and quite a few others out of town. Not even the peripatetic Chi to come around and pick from her fridge without asking.

A New Year party at our place

We've invited the friends we've made here, as a kind of thank you to them, and the beginnings of a farewell. It's interesting to see who turns up—Pat Lowe, Mary and her ex-husband (they keep separate houses but still see a bit of each other), Perpetua, Lyn, Bill Reed, Kerry Stokes, and a few others. Even Gordy shows up, although he's unusually subdued. He spends most of his time inside in the air-con with Boy on his lap. No Damien.

It's a stinking hot night. When Kerry starts talking about the challenges of the new millennium, I can't concentrate, the sweat is running down my face so much. The chips are soggy within half an hour. The only food people eat with any enthusiasm is the cool fruit from the fridge.

I end up on the tiles, literally. From my prone position I'm quite enjoying myself, listening in, indicating every now and again that I'm still alive and compos mentis. Anne and Boy both check on me occasionally.

The hangover next day has to be carefully nursed.

Back row: Lyn, Mary, Perpetua, Susan
Front row: Kerry Stokes, Pat Lowe, Anne

The heat on New Year's Eve! We were on the side terrace under the fan but everyone was literally dripping sweat. At 1 a.m. people looked like they'd just stepped out of the shower.

Most of the party is a blur, but a few things I remember: a long talk about Kevin Fong's chances in the coming Shire elections, thankfully *before* Lyn Page arrived; the New Year's resolution game that someone suggested (we all had to make up a resolution and put it in a hat) and the surprising appositeness of some of them—Mary's injunction 'to have more fun', Gordy's 'to thine own self be true', mine to swim ten laps a day. Then there was Perpetua and Mary's little commune, calling each other 'family'—Paddy Djiagween's father-in-law worked at the Durack stations. And Mary and Lyn doing some bridge-building, declaring that their positions weren't so very far apart. As Lyn's mantra goes, 'heritage and development can go together'.

Trouble at Goolarri

Monday, January 4

In the reception area at Goolarri there's a petition for people to sign, asking ATSIC to grant Goolarri funding to enable it to continue. The place is running on a skeleton staff. A sign at reception says, 'Save Mary Geddardyu'. Her show is currently off-air. Mark has been doing it for five years but has never been paid for it.

I'm told Mark is on the set at the Uniting Church, shooting a sequence for his film, *Peeping Through the Louvres*, so I go down to watch. The town is quiet; there's hardly anyone around.

A girl of about ten, one of David Pigram's daughters, is playing young Phyllis at the orphanage. She sweeps the verandah, wearing an old-fashioned flowered dress several sizes too big for her. Mark asks 'young Phyllis' to pause and look into the distance, wistfully.

In the afternoon another scene, at Morgan's camp this time, the marshy area beyond Chinatown where the pearling crews used to live. There were many houses here once. Now it's a desolate wasteland, only one place still standing. It's a little ramshackle house, one of those typical old Broome

houses on low concrete stumps, with a couple of push-out storm shutters and a wide verandah at the back overlooking the mangroves. A few scrawny mutts sprawl in the shade of an old caravan. Nearby are a couple of tatty runabout dinghies. Two hundred yards away looms the big shiny roof of the Paspaley shopping centre.

Mark and his crew are filming a re-enactment of the only occasion when Phyllis saw her mother, after being taken from her at three years of age. Outside the house is an ancient 'International' truck painted bright green with a bright yellow bumper, driven by an old Aboriginal chap called Paulie Phillips. (Paulie, it turns out, is Damien's father). The woman passenger is playing Phyllis's mother. The truck drives up to the house and pulls up. The old man calls 'Phyllis!', A teenage girl—played by one of the older Pigram offspring—comes out of the house and hesitates when she sees the woman. 'It's yer mother,' the old man says. The girl steps forward awkwardly and hugs her. The mother looks at her and says, in a tone halfway between hardness and sadness: 'You're not my daughter. You belong to the white habits.' And turns away.

Thursday

Mark has shown me roughs of a couple of scenes from his film: Phyllis meeting her uncles, seeing her mother's country for the first time, finding the tree under which she was born. The material is potentially so powerful, yet there's a strange feeling of remove about it, of alienation and coldness. It's not a fault in the film-making so much as inherent in the material. The dislocation has been too great. There can be no happy reunions, no happy endings.

'I did it for the kids' sake,' Phyllis tells me. 'To show them what I've been through. If you don't talk about these things, no-one is going to know about them. It's hard to talk about. It brings tears to your eyes. And we never ever talked about it. We were quiet people.'

Did Mark push her into it?

'No, he didn't push me. He just said, "Mum I think it would be a good idea. I want to make a film. For the kids, for the grandchildren, too."'

She pronounces 'film' as 'filum', in the manner of the Irish nuns.

What of the family she had met, I ask. Wasn't that a tremendous thing?

'Yes,' she says listlessly. 'They were happy to see me after that long.' But it also served to remind her of the gap between them.

Phyllis and the film crew had to fly out to the Margaret River by helicopter because of the big Wet.

'I just trusted myself and said my prayers.'

Friday, January 15

Only a couple of weeks before we leave for home. We walk over to say hello to Bishop Chris who's back from Rome. We tell each other we won't take in much—we're worn out.

The bishop seems a little more bishoplike since his stint in Rome, more full of the theology and orthodoxy. Maybe that's why they have these synods, to pull them all into line. This time the Australian bishops were wrapped over the knuckles, basically for being too informal. Chris told us it was all misreported in the Australian papers, and he certainly wouldn't be changing the way things are done here.

*

Gordy needs a holiday. He looks tired, almost too tired to make the effort to go. The Wet is starting to get to everyone. Damien is set on going to Queensland for five weeks. Sea World and lots of iced champagne is what he has in mind.

Gordon says the whole of last weekend was taken up with a video of *Jaws*.' 'If Damien likes a video, he plays it over and over again, till I feel I'm going mad and forbid any more.'

While Gordy is out getting us some beers, Damien tells us he was worried he might have broken Gordy's ribs when he kicked him one drunken night just after Christmas. He's thrown away his heavy boots which did the damage. 'But he knows the rules, and he broke them.'

What are the rules?

'If he comes home late and drunk he's not to start an argument.'

'I've never managed to stay up long enough to see Gordon badly pissed,' I say.

'He's bad,' says Damien in a resigned voice. 'He just goes on and on and on.'

Vanessa's dream

Vanessa was looking sassy in a short orange skirt, white shirt and her array of necklaces—the large blister pearl that she found in the mudflats, a little MOP turtle and another trinket. She always manages to look stylish on very little, and no make-up.

She waved at every second car or person as we sat on the terrace of Ederby's. She handled a drunk guy with ease, gave him the dollar he wanted, let him sit down. They discovered mutual family. 'I'm Watson mob,' she said. 'My mother was a Watson.' He almost fell into her arms, pumped her hand. She tolerated him for another few minutes, then extricated herself without making him appear small.

She's leaving her job. She's setting about making her dream come true—to go back to her mother's country on the Lower Liveringa and set up a self-sufficient community there. She'll return to Broome only periodically, but she'll still be on the committee planning a memorial to the pearl divers, to be ready for next year's Shinju festival. She wants to make sure that the lugger divers are properly remembered.

Next year the Chinese community will be the theme. Vanessa is amiably contemp-

tuous of that: 'What did the Chinese ever do?' she demands, grinning. 'They just kept the shops and made the food!'

*

We went for a walk on the beach with Lyn on Sunday evening. Boy probably had the best time ever of his short life. Lyn's dog, large jovial Georgie, was charging around the edges of the water after her ball and Boy was lolloping everywhere after her, just adoring everything, and imitating her every move. He raced after her into the surf, trying to jump over the waves, but suddenly he had to swim, which he did with quick panicked movements, a surprised look on his face.

Lyn did her usual range of talk, from the very personal to the political. She's off to Sydney for her son's engagement party and planning, of course, to be the best turned-out woman there.

Will she take the black toy boy, just to shock the Sydney social set? Probably not, on second thoughts.

Tuesday, January 19

Less than a week before we leave for home and I'm worried that we're running out of time. But whenever it is, the cut-off point will be arbitrary and painful.

I know the wonder of this place will always be with us. The incomparable colour of the pindah roads at dusk, even redder after a shower of rain. The tin roofs glittering in the sun. The way Guy Street runs flat and long into the smooth aqua bay...tide in, the mangroves submerged; tide out, the mangroves emerge. And everywhere the sea, the sea so bright that we always exclaim, 'Look how blue it is today!'

Perhaps our last sight of Gordy and Damien. On impulse we drop in at the ALS office. Gordy is in black singlet and shorts, at his desk in the bare room, files on the floor, a pile of 'Records of Interview' videos on the desk, three or four criminal law books on the shelf. He gives us a tired half-smile.

He says he's giving up on the women's clothing kick—part of a New Year resolution—and even on the constant leg-shaving. He shows us his day-old growth to prove it. He even seems to be thinking, vaguely, of returning to his family. A 'normal' life is beginning to look attractive again. He's sick of the way things are. No change. Same old round.

Damien is looking dispirited, too. His dream of the Gold Coast and Sea World is fading.

I wonder if we'll see Gordon again, out of this Broome context. I somehow think so. Another Gordon may yet be invented.

Lyn is feeling at a loose end. She's been entertaining herself by flying the idea that the Kimberley adopt Central Time, which would put it a couple of hours ahead of the rest of Western Australia. She reckons longer days would be good for tourism.

'I'm expecting a call from Richard Court any moment, asking me what the hell I think I'm up to!' she chortled, swinging a leg over the side of the cane chair. 'A stockbroker with any sense would set up right here. We could have our own stock exchange! Now that'd be fun.'

Friday

At last light we take Boy to the beach for a walk and a swim. Perhaps the last? Everything now is beginning to be 'the last'. He dives through the waves but is not quite brave enough to go beyond his depth without the company of a larger dog. There are great shoals of shells along the high tide mark, which I never saw during the cooler months—a thick, wide band that we crunch over before getting to softer sand.

Now, deep into the Wet, the sea is a more ordinary colour, no longer aqua, more grey-green or simple deep blue. But the clouds! Overhead they're mauvy pink; in the west, gold and yellow. And between them the sky is a bright, bright blue, even after the sun has set. With the tide going out, the golds and mauves from the sky are reflected on the wet sand. The water is as warm as a bath.

Last night at the movies

Susan wants to take a light jacket to the movies. She still can't believe it won't get cool in the evenings! I persuade her not to. But she still puts on heavy linen trousers. We get to Sun Pictures. It's sweltering in the canvas deck chairs. She's sweating in the linen trousers. I know she'll fidget and complain and ruin the movie, so I offer to change pants with her. We cross the lawn to the 'ladies' behind the screen. She puts on my light, white cotton drawstrings, and I put on her pants. I cope, just, although they are so scratchy around my hips that I undo them.

Anthony, the manager of Matso's, is sitting next to us. 'Take them off,' he says, 'No-one will notice.'

Mary's farewell

In the end our farewell picnic was just us, Perpetua and Mary. The day had been hellishly hot but by the time we got to Gantheaume there was just enough breeze coming off the sea. We met Mary down on the rocks—her special place. She often goes there alone, has been going there since she was a small child. She had already caught one fish but thrown it back and was fossicking for oysters. She gave me two juicy ones, instructing me to wash them first. We pottered about, she telling us what was edible, pulling up big rocks to show the tiny creatures and growths underneath.

We made our way around to the small beach beyond the rocks. This is a place for the spirit children, Mary told us. The spirits sometimes pick their father-to-be from those who come down here, and sometimes they just decide to be your companion or 'good fairy'.

Roy and his girlfriend Sharon came by, walking their dog Pearl. Perpetua offered them a beer and we chatted while the sun set, then they wandered off…It was so easy, this meeting, chatting, strolling on—somehow the essence of all that is lovely about Broome.

We settled ourselves with picnic bits and pieces provided by Mary and Perpetua. Mary talked about the place and its stories—the names for the sea, fish, stones and sand. She saw Boy go bravely out into the dark, unconcerned by the newness and strangeness, and said, 'He feels safe. The big spirit dogs go through here; they're keeping an eye on him.' Indeed Boy was remarkably content and far less nervous than on a walk up Guy Street.

'Maybe we should leave him in Broome,' I wondered.

'No,' Mary said calmly, 'take him with you. He'll look after you.'

Perpetua said, gently hinting, 'Pat Torres tells stories about this place, too.'

'Let her tell them, if she feels comfortable,' said Mary with the same gentle slyness.

Perpetua and Mary handled each other with much mutual consideration. Perhaps their connected histories have given them clues as to how to deal with each other. Mary asked Perpetua if she would come on the culture centre working party, and Perpetua said, in that hesitant–direct way of hers, 'Mary, that...ah...that is wonderful of you...to ask me. I would be honoured, ah...proud. Thank you. Thank you.'

Mary is feeling pretty confident that they'll have the land for the culture centre at least by the year 2000. She's aware that the 'power boys', as she calls them, might try to take over the centre now that it is looking more promising. But she knows that her trump card is the country, and that's more important than male–female games.

It was a night of strange phenomena. What we thought was the evening star disappeared too quickly below the horizon. At the other end of the beach, towards Cable, there was a constant show of sheet lightning. Then the moon appeared without warning and took strange shapes through the clouds.

Anne said the moon looked like cat's eyes.

'Serpent's eyes,' Mary said.

All evening it felt as if Mary were giving us a gift; letting us have a glimpse of what this place means to her, how alive it is with association, story, life experience, family. Her children already know it well. We ate and drank and talked, or rather listened to Mary talk—she was quietly insistent on her agenda—and were content with each other's company.

Mary said that the Law ceremonies, always held at this time of year, are nearly over. No-one is supposed to travel or do anything until they are finished.

'Will your little fella, Laib, go through the ceremonies?'

'Of course.'

Mary sang a song in Yawuru. She speaks the Yawuru words so lovingly, as if their spiritual import was implicit in words.

> I'm happy in my heart
> here in my country
> from the sea to the land.

We blew out Roy's lantern and sat watching the lightning. We fantasised about staying on the little beach all night. I could imagine the evening slipping into sleep, how one would just curl up on the sand. But Perpetua and Mary said the crabs would come out and nibble our toes.

When we got back to our place, Mary started to sneeze. Probably just a summer cold, we said. But she thought it meant that she was not supposed to be swimming earlier, only fishing, and that the waves were reminding her of that. Or maybe that the ceremonies weren't over yet, and we shouldn't have been out there at all.

We talked on, rolled a joint. Mary was just beginning—letting us in, telling herself to us so we'd understand better. But we were tired. We finally pushed her out the door, half a joint in hand, saying, 'Smoke it at home.'

She rang ten minutes later.

'Just to tell you I got home safely.'

Last morning

A big storm broke while I was at the pool. Rain in torrents. In fifteen minutes the gutters in Guy Street were running eight feet wide. Young boys stood on the roundabout at Dora Street, yelling with glee as the cars swished past, drenching them.

Cleansing rain prior to a journey, our journey and the end of the Law time. While the men are out bush doing Law, the women and children stay put. Now it's over, people will be on the move again. And so will we. It's a good time to be leaving—everything fresh, and fat green pawpaws ripening on the trees.

Postscript

In the May Shire elections Kevin was elected to Council. A week later he became Shire President.

Lyn fell out with Greg Powell and found herself in the minority faction on the new council. She defied the Shire and published her own *Business and Community Directory*.

Towards the end of the year, Damien ran off to Perth with a German tourist. A couple of months later he was back in Broome. Life in the flat above Sheba Lane returned to normal.

Mary finally got some funding from ATSIC and an assistant to help her run the culture centre campaign.

Vanessa moved back to her mother's country on the Lower Liveringa River.

The second stage of The Catalinas was completed, blocking out the view of Roebuck Bay. Bob sold his place next door to a developer and said he was retiring to Perth.

The old Seaview supermarket closed down, driven out of business by the supercentres.

In April 2000, Broome was hit by Tropical Cyclone Rosita. Eco Beach, 35 kilometres across the bay, was completely destroyed. The people of Broome were lucky—the only fatalities were the giant tamarind trees.

the cast (continued)

Wendy Albert—bookshop proprietor and Baamba's first wife
Theresa Barker—founder, Jarndu Yawuru women's co-op
Aunty Bella—'mother' to a Broome generation; Pearl's aunt
Esther Bevan—member of the board of the University of Notre Dame; Tom Wiggan's wife
Peter Bibby—writer, editor and Broome perennial
Angela Bolger—refugee from Melbourne; Legal Aid lawyer
Gwen and John Bucknall—Labor Party activists; Aboriginal education consultants
Clare Chang—events co-ordinator for the Shire
Chi—new-age seer
Maxine Chi—post-graduate scholar; Jimmy Chi's sister
Phillipa Cook—one of Broome's powerhouse women
Samantha Cook—designer, Magabala Books; Phillipa's daughter
Donny D'Antoine—our first landlord
Sally Demin—sister of Pearl Hamaguchi
Lyn Devereaux—the Shire's community development officer
Anne Deveson—Sydney writer
Cissy Djiagween—Yawuru elder and Mary's mother
Paddy Djiagween—late esteemed Yawuru elder and Mary's grandfather
Patrick Dodson—prominent Aboriginal activist and Broome resident
Malcolm Douglas—ex-crocodile hunter
Elizabeth Durack, aka Eddie Burrup—artist
Dave Dureau—odd-job man and intellectual

Anthony Ellis—manager of Matso's
Pam Farrell—Baamba Albert's wife
Ahmat Fidel—Malay community leader; Sally Demin's partner
Corrie Fong—owner of the infamous house on Gantheaume Point;
   Bev Kinney's sister
Alison Fong—Kevin Fong's wife
Joyce Fong—Bev Kinney's mother
Elsta Foy—Aboriginal Shire councillor and Dave Dureau's wife
Glenys Gill—Uniting Church minister
Hiroshi Hamaguchi (Hama)—Pearl's husband and former pearl farmer
Dale and Craig Hamaguchi—two of Pearl and Hama's six sons
Harvey the Painter—Broome eccentric
Joyce Hudson—linguist
Tony Hutchinson—local real estate agent
Howard Jacobson—English writer
Jeanie—Lyn Page's friend
Sos (Ron) Johnston—ex-Shire President
Coralie Kennedy—Bob Noble's daughter
Peggy Kerr—Damien's mother
Uncle Kiddo—harmonica player extraordinaire
Beverley Kinney—pearl farm owner; the 'Queen of Broome'
Dave Lavery—KLC lawyer
Alison Lawrence—school librarian and community stalwart
Maria Mann—journalist, photographer, long-term Broome resident
Lord Alistair McAlpine—British peer, Broome enthusiast and former resident
Kimberley (Kim) Male—scion of the Broome aristocracy
Magda Male—Kim's Hungarian-born wife
Ian Moore—Lyn's rival for the Shire Directory
Ken Oobagooma—Kimberley elder
Pigram Brothers—Broome's leading musical family
Carl Plunkett—operator of Eco Beach; Lyn's ex-husband
Simon Poelina—Vanessa's late father
Greg Powell—chief executive officer of Broome Shire Council
Col Roberts—Broome magistrate
Paddy Roe—well-known elder
Rosalin Sadler—art critic, writer and Howard Jacobson's wife
Bruce Sims—our friend; editor at Magabala Books
Harp Singh—doctor
Kerry Stokes—artist (not the media magnate)
Pat Torres—Aboriginal artist, writer and activist
Vedant—ex-opera singer, masseur
Tom Wiggan—Bardi elder
Sharon Wigan—a relative of Damien's
Roy Wilkinson—The Lantern Man
Sarah Yu—anthropologist and Peter's wife